Red Hat® Linux® 9 For Dummies®

Cheat Sheet

vi commands

The Visual Editor, vi, is almost as old as the Unix operating system and is much older than Linux. This straightforward text editor is nothing fancy, like OpenOffice, but is nonetheless useful and powerful. You can start vi by entering the command, vi, from the GNOME Terminal shell prompt:

[username@somemachine username]$ vi somefile

You enter these commands from the vi editor:

Command	Description
vi filename	Open filename in vi
I	Enter insert mode, inserting before the current position
Shift+I	Enter insert mode, inserting at the beginning of the current line
a	Enter insert mode, inserting after the current position
Shift+A	Enter insert mode, inserting at the end of the current line
Esc	Return from insert mode to command mode
a	Delete a character while in command mode
cw	Delete the word to the left of the cursor and put the editor in input mode
:w	Write out the file
:q	Quit with no additional writes to the disk
:wq	Write back the file and then quit
Shift+ZZ	Write back the file and then quit
:q!	Quit the file with impending changes unwritten
/string	Search forward through the file for a string
?string	Search backward through the file for a string
n	Find the next string (either forward or backward)
u	Undo the last command

System administration commands

This list shows several commonly used Linux commands that help you to manage disks, shut down your computer, and gather information about your computer system. Enter these commands from a GNOME Terminal shell prompt (see Chapter 4):

Command	Description
mount [options] device file_system	Mount a file system
umount [option] file_system	Unmount a file system
fsck [options] file_system	Check the structure and integrity of a specified file system
mkfs [options] file_system	Put a directory structure on a low-level formatted disk
shutdown	Shut down the system now rather than wait for a message to be sent (Ctrl+Del does the same thing)
vmstat [options]	Look at the virtual memory performance
procinfo	

D1508421

File per...

These examples show different file permission combinations. Please consult Appendixes B and C for more information about files and file permissions.

Permission	Description
-rwxrwxrwx	Create read, write, and execute permissions for user, group, and rest-of-the-world (mode 777)
drwxr-xr--	Create a directory that is completely open to its owner and that can be read and searched by the group and read (but not searched) by the world (mode 754)
crw-r--r--	Create a character-special file that the owner can read or write to but that the group and the world can only read (mode 644)
brw-------	Create a block-special file; only the owner can read and write to it (mode 600)

Red Hat® Linux® 9 For Dummies®

Cheat Sheet

A few good commands

Some commonly used and useful commands are listed here. You enter these commands from a shell prompt:

Command	Description
`cd directory`	Change the current directory to *directory*
`ls [options] [directory]`	List the current directory's contents
`ls -l`	List the current directory's contents along with sizes, permissions, ownerships, and dates of files
`ls -a`	List all files, including invisible files (files whose names begin with a period)
`pwd [option]`	Print the working directory (the one you're in)
`rm [options] filename`	Remove filename
`mkdir [options] directory_name`	Make a new (empty) directory
`rmdir [options] directory_name`	Remove an empty directory
`cp [options] src_filename dst_filename`	Copy a file
`mv [options] src_filename dst_filename(s)`	Move (or rename) a file
`cat [options] filename`	Concatenate a file to the standard output (display the file)
`more [options] filename`	Paginate a file
`less [options] filename`	Paginate a file
`touch [option] filename`	Make a new (empty) file, changing the access date of an existing file
`chown [options] filename`	Change the owner of a file or a directory
`chgrp [options] filename`	Change the group of a file or a directory
`chmod [options] filename`	Change the permissions of a file or directory
`sort [options] filename`	Sort a file in a particular order (depending on the option)
`echo [options] text string`	Echo back to the screen what is typed after the command
`date [options] text string`	Read the date and time (without an argument); set the date and time (with an argument)
`cut [options] filename`	Break a wide file into multiple narrow files
`sed [options] filename`	Stream editor for large files or real-time editing
`ln [options] source_filename/directory target_filename/directory`	Link a filename to another file
`grep [options] filename`	Use this searching program, which uses general regular expressions to find data and then prints it to its output

For Dummies: Bestselling Book Series for Beginners

Red Hat® Linux® 9

FOR

DUMMIES®

Red Hat® Linux® 9

FOR
DUMMIES®

by Jon "maddog" Hall
and Paul G. Sery

WILEY

Wiley Publishing, Inc.

Red Hat® Linux® 9 For Dummies®

Published by
Wiley Publishing, Inc.
909 Third Avenue
New York, NY 10022

www.wiley.com

About the Authors

Jon "maddog" Hall is the executive director of Linux International, a vendor organization dedicated to promoting the use of the Linux operating system. He has been in the computer industry for more than a quarter of a century (somehow, that sounds more impressive than just "25 years"), the past 18 years of which have been spent using, programming, and admiring the Unix operating system. Jon works for Compaq Computer Corporation, where he is helping to shape Compaq's strategy with respect to Linux. Previously, Jon was the department head of computer science at Hartford State Technical College, where his students lovingly (he hopes) gave him the nickname "maddog" as he tried to teach them operating system design, compiler theory, and how to live an honorable life.

While working for Digital Equipment Corporation in May of 1994, "maddog" met Linus Torvalds, and was intelligent enough (his critics say "maddog" was just lucky) to recognize the potential of the Linux operating system. Linux changed his life, mostly by providing him with 22-hour workdays. Since "maddog" has started working with Linux, however, he has also started meeting more girls (in particular, his two godchildren). You can usually find Jon speaking at various Linux conferences and events ("maddog" just barks), and he has also been known to travel long distances to speak to local Linux user groups.

Paul G. Sery is a computer systems engineer employed by Sandia National Laboratories in Albuquerque, New Mexico. He is a member of the Computer Support Unit, Special Projects, which specializes in managing and trouble-shooting Unix and Linux systems.

When he is not beating his head against systems administration problems, Paul and his wife, Lidia, enjoy riding their tandem bicycle through the Rio Grande valley. They also enjoy traveling throughout Mexico. Paul is the author of *Linux Network Toolkit* and the co-author of several other books. He has a bachelor's degree in electrical engineering from the University of New Mexico.

Dedication

Jon "maddog" Hall: To Mom & Pop™, whose aversion to things electronic is well known, and who can still call their son Jon rather than maddog.

Paul G. Sery: To my wife, Lidia Maura Vazquez de Sery.

Author's Acknowledgments

I want to thank my wife, Lidia, for her patience, support, and good advice, all of which have made writing this book possible. Without her, I would still be the pocket-protector-inserted-into-shirt, busted-eyeglass-fixed-with-tape-wearing, "Star Trek"-watching, wrinkled-shirt-suffering, spaghetti-in-the-pot-over-the-sink-eating, Saturday-night-hacking sorry-sack sorta guy. Well, I never was into "Star Trek," and I *am* pecking at this keyboard on Saturday night, but my wonderful and beautiful wife certainly has made me a better man.

And, of course, I want to thank the staff at Wiley Publishing, who provided considerable and essential help, too. Terri Varveris and Rebecca Whitney provided constant and essential assistance. Their patience with me was truly vital.

I also want to thank Laura Lewin, who gave me the chance to help write this book. She showed great confidence and patience in me. I'm also in debt to Anne Hamilton (now working for, er, the other guy), who gave me my first Linux gig. I'm truly grateful and wish them success in their new ventures.

I also want to acknowledge a total lack of assistance in writing this book from my dog, the infamous Oso Maloso; eater of many things that should have ended his long career early, including but not limited to: ant poison, Advil, pounds of tootsie rolls one Halloween, several bags of chicken bones during one party, beer and other assorted items; escaper of many fences and gates; and friend of the late, great Paunchy (former demidog of Albuquerque).

How useful was Oso? Well, one night while working on this book, I got a phone call. Leaving my apple pie behind next to the keyboard, I went downstairs to take the call and passed him on his way up. I should have known something was up because he had a cell phone with him and no one answered when I picked up to take the call. I went up the stairs while he went down. The apple pie was gone. Oso 1, human 0.

— *Paul G. Sery*

Publisher's Acknowledgments

We're proud of this book; please send us your comments through our online registration form located at www.dummies.com/register/.

Some of the people who helped bring this book to market include the following:

Acquisitions, Editorial, and Media Development

Project Editor: Rebecca Whitney

Acquisitions Editor: Terri Varveris

Technical Editor: Terry Collings

Editorial Manager: Carol Sheehan

Media Development Manager: Laura VanWinkle

Media Development Supervisor: Richard Graves

Editorial Assistant: Amanda M. Foxworth

Cartoons: Rich Tennant (www.the5thwave.com)

Production

Project Coordinator: Kristie Rees

Layout and Graphics: Amanda Carter, Jennifer Click, Sean Decker, Michael Kruzil, Kristin McMullan, Jackie Nicholas, Jeremey Unger

Proofreaders: John Tyler Connoley, John Greenough, Susan Moritz, Charles Spencer, TECHBOOKS Production Services

Indexer: TECHBOOKS Production Services

Publishing and Editorial for Technology Dummies

    Richard Swadley, Vice President and Executive Group Publisher

    Andy Cummings, Vice President and Publisher

    Mary C. Corder, Editorial Director

Publishing for Consumer Dummies

    Diane Graves Steele, Vice President and Publisher

    Joyce Pepple, Acquisitions Director

Composition Services

    Gerry Fahey, Vice President of Production Services

    Debbie Stailey, Director of Composition Services

Contents at a Glance

Table of Contents

Introduction

● ●

*R*ed Hat Linux 9 For Dummies is designed to help you install and use Red Hat Linux. This book shows you how to do fun and interesting — to say nothing of useful — things with Red Hat Linux. The book is also designed to be an effective doorstop or coffee cup coaster. Whatever you use it for, we hope that you have fun.

About This Book

This book is designed to be a helping-hands tutorial. It provides a place to turn for help and solace in those moments when, after two hours of trying to get your network connection working, your dog bumps into the cable and it magically starts working.

We tried our hardest to fill up this book with the things you need to know about, such as how to

- ✔ Install Red Hat Linux
- ✔ Get connected to the Internet via broadband DSL and cable modems or old-fashioned dial-up modems
- ✔ Get connected to your Local Area Network (LAN)
- ✔ Build a simple firewall
- ✔ Build simple Internet and LAN services, such as Web pages and print servers
- ✔ Use Red Hat Linux to play CDs, and MP3s and listen to radio stations
- ✔ Use the GNOME desktop environment
- ✔ Use useful and usable applications, such as the OpenOffice desktop productivity suite, Evolution desktop organizer/ and e-mail client, and the streaming multimedia MPlayer
- ✔ Work with the OpenOffice desktop productivity suite to satisfy your word processing, spreadsheet, and presentation needs
- ✔ Upgrade your computer and network security
- ✔ Know where to go for help
- ✔ Manage your Red Hat Linux workstation

You see troubleshooting tips throughout this book, but Chapter 17 is devoted to the subject. It's not that Red Hat Linux is all that much trouble, but we want you to be prepared in case you run into bad luck.

The instructions in this book are designed to work with the version of Red Hat Linux that's on the companion CD-ROMs; we also describe how to download several software packages not found on the companion CD-ROMS. Feel free to use other versions of Red Hat Linux or even other Linux distributions, but be aware that our instructions may not work exactly or even at all. Good luck!

Foolish Assumptions

You know what they say about people who make assumptions, but this book would never have been written if we didn't make a few. This book *is* for you if

- **You're building a Red Hat Linux workstation.** You want to use the Linux operating system to build your personal workstation. Surprise! — the CD-ROMs included with this book contain the Red Hat Linux distribution.
- **You have a computer.**
- **You have no duct tape?** You want to put the Red Hat Linux operating system and the computer together, and using duct tape hasn't worked.
- **You want to be a guru.** You don't want to become a Red Hat Linux guru — at least not yet.

However, this book is *not* for you if you're

- **Looking for a reference-style book.** We simply don't have enough space to provide a comprehensive range of topics. We concentrate on providing help on getting popular and useful stuff up and running. We devote more space on, for example, getting your DSL or cable modem working.
- **Looking for a systems administration book.** Again, we don't have enough space to do the subject justice. We provide instructions on how to perform certain essential tasks, like adding users, packages, and network connections. This book selects certain topics to focus on and leaves the rest for other books.

Conventions Used in This Book

At computer conventions, thousands of computer people get together and talk about deep technical issues, such as

✔ What is the best hardware for running Red Hat Linux?

✔ Is Coke better than Pepsi?

✔ Could Superman beat Batman?

✔ Could Superman, Batman, and Spiderman beat The Punisher?

But these aren't the types of conventions we're talking about here. Our conventions are shorthand ways of designating specific information, such as what is and isn't a command or the meaning of certain funny-looking symbols.

Typing code

Commands in the text are shown like this. Commands not shown in the text, but set off on lines by themselves, look like this:

```
[lidia@cancun lidia]$pwd
/home/lidia
```

See the [lidia@cancun lidia] part of the preceding lines? You don't necessarily see that on your system, unless you happen to be my wife's mirror image who also likes Cancun, Mexico, very much. But you see something similar depending on what your computer and user name are. The first name, lidia, is replaced by whatever your user name is. The second name is your computer name. The final one is the directory in which you're working, which in this case is the lidia home directory. Therefore, if your user name is zoot and your computer name is wishbone, your prompt is

```
[zoot@wishbone zoot]$.
```

When you see stuff in boldface, it means it's something you should type. For example:

Type **man chown** at the command prompt and press Enter.

If we tell you to type something in a bolded step, the text you type isn't in bold, as in this step:

1. Type man chown **at the command prompt and press Enter.**

Here's a rundown of the command syntax in Linux:

✔ **Text *not* surrounded by [ ] or { } brackets must be typed exactly as shown.**

✔ **Text inside brackets [ ] is optional.**

✔ **Text in *italics* must be replaced with appropriate text.**

✔ Text inside braces { } indicates that you must choose one of the values inside the braces and separated by the | sign.

✔ An ellipsis (. . .) means "and so on" or to repeat the preceding command line as needed.

Don't concern yourself too much with this information now. For most of this book, you don't need to know these particulars. When you do need to know something about a particular syntax, come back here for a refresher course.

Keystrokes and such

Keystrokes are shown with a plus sign between the keys. For example, Ctrl+Alt+Delete means that you should press the Ctrl key, Alt key, and Delete key all at the same time. (No, we don't make you press any more than three keys at the same time.)

Most applications and utilities we describe in this book use graphical user interfaces (GUIs), such as GNOME, which allow you to control your computer by pointing and clicking with your mouse. Occasionally, however, we give nongraphical instructions that require pressing keys on your keyboard. In those situations, we often simplify the instructions by saying "Select OK." That generally means that you press the Tab key, which moves the cursor to the OK button, and then press the Enter key. That two-step process is equivalent to clicking an OK button in a GUI.

How This Book Is Organized

Like all proper *Dummies* books, this book is organized into independent parts. You can read the parts in any order. Heck, try reading them backward for a real challenge. This book is not meant to be read from front cover to back; rather, it's meant to be a reference book that helps you find what you're looking for when you're looking for it. Between the Contents at a Glance page, the table of contents, and the index, you should have no problem finding what you need.

If you do read the book in order, you encounter the useful and interesting things first and the more technical items last. For instance, after installing Red Hat Linux in Part I, you may want to immediately proceed to Part II to see how to connect Linux to the Internet or your local network. From there, you can use your new workstation to surf the Internet and use e-mail.

The following sections describe each part.

Martha Stewart we're not:
Other uses for CD-ROMs

Where computers abound, so do CD-ROMs. Eventually, these CD-ROMs become obsolete or are never installed — that's the case with software products that arrive as unwanted advertising. What can ecologically minded people do with these CDs so that they don't fill up landfills?

✔ Try using those defunct CDs as coasters for drinks.

✔ Make pretty mobiles from castaway CDs. (The sun shining off the CD-ROMs makes wonderful rainbows on the wall.)

✔ Make CD-ROM clocks and give them to all your friends at the holidays. Just purchase inexpensive quartz-crystal clock motors (complete with hands) and use the CD-ROM as the face of the clock. I have four of these

clocks made from Windows NT CD-ROMs — hey, can you imagine a better use for them?

✔ Make a nice flowerpot. Just use a high heat to melt a CD-ROM around the base of a water tumbler. Of course, if you try this at work, you could cause some consternation among members of management, particularly after they find out that one of the more expensive programs they've purchased has ended up at the bottom of a flowerpot.

✔ Make an ashtray by plugging the hole.

For now, please keep your *Red Hat Linux 9 For Dummies* CD-ROMs in a safe place, such as the sleeve in the back of this book, when you're not using it.

Part I: Installing Red Hat Linux

In Part I, you find out what Linux is and how to prepare your computer to install Red Hat Linux. We then walk you through the installation and show you the basics of working with Red Hat Linux.

Part II: Got Net?

In Part II, you find out about connecting to the Internet and local networks. You see how to jump on the Internet with your everyday modem or high-speed (broadband) DSL or cable modem. We also show you how to connect to an existing network. If that local network has a high-speed Internet connection, you can use it as your portal to the wonderful world of surfing. The Internet can be dangerous, so we include instructions on creating your own firewall. Finally, we show you how to use Mozilla to satisfy your browsing and e-mail needs.

Part III: Linux, Huh! What Is It Good For? Absolutely Everything!

Part III guides you through the glorious particulars of *doing* something with Red Hat Linux. You're introduced to the GNOME desktop window environment. You're taken through its paces by moving, resizing, hiding, and closing windows; using the file manager; and much more. Two chapters are devoted to using the Red Hat Linux multimedia capabilities, such as listening to CDs and MP3s, as well as to rip and record them. The world's radio stations are now available to you with streaming media technology. We describe the full-featured OpenOffice desktop productivity suite in some detail. You can use OpenOffice with your Red Hat Linux machine to do all your writing and other work-related functions. You can even write a book with it! Finally, you see how to get organized with Red Hat Linux.

Part IV: Revenge of the Nerds

In Part IV, you're guided through using your Red Hat Linux computer's network capabilities. It's Nerd City but also fun and useful. We start by building a simple network. After the network is up and running, we describe how to build network services, such as an Apache Web server, Samba, and a printer server. The last two chapters are devoted to exploring the art of network computer security and troubleshooting network problems. Insert your pocket protector, strap the ol' HP calculator to your hip, retape your glasses, and get ready for Saturday night!

Part V: The Part of Tens

A *Dummies* book just isn't complete without The Part of Tens, where you can find ten all-important resources and answers to the ten most bothersome questions people have after installing Red Hat Linux. (The folks at Red Hat Software provided these questions.) We introduce the ten most important security concerns too.

Part VI: Appendixes

Finally, you get the appendixes. Appendix A describes how to find out about the details of your computer's individual pieces of hardware; this information is sometimes helpful when you're installing Red Hat Linux. Appendixes B and C introduces you to using and managing the Linux file system. Appendix D shows how to use the Red Hat Package Manager (RPM). Appendix E finishes by describing what you can find on the companion CD-ROMs.

What You're Not to Read

Heck, you don't have to read any of the book if you don't want to, but why did you buy it? (Not that we're complaining.) Part I has background information. If you don't want it, don't read it. Also, the text in sidebars is optional, although often helpful. If you're on the fast track to using Linux, you could skip the sidebars and the text with a Technical Stuff icon. But we suggest instead that you slow down a bit and enjoy the experience.

Icons in This Book

These are nifty little shortcuts and timesavers. Red Hat Linux is a powerful operating system, and you can save unbelievable amounts of time and energy by utilizing its tools and programs. We hope that our tips show you how.

Don't let this happen to you! We hope that our experiences with Red Hat Linux will help you avoid the mistakes we made.

Recall for later use the information given here.

This stuff is particularly nerdy technical information. You may skip it, but you may find it interesting if you're of a geekier bent.

Where to Go from Here

You're about to join the legions of people who have been using and developing Linux. We have been using Unix for more than 20 years, Linux for more than 10 years, and Red Hat Linux for 8 years. We've found Red Hat Linux to be a flexible, powerful operating system, capable of solving most problems even without a large set of commercial software. The future of the Linux — and Red Hat Linux in particular — operating system is bright. The time and energy you expend in becoming familiar with it will be worthwhile. Carpe Linuxum.

Part I
Installing Red Hat Linux

The 5th Wave   By Rich Tennant

"It's called Linux Poker. Everyone gets to see everyone else's cards, everything's wild, you can play off your opponent's hands, and everyone wins except Bill Gates, whose face appears on the Jokers."

In this part . . .

You're about to embark on a journey through the Red Hat Linux installation program. Perhaps you know nothing about setting up an operating system on your computer. That's okay. The Red Hat Linux installation system is easygoing by nature and straightforward to use. Plus, we help guide you through the installation.

In Chapter 1, you begin to discover what Red Hat Linux is all about and what it can do for you. Chapter 2 helps you to get ready to install Red Hat Linux and repartition your hard drive if necessary. The real fun begins in Chapter 3, when you install your own Penguin. (Linus Torvalds, the inventor of Linux. loves penguins, and they have been adopted as the Linux mascot.) Finally, Chapter 4 gives you a brief, but important, introduction to working with Red Hat Linux.

Chapter 1

And in the Opposite Corner . . . a Penguin?

*W*e see a penguin in your future. He's an unassuming fellow who's taking on a rather big competitor — that other operating system — in the battle for the hearts, minds, and desktops of computer users. Red Hat Linux, with its splashy brand name and recognizable logo, is undeniably one of the driving forces behind the Linux revolution — and is by far the most popular Linux brand.

This chapter introduces you to the latest and greatest Red Hat release, Red Hat Linux 9. This book covers all the bases — a good number of bases, at least — about how to use Red Hat Linux as a desktop productivity tool, Internet portal, multimedia workstation, and basic network server. You can do lots of things with Red Hat Linux, and this chapter gives you an overview of the possibilities in addition to a brief look at the history of Linux.

History of the World — Er, Linux – Part II

In the beginning of computerdom (said in a booming, thunderous voice), the world was filled with hulking mainframes. These slothful beasts lumbered through large corporations; required a special species of ultranerds to keep them happy; and ate up huge chunks of space, power, and money. Then came the IBM PC and Microsoft Windows, and the world changed. Power to the people — sort of.

In 1991, a student at the University of Helsinki named Linus Torvalds found himself dissatisfied with his operating system. Torvalds thought that the Unix operating system might be better suited to help him accomplish his work. Unix was invented in the 1970s and, although powerful, was expensive, so he began writing his own version of Unix. Now that's a simple task — *not!* After formulating the basic parts, Torvalds recruited a team of talented programmers through the Internet, and together they created a new operating system, or *kernel,* now named Linux.

One of the most important decisions Torvalds made in the early days of Linux was to freely distribute the Linux kernel code for anyone to do with as they wanted. These free Linux distributions were and still are available in several forms, mainly online.

The only restriction Linus imposed on the free distribution of his creation was that no version of the software can be made proprietary. (*Proprietary* software is owned and developed under wraps by private companies. *Open source* code is for "the people" — anyone can develop it without breaking the law.) You can modify the heck out of it and distribute it for fun (and for profit, if you want). What you can't do is stop anyone else from using, modifying, and distributing even your modified version of the software — either freely or for profit.

The lack of proprietary restrictions on Linux has led to drastic improvements in the technology. We can't overstress how important it has been to the Linux operating system that its source code is freely available; the Linux operating system continues to improve rapidly — even organically — because it is continually being tweaked by lots of really smart people. (In contrast, proprietary operating systems, like Microsoft Windows, are tweaked every once in a while by a smaller group of smart people.)

By the early spring of 1994, the first real version of Linux (Version 1.0) was available for public use. Even then it was an impressive operating system that ran smartly on computers with less than 2MB of RAM and a simple 386 microprocessor. Linux 1.0 also included free features for which other operating systems charged hundreds of dollars. Nowadays, tens of millions of users enjoy Linux at home and work.

By the way, if you're wondering about the whole penguin thing, the answer is disappointingly simple. The reason the friendly penguin (whose name is Tux, by the way) symbolizes All Things Linux is that Linus Torvalds, the inventor of the Linux operating system, loves penguins. Some mystery, eh?

Knowing What You Can Do with Red Hat Linux

Linux is freely available software. The source code for Linux, which is the heart and soul of the operating system, is also publicly available. The Free Software Foundation (FSF) contributes much of the utilitarian software that makes using Linux much easier — FSF is the brainchild of the great Richard Stallman.

Red Hat Linux combines all those pieces plus some additional applications and then goes another step and adds a few of its own to create an *integrated product.* Red Hat, Inc., combines the basic Linux operating system with software (some made by other companies and some made by Red Hat) to produce a package with a value that's greater than the sum of its parts. That combination is known as a *distribution,* or *flavor,* of Linux.

So that you can get up and running with Red Hat Linux 9 as quickly as possible, we've been sweet enough to include the Publisher's Edition operating system on the CDs that come with this book. The Publisher's Edition contains all the major parts of the full Red Hat distribution except the source code and some MS-DOS utilities (for example, the Windows File Allocation Table, or FAT, repartitioning program First nondestructive Interactive Partitions Splitting — FIPS — isn't included).

Initially used almost solely to provide network services, Red Hat Linux is now used by businesses, individuals, and governments to cut costs, improve performance, and just plain get work done. You can use Red Hat Linux as a desktop workstation, a network server, an Internet gateway, a firewall, the basis of an embedded system (such as a smart VCR or a robot), or even as a multiprocessor supercomputer. And thanks to the thousands of people who continually refine different parts of Linux, Red Hat Linux continues to become more flexible and capable with each release.

This list shows some of the cool Red Hat Linux features you can use:

  ✔ **Desktop productivity tools:** Red Hat has successfully worked overtime over the past few years to make Linux work on your desktop. Red Hat bundles software, such as the OpenOffice suite of productivity tools, so that you can get your everyday work done. The OpenOffice suite includes a full-function word processor plus spreadsheet, presentation, graphical drawing, and Web page creation tools. The word processor can read and write all the Windows Office formats plus many others, such as WordPerfect. When you install Red Hat Linux, OpenOffice is installed and icons are placed on the menu bar to make accessing it easy.

✔ **Multimedia stuff:** Red Hat Linux packs numerous multimedia tools for you to use. You can play, record, and rip audio tracks from CDs and DVDs. You can listen to streamed media sources, such as radio stations, over the Internet. Linux also lets you transfer photos and other items from your own cameras and MP3 players, for example.

✔ **Network services:** Red Hat Linux works as a network-based server too. Linux found its initial popularity performing jobs like Web serving and file and printer sharing and hasn't missed a beat. We show you how to create several network services.

Boosting your personal workstation

We can't emphasize enough how well Red Hat Linux works as a personal workstation. With Red Hat Linux, you can easily create your own, inexpensive, flexible, and powerful personal workstation. Linux provides the platform for most of the applications you need to get your work done. Many applications come bundled with Red Hat Linux, from address books and text editors to checkbook balancers and Web browsers.

The following list describes just a few of the major categories of free software that are available for Linux, along with some examples of popular programs:

✔ **Office suites:** Complete desktop productivity suites — such as OpenOffice, StarOffice, and Koffice — include advanced word processors that can read and write Microsoft Word files (as can the Open Source AbiWord word processor), HTML editors, spreadsheet editors, and graphics editors. For simple, no-frills word processing, you can use the well-known AbiWord word processor.

OpenOffice is Microsoft Office 97, Office 2000, and Office XP compatible. Check out the site at `www.openoffice.org`.

✔ **Streaming multimedia players:** Red Hat packages and installs the Open Source XMMS MP3 player. You can use XMMS to play downloaded MP3 files or continuous MP3 streams. You can also download a free version of the RealNetwork RealPlayer to listen to radio stations across the world and also watch video streams. The Internet is going multimedia, and streaming players let you get in on the action.

✔ **Freely distributable Open Source programs:** You can download these programs from the Internet and use them without paying to register the product. Literally dozens and dozens of software packages are available on the CDs that come with this book, including (but by no means limited to) the `pine` text-based e-mail reader, the zip data-compression program (which compresses files using the same format as WinZip), the Gimp graphics manipulation program, and many more.

✔ **Virtual machines:** The commercial VMware workstation creates a virtual computer within your Linux PC. The virtual machine looks, acts, smells, and performs just like a real computer, but is really just a program running under the Linux operating system. You can install Linux or Windows or both on the virtual machine. VMware helps bridge the world between Linux and Windows and gives you the best of both worlds.

✔ **Web browsers and e-mail clients:** The Open Source browser, Mozilla, is included with Red Hat Linux 9. Red Hat Linux also provides the Galleon Web browser. The nongraphical, text-based lynx browsers are included too and come in handy if you're using an older, slower modem because they don't require as much speed as Mozilla does. You can use the Mozilla or the new Ximian Evolution personal organizer, calendar, and e-mail client.

Not all the software in the preceding list is included on the CDs with this book. RealPlayer, for example, is available for download only over the Internet. You can obtain StarOffice by downloading it from the Internet or ordering it on CD from www.sun.com.

Linux is for nerds too

The Linux operating system has been *ported* (or converted) from the 32-bit Intel architecture to a number of other architectures, including Alpha, MIPS, PowerPC, and SPARC. This conversion gives users a choice of hardware manufacturers and keeps the Linux kernel flexible for new processors. Linux handles *symmetric multiprocessing* (it can take on more than one CPU or mathematical and logical programming unit per system box). In addition, projects are in the works to provide sophisticated processing capabilities, such as

Real-time programming: Controlling machinery or testing equipment.

High availability: Running a reliable computer all the time.

Journaled file systems: Using journaled file systems that can "heal" much more quickly and reliably than nonjournaled ones.

Parallel processing: Amplifying the problem-solving power of computer by using multiple processors to work in parallel. Parallel processing systems come in various flavors, such as Symmetric Multi Processing (SMP), extreme Linux systems, and Beowulf clusters. Research organizations and even individuals can create machines with supercomputer capabilities at a fraction of the price of supercomputers. In certain cases, extreme Linux systems have been made from obsolete PCs, costing the organizations that make them nothing in material costs.

Using Linux network tools and services

Linux computers can provide many powerful and flexible network services. Your two Red Hat Linux Publisher Edition CDs come packed with the tools to provide these services:

✔ **Apache Web server:** Of all the Web servers on the Internet, the majority are run by the Open Source Apache Web server. You can start a simple Web server by simply installing the bundled Apache software from the companion CD.

✔ **OpenSSH:** The Open Source version of Secure Shell enables you to communicate securely across the Internet. Secure Shell is much safer than Telnet because Secure Shell encrypts your communication when you log in (even when you log in to other computers), making much slimmer the chance that others can discover your passwords and other sensitive information. OpenSSH also provides other authentication and security features and enables you to securely copy files from machine to machine. With OpenSSH, you can prevent people from listening to your communication.

✔ **VPN (Virtual Private Network):** VPNs encrypt connections across insecure networks, such as the Internet, to create in effect private networks. Red Hat Linux packages the tools necessary to securely connect two computer or private networks across the Internet.

✔ **Internet accessing utilities:** Red Hat Linux provides several configuration utilities that help you connect to the Internet. The utilities help you to configure DSL, cable modems, and plain old telephone modems to connect to the Internet. They also help you to connect to Local Area Networks (LAN) using Ethernet adapters.

✔ **Firewalls:** A *firewall* is a system that controls access to your private network from any outside network (in this case, the Internet) and to control access from your private network to the outside world. To keep the bad guys out, Red Hat Linux provides protection by giving you the tools to build your own firewall. Red Hat Linux is flexible in this regard, and many software packages are available, including the popular and simple-to-use `netfilter/iptables` filtering software, which is included on the accompanying CD-ROMs. Building a firewall is covered in Chapter 8.

This list is just a sample of the networky things you can do with Red Hat Linux. We describe many of them in this book, but it takes much more exploration to find them all!

Chapter 2

Getting Ready for Red Hat Linux

. . . .

In This Chapter

▶ Preparing to install Red Hat Linux

▶ Resizing Windows 9*x* and Windows Me FAT partitions

▶ Defragmenting your hard drive

▶ Resizing Windows NT, Windows 2000, and Windows XP NTFS partitions

. . . .

*A*ll major personal computer (PC) manufacturers now install Microsoft Windows on their machines by default. However, you can still purchase computers without Windows from local, nonbrand stores.

What does that mean? Basically, you can skip this chapter if you have a computer with no preinstalled operating system. You can also skip this chapter if you have a Windows computer and are willing to completely reformat your hard disk, permanently erasing it contents. Finally, some Windows computers include secondary Windows partitions that you can use on which to install Linux.

A *partition* is a portion of a disk drive used to organize files and directories. For example, the famous Windows C: drive is installed on its own partition. A partition can use all or part of a disk. Most systems use one large partition that hogs up an entire hard drive.

Otherwise, you have to make accommodations for Red Hat Linux to live alongside Windows. But Linux is an easygoing fellow who gets along well with others. You can install Red Hat Linux on the same hard drive with Windows. This type of configuration is a *dual boot system,* meaning that you choose which operating system to use when you power up, or boot, your computer.

This chapter shows you how to properly tenderize and marinate your hard drive so that Linux and Windows can live in harmony. It's going to be a love-fest.

Preparing Your Hard Drive for Red Hat Linux

Before you install Red Hat Linux alongside Windows, you need to get your hard drive ready. This list provides an overview of the disk preparation process:

1. **Put on a red fedora.**

2. **Back up your computer.**

   The processes we describe in this chapter should not affect your existing Windows installation. However, you can never be too safe in dealing with your precious files, so you should back them up. It's beyond the scope of this book to describe how to back up a Windows computer, so we leave it up to you to get it done. Several good Windows products are available for making backups. One good product that both backs up and repartitions your computer is Norton Ghost 2002. A side benefit of Ghost is that you can use it to repartition your hard drive.

3. **Determine how your Windows computer's hard drive is formatted.**

   Windows uses two types of formatting: FAT (File Access Table) and NTFS (NT File System). FAT is older and less advanced than NTFS. However, free tools are available for resizing FAT-based disks to make room for Linux. You have to purchase commercial software to repartition NTFS systems.

4. **Defragment your disk.**

   All resizing programs require you to defragment your disk before proceeding. Over time, the bits and bytes that comprise your files tend to get scattered around your hard drive. Resizing may not work or may even cause problems if your computer has too much fragmentation.

5. **Repartition your computer's hard drive to make room to install Red Hat Linux if you want to install it alongside Windows (or another operating system).**

   You can use either destructive or nondestructive resizing to make room for Linux. *Destructive* resizing wipes everything off your hard drive and starts fresh. *Nondestructive* resizing uses Windows utilities to dynamically shrink the existing partition and then uses the freed space to make a new Linux partition.

The Open Source — FIPS (First nondestructive Interactive Partition Splitting) program is supplied with the full Red Hat Linux distribution to repartition FAT disks. You need to use commercial utilities, like PartitionMagic or Norton Ghost, to repartition NTFS disks; both these programs also work on FAT systems.

Am I Fat or Just NTFS?

Determining your partition type is straightforward. These instructions describe how to use the tools provided by Windows (Windows 9*x*, Windows Me, Windows NT, Windows 2000, and Windows XP) to show the partition type.

Follow these instructions on all Windows systems:

1. **Start your computer.**

2. **Open the My Computer icon.**

3. **Right-click the C:\ drive icon.**

4. **Click the Properties button. You should see information displayed about the partition, as shown in Figure 2-1.**

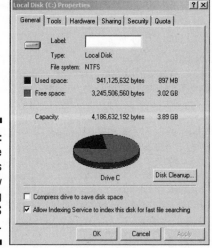

Figure 2-1:
The Properties window showing an NTFS partition.

Figure 2-1 shows the information about drive C:\ (partition). The upper-middle part of the figure shows, in this case, that the partition uses the FAT.

The following section describes how to defragment both FAT and NTFS partitions.

Defragmenting Your Hard Drive

Defragmenting consolidates all files on your hard drive into contiguous portions. This task is necessary because Windows is a slob as operating systems go, scattering data all over the hard drive rather than in any sort of logical order.

These steps show how to defragment your Windows partition:

1. **Close all programs and windows on your computer, leaving just the desktop and icon bar.**

2. **Double-click the My Computer icon on the desktop.**

3. **Select your C: drive by clicking it and then choose File➪ Properties➪Tools.**

4. **Click the Defragment Now button.**

   The defragmentation program looks at the drive to determine whether it needs defragmentation.

   You may get a message telling you that you don't need to defragment because your hard drive is not very fragmented; don't believe it. Under ordinary circumstances, this statement may be true. But resizing isn't an ordinary occurrence; defragmenting your hard drive is necessary because you're going to move the end of the partition file system and make the partition smaller, erasing any data outside that barrier.

5. **Click Start.**

The defragmentation window appears and the defrag process begins. Defragmenting can take a long time, depending on the size of your hard drive and the number of errors to be corrected.

By clicking the Show Details button, you can scroll up and down the large window to watch the defragmentation process in action, as shown in Figure 2-2.

The colored blocks represent programs and data, and the white space represents free space on your hard drive that FIPS can allocate to the Linux file system. The movement of the blocks around the screen shows that the data is being moved forward on the drive. Expect to see white space appear toward the bottom of the window, which represents the end of your drive. At the end of the defragmentation process, no colored blocks appear at the bottom of the window, and all the blocks are compressed toward the top of the window. After what may seem like quite a long time, defragmentation finishes. All useful blocks of information are now at the beginning of the drive, making it ready for the resizing program.

These instructions describe how to defragment your Windows NT, Windows 2000, or Windows XP (NTFS) computer:

1. **Close all programs and windows on your computer.**

2. **Click Start➪Programs➪Accessories➪System Tools➪Disk defragmenter.**

3. **Select the partition to defragment. Most computers use a single partition labeled C:\ (the ubiquitous "C drive"). Click the Defragment
   button and the process starts. Figures 2-2 and 2-3 show a typical
   defragmentation process for a FAT and NTFS partition, respectively.**

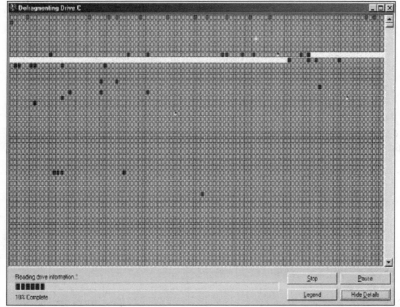

Figure 2-2:
Defrag-
menting
a FAT
partition.

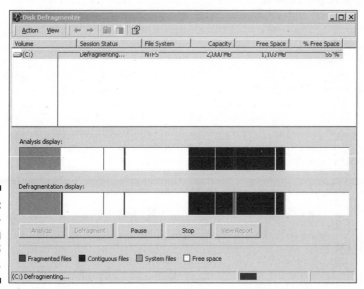

Figure 2-3:
Defrag-
menting
an NTFS
partition.

Move Over, Windows — Here Comes Linux

You need to make room for Linux. This section describes how to repartition your Windows computer to make the necessary room. You can use the Open Source FIPS program to repartition FAT partitions. FIPS doesn't work on NTFS partitions, so you need to purchase a commercial tool. The next section is dedicated to using FIPS on FAT. The subsequent section describes using the commercial PartitionMagic program.

We strongly suggest backing up your entire computer before proceeding. If that is impractical or impossible, you should back up all-important files. You can generally reinstall your operating system and applications from your systems discs, but you can't do that for your data. You don't want to lose any data or programs that you worked hard to create. Refer to your system's owners' manual to find out how to back up your system and how to restore the data if necessary.

Resizing Windows 9x and Windows Me FAT partitions with FIPS

FIPS resizes your FAT-based Windows partitions. Newer versions of Windows (some versions of Windows 95, Windows 98, and Windows Me) use a 32-bit file allocation table (called FAT32) and drive management tools that provide for single-drive configurations larger than 2GB. Older versions of Windows 95 use a 16-bit FAT (called FAT16, oddly enough); to use more space over and above 2GB, the hard drive has to be partitioned into logical drives of 2GB or less. Newer computers have hard drives much larger than the old 2GB limit. If the drive is repartitioned, the large drive management system is disabled, and DOS and Windows partitions are once again limited to 2GB.

You need to use the ancient MS-DOS (Microsoft Disk Operating System) operating system — yes, one way or another, all of Windows-dom owes its existence to MS-DOS. The following instructions describe how to create an MS-DOS boot floppy disk, which you use to run FIPS:

1. **Boot your Windows 9x or Me computer.**

2. **Insert a floppy disk and click the My Computer icon.**

Be aware that these instructions permanently erase all information from the disk.

3. **Right-click the 3-1/2 Floppy (A:) icon and choose the Format option.**

4. **The Format A:\ window appears.**

   Click the Make a bootable disk option and then click the Start button.

5. **Insert CD1 in the CD-ROM drive.**

6. **Copy the fips.exe program from the** \dosutils\fips20 **directory on CD1 to the floppy disk.**

   The fips.exe program in the dosutils\fips20 directory works with the FAT32 file partitions. Windows 98, Me and newer versions of Windows 95 use FAT32.

   You need to use the FAT16 version of fips.exe for early versions of Windows 95. That version is stored in the \dosutils\fips15c directory.

   You need to reboot your Windows computer into MS-DOS mode (in this nongraphical mode, you need to type in commands at the *DOS prompt*. Because you're booting from the floppy disk you just made, the DOS prompt looks like this: A:\.

These instructions describe how to use FIPS to repartition your Windows FAT partition:

1. **Reboot your computer from the floppy disk.**

   The computer restarts in MS-DOS mode.

   If your computer can't boot into MS-DOS mode, you have one other option: Obtain an MS-DOS boot floppy (one that contains CD-ROM drivers) and boot from it; the CD-ROM drivers are necessary because you have to access the fips program on CD1.

2. **Type** cd a: **at the DOS prompt and press Enter.**

3. **Type** fips **at the prompt and press Enter.**

   Some messages appear and flash by, but you can ignore them all except the last one, which asks you to press any key.

4. **When you see the** Press any key **message, do so.**

   You see all existing partitions on the hard drive.

5. **When you see the** Press any key **message, do so again.**

   You're getting pretty good at this! A description of the drive and a series of messages flash by. Then FIPS finds the free space in the first partition.

6. **When you're asked whether you want to make a backup copy of sectors, press** y **for yes.**

   The screen asks whether a floppy disk is in Drive A.

7. **Place a formatted floppy disk in Drive A and press** y.

   A message similar to `Writing file a:\rootboot.000` appears, followed by other messages and then the message `Use cursor key to choose the cylinder, enter to continue`.

   Three columns appear on the screen: Old Partition, Cylinder, and New Partition. The Old Partition number is the number of megabytes in the main partition of your hard drive. The New Partition number is the number of megabytes in the new partition that you're making for the Red Hat Linux operating system.

8. **Use the left- and right-arrow keys to change the numbers in the Old Partition and New Partition fields to create the space you need for both the Windows operating system and Linux (see Figure 2-4).**

   See Chapter 3 for installation requirements.

Figure 2-4: The FIPS program carves up a hard drive.

9. **When you have the correct amount of hard drive space in each field, press the Enter key.**

   The partition table is displayed again, showing you the new partition that has been created for the Linux operating system. This new partition is probably partition 2; your C: drive is probably partition 1.

   You also see a message at the bottom of the screen asking whether you want to continue or make changes.

10. **If you're satisfied with the size of your partitions, press** c **to continue (if you** *aren't* **satisfied, press** r**, which takes you back a couple of steps).**

    Many more messages about your hard drive flash by. A message then appears, stating that the system is ready to write the new partition scheme to disk and asking whether you want to proceed.

11. **Press** y **to make FIPS write the new partition information to the hard drive.**

    The partitioning process begins.

    If you press **n**, FIPS exits without changing anything on your hard drive, leaving your hard drive exactly the way it was after you defragmented it.

12. **To test that nondestructive partitioning worked properly, remove the boot floppy disk and reboot your system by pressing Ctrl+Alt+Delete.**

13. **When Windows starts, run ScanDisk by clicking the Start button and choosing Programs**➪**Accessories**➪**System Tools**➪**ScanDisk.**

    ScanDisk indicates whether you have all the files and folders you started with and whether anything was lost. Even if everything is found to be okay, consider keeping any backup files around for a while, to be on the safe side.

Now you're ready to install Red Hat Linux 9, which we explain how to do in Chapter 3. The Red Hat Linux installation process can use the newly created space to create its own partitions. Chapter 3 describes how to use the new space without stepping on the existing Windows partition.

Resizing Windows NT, Windows 2000, and Windows XP NTFS partitions with a little PartitionMagic

Resizing NTFS requires the use of commercial tools, such as Norton Ghost (www.norton.com) or PartitionMagic (www.powerquest.com). PartitionMagic works by shrinking the Windows partition, leaving free space for a new partition. Ghost 2002, however, doesn't dynamically modify your existing NTFS file system. Instead, it backs up your existing Windows disk, erases the current disk partitions, and then creates new partitions on which it writes the Windows image back to the new partition. Ghost requires a storage device on which to save the snapshot image. If your Windows installation is relatively small (less than 2GB), you may be able to use a Jaz drive or Zip drive as a storage device. However, you have to use a second hard drive, tape backup, or other backup mechanism for larger installations.

We describe how to use PartitionMagic in this section. Norton Ghost is an excellent tool, but is beyond the scope of this book because we can't assume that you have the resources to use it. (You need backup media large enough to store your entire Windows installation.) PartitionMagic doesn't give you the warm fuzzies of getting a backup along with your resizing, but it still works well. We have used it a number of times with good results.

These steps describe how to install PartitionMagic:

1. **Get out your credit card and go to your friendly computer store and buy PartitionMagic 8 or higher; or, alternatively, go to your friendly Internet store, and so on.**

   This statement is uncomfortable to make in a book devoted to the free, Open Source Linux operating system. However, the name of the game is getting the job done, and in this case we have no noncommercial alternative. So until an Open Source NTFS resizing utility breaks out into the light, go ahead and make the purchase.

   Three NTFS variations are available. Older Windows $9x$ systems used one type, Windows NT used another, and the third version is used by current Windows versions. You must use PartitionMagic 8, the current version, because it's capable of recognizing and handling all three NTFS versions.

2. **Start the PartitionMagic installation by inserting the disc into your CD-ROM drive.**

3. **Click the PartitionMagic button when the installation window opens.**

4. **Click the Install option when the subsequent screen opens.**

5. **An installation wizard starts. Answer the questions depending on how your computer is configured.**

   In general, you should be able to use the default options.

6. **Create a rescue disk. The installation wizard guides you through the process.**

After you install PartitionMagic, you can use it to repartition your drive. The following instructions show how to select an existing partition, shrink it, and then create a second one from the new space:

1. **Start PartitionMagic, and you see a screen like the one shown in Figure 2-5.**

2. **Click the partition you want to reallocate.**

3. **Click the Create a new partition option in the upper-left corner of the screen.**

   The Create New Partition window opens, as shown in Figure 2-6. This wizard guides you through the process of shrinking the existing partition and creating a second one from the new space.

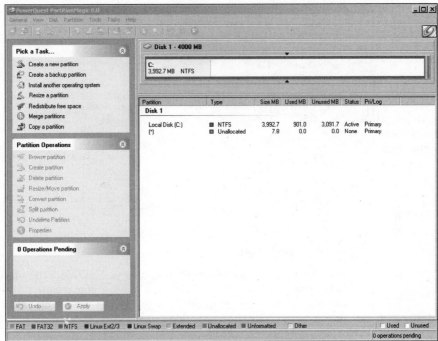

Figure 2-5:
The initial
Partition-
Magic
screen.

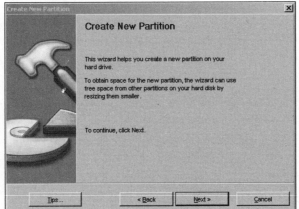

Figure 2-6:
The Create
New
Partition
window.

4. Click the Next button.

The Where to Create window opens. You need to tell PartitionMagic
which partition to repartition. In this example, we assume that you have
the typical single-partition Windows computer (the ubiquitous C: drive),
as shown in Figure 2-7.

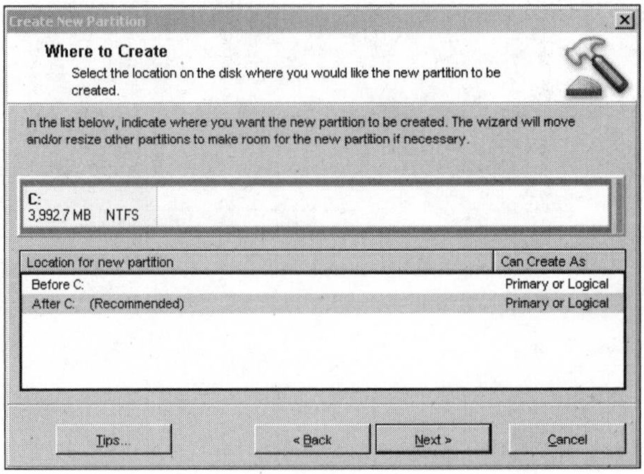

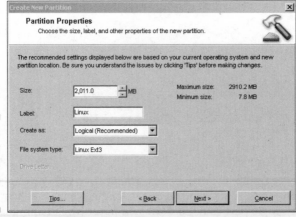

Figure 2-7:
The Where
to Create
window.

5. Click the Next button.

The Partition Properties window allows you to select the options for your new partition. Figure 2-8 shows the settings we have entered for our new partition (this example is 2GB, has a `linux` label, is a logical partition, and uses the `ext3` file system):

- **Size:** The size of the partition depends on the size of your disk.

- **Label:** The label is optional and arbitrary. Use any description you want.

- **Create as:** You have two options: Logical and Primary. PC drives can have as many as four primary partitions and any number of logical ones.

Figure 2-8:
The
Partition
Properties
window.

6. **Click the Next button and the Confirm Choices window opens, as shown in Figure 2-9.**

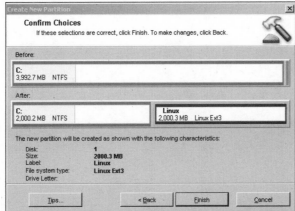

Figure 2-9: The Confirm Choices window.

7. **PartitionMagic wants you to be sure about the new partitions you're about to create and summarizes the potential new configuration. Inspect the information and click the Finish button if you're satisfied with the selection.**

   If you don't want to repartition with the current choices, click the Back button to return to the preceding window, where you make new choices.

8. **After you click the Finish button, the new partition-to-be is displayed in the main window. However, your disk isn't repartitioned until you click the Apply button in the lower-left corner of the PartitionMagic window.**

   Click the Apply button, and a final confirmation window opens.

9. **Click the OK button in the confirmation window, and your disk is repartitioned.**

   The new partitions aren't put into place until you reboot your computer.

10. **Reboot your computer.**

   PartitionMagic applies the changes to make the new partition while your computer boots.

Chapter 3

Ready, Set, Install!

*I*nstalling Red Hat Linux isn't rocket science — it's more like astrophysics. No, no — just kidding. Don't run — just relax, sit down, grab your favorite drink, and contemplate the fun you'll have installing Red Hat Linux. After you're done, you'll have a powerful computer that's capable of performing most, if not all, of your daily computing chores — all for the cost of this book! That's pretty amazing when you think about it: For a few dollars, you get the same amount of operating power that cost megabucks just a few years ago.

This chapter walks you through the process of using the Workstation installation of Red Hat Linux. (You can use the Personal Desktop installation type, but you may have to manually install the software development tools later on.)

Before getting started, you should know that you can easily change your configuration choices. If you realize that you have made a mistake, you can click the Back button to retrace your steps and redo your choices. And, if you ever want to stop the installation process, you can simply reboot your computer.

The point of no return comes at the end of the process, when the configuration is written to your hard drive (see the later section "Installation Stage 5: The Point of No Return!") and the installation software starts to partition your hard drive and write Red Hat Linux to it. If you stop at that point, you need to reinstall an operating system before you can use the computer again.

For installation masochists and text snobs only

You can run the Red Hat Linux installation system from either a graphical or text-based interface. If the installation process successfully detects your graphics hardware, the graphical method is selected automatically, and that's what we discuss in this chapter. In addition to the ease of using a mouse to point and click, the graphical method groups similar configuration choices. For example, the keyboard and mouse selections are presented within one window, not two, as in the text-based installation.

You may have to use the text-based installation, for these reasons:

✔ Your mother told you never to point and click.

✔ The Red Hat Linux installation system can't use your graphics adapter. You figure this out when the graphical installation window doesn't appear, but a text-based window does appear; with the text-based system, you use the keyboard to enter information and the cursor (arrow) keys to move from step to step. This doesn't happen often any more because the folks at Red Hat have done their homework and refined the installation process, but your computer may prove to be the exception.

You can select the text-based installation method by typing **text** at the boot: prompt.

Choosing an Installation Type

Red Hat provides several installation types to choose from. Although we think that you can probably get away with having less space on your system, we decided to give you the minimum system requirements Red Hat suggests for each installation option:

✔ **Server:** Creates an operating system environment for computers that provide services such as hosting Web pages. This installation requires 1.3GB of free space if you want only minimal bells and whistles, at least 1.4GB of free space if you want to install all the bells and whistles except X, and at least 2.1GB to install all the bells and all the whistles and throw in the Acme Bell and Whistle Factory (which includes both GNOME and KDE).

✔ **Custom:** Installs a minimum base of software and requires you to select additional services, utilities, and applications. You need 350MB of free space for a minimal installation and at least 3.7GB of free space if you want to install all the bells and whistles.

✔ **Upgrade:** Updates the Red Hat Linux software that's already installed on a computer but leaves all existing settings, users, and data alone.

✔ **Personal Desktop:** Installs Red Hat Linux but excludes the software development tools. (You have many of the bells and whistles, but you may not be able to use some applications.) If you install either GNOME or KDE, you need at least 1.7GB of free space. If you want both, you need 1.8GB.

✔ **Workstation:** Creates an operating system environment for computers and laptops used as workstations for personal use. This version includes the software development tools you need to run certain applications. If you install either GNOME or KDE, you need at least 2.1GB of free space. To install both, you need at least 2.2GB.

The primary difference between the Workstation and Personal Desktop installation types is that Workstation installs software development tools and Personal Desktop doesn't. We encourage you to use the Workstation installation option because you need some of the software development tools to configure many of the applications described in this book.

Both the Workstation and Personal Desktop installation types automate otherwise horrifically complicated decisions that no sane person would want to haggle with, such as how to partition your hard drive and select software. The installation includes the GNOME graphical user interface (GUI) and all the tools that an average computer user (that's you) needs to survive. If you want software that the installation doesn't provide, you can always add packages later.

Installation Stage 1: Starting the Installation

Before you install Red Hat Linux, you need to boot or reboot your computer with the CD that comes with this book in your CD-ROM drive. The instructions in this section describe how to start installing Red Hat Linux on your computer.

This section gets you started with the Red Hat Linux installation process. Use these initial steps to start the installation and perform some basic configuration:

1. **Insert CD1 that came with this book (or a boot floppy disk if you're using one) and boot or reboot your computer.**

   After your computer thinks for a while, the first installation screen appears, displaying a welcome message, some options, and the `boot`: prompt.

Checking your discs

Red Hat provides a validation mechanism for checking its CDs. Red Hat inserts numeric keys into its CDs to help verify that they aren't corrupted. If you enter **linux mediacheck** at the `boot:` prompt, the installation process starts up and shows the CD Found window. Follow these steps to verify that your CDs are in working order.

1. **Select the OK option by pressing the Enter key if you want to verify that your CD is okay.**

   If you have already verified your media, perhaps you have already checked them during a previous installation —you can select the Skip option to return to the Red Hat installation process without checking the media.

   The Media Check window opens.

2. **If you're installing Red Hat Linux from a set of CDs you have never tested, select the Test option and the CD test starts.**

Alternatively, select the Eject option, insert another CD, and select Test to inspect the new CD.

The media check system displays a progress meter and then shows the results when it's finished.

3. **If the CD is okay, select Continue.**

   The current CD is ejected, and you can insert the second CD or choose to continue with the Red Hat installation process.

   If the CD doesn't pass the test, you shouldn't use it. You should buy another copy of this book. No, no — just kidding. Contact the Wiley Media Development department at MediaDev@wiley.com to find out how to get a replacement CD.

4. **Repeat Steps 3 and 4 for CD2. When you finish testing the second CD, select Continue to start installing Red Hat Linux.**

2. **Press Enter.**

   A series of messages scrolls by, indicating the hardware that the Red Hat Linux kernel detects on your computer. Most of the time, particularly with newer systems, Red Hat Linux detects all the basic hardware, and then a CD Found window appears. If you want to check your CDs, refer to the nearby "Checking your discs" sidebar.

3. **When Red Hat Linux has detected your hardware, the Red Hat installation process starts and the Welcome message is displayed onscreen. Click the Next button to proceed to the next window.**

   You can view information about your Red Hat installation by clicking the Release Notes button, in the lower-left corner of the screen.

   After the Welcome message screen disappears, the Language Selection window appears.

4. **Select a language and click Next.**

   Choose the language you speak or, if you're feeling adventurous, one that you don't (not recommended).

   The Keyboard Configuration window appears.

5. **Select the keyboard configuration and then click Next.**

   The Mouse Configuration window appears.

6. **Select your mouse (squeak!) and click Next.**

   Red Hat generally automatically detects your mouse. However, in case Red Hat fails to find your mouse, you can select your mouse manually from the slew of mice shown. If you have a PS/2 mouse, all you have to do is select the manufacturer and number of buttons. If you have the older style of mouse that connects via a serial port, you have to select the manufacturer, number of buttons, and the serial port to which it's connected; you have only four serial ports to select from, and in many cases it's either ttyS0 or ttyS1.

   If you have a two-button mouse (either serial or PS/2), you can choose to have it emulate three buttons by clicking the Emulate 3 Buttons option. You emulate the third (middle) button by pressing both mouse buttons at one time.

7. **Click Next.**

   The Installation Type window appears. (However, if you have already installed Linux on your computer, you're asked whether you want to upgrade or make a fresh installation. Go ahead and upgrade if you want; your current software is updated to newer versions. However, this book is oriented toward installing Red Hat Linux for the first time.)

See the following section, "Installation Stage 2: Slicing and Dicing the Pie," to choose an installation option, and then continue.

Installation Stage 2: Slicing and Dicing the Pie

You must decide where on your hard disk to install Red Hat Linux, a process called disk partitioning. *Disk partitioning* divides a disk into multiple sections, or slices. Red Hat Linux is then installed on the partitions, typically three to seven partitions.

Red Hat provides automatic and manual methods for creating disk partitions. We use the Red Hat automatic method because it's easy to use. The automatic method erases any existing Red Hat Linux partitions, but leaves alone any existing Windows partitions. If you don't have any existing Red Hat partitions or unused space on your disk, you have to make some free space. Refer to Chapter 2 for instructions on shrinking Windows partitions to make space for Linux.

Linux disk partitions are analogous to Windows disk partitions. The well-known C: drive is placed on a disk partition. The Linux equivalent is the root (/) partition. The two operating systems use different terminology, and the analogy eventually ends, although the concept is the same.

Follow these steps to continue the installation:

1. **Select the Workstation option in the Installation Type window and click the Next button.**

   The Disk Partitioning Setup window appears, as shown in Figure 3-1. The Red Hat Linux installation system must partition your hard drive in order to install its software. Partitions divide a hard drive into one or more parts. The divisions are used to organize the software and data (user files, for example) that comprise the operating system.

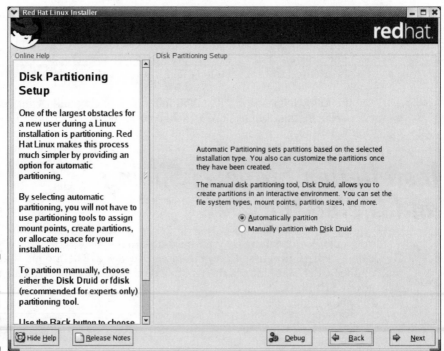

Figure 3-1: The Disk Partitioning Setup window.

Red Hat provides two partitioning methods: automatic and manual using the Red Hat Disk Druid. Using Disk Druid requires you to make several decisions to select your disk partitions, so we use the automatic method, which is simpler to use. The automatic method is the easier to use, and we recommend it unless you're feeling ambitious and want to experiment or have the experience of manually partitioning your hard drive.

2. **Select the Automatically Partition option.**

The Automatic Partitioning window appears, as shown in Figure 3-2. You have three options:

- **Remove all Linux partitions on this system:** This option leaves any Windows partitions (FAT, VFAT, and NTFS) unmodified while erasing any existing Linux partitions. Use this option if you're reinstalling Red Hat Linux (in either a dual boot or solo configuration).

- **Remove all partitions on this system:** This option is the most dangerous one because it erases everything on your hard disk. Use this option only if you're absolutely sure that you don't have, or don't want to save, anything on your disk. Your new Red Hat Linux installation is the only operating system on the hard disk if you use this option.

- **Keep all partitions and use existing free space:** Use this option if you used the nondestructive repartitioning (using FIPS, Norton Ghost, or PartitionMagic, for example) described in Chapter 2 to shrink your Windows partition.

You can use commercial products, like Norton Ghost 2002, to shrink NTFS partitions. Shrinking a Windows partition frees up disk space that you can use to install Red Hat Linux. Using this option creates a dual boot configuration if Windows already exists on your computer.

Never use the Remove All Partitions on This System option unless you want to erase everything on your disk. Use extreme caution because this action destroys all installed operating systems (Windows and Red Hat Linux) and data. You may use this option, for example, if your computer came with Windows preinstalled and you want to convert it to a Red Hat Linux–only workstation.

Use the Keep All Partitions and Use Existing Free Space option if you want to install Red Hat Linux on extra, unused space on your hard drive (for example, if you have shrunk an existing Windows FAT or NTFS partition, as described in Chapter 2).

3. **Select the partitioning option most appropriate for you.**

If you repartitioned your Windows disk in Chapter 2 to make room for Linux, click the Keep All Partitions and Use Existing Free Space button. The Red Hat Linux installation system uses the extra space on the disk to install.

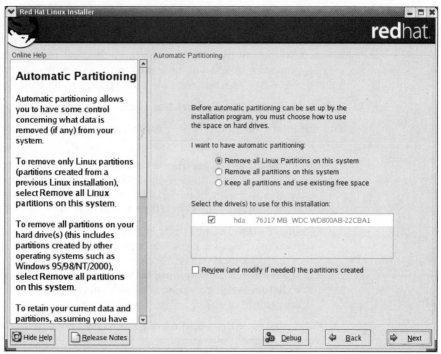

Figure 3-2:
The
Automatic
Partitioning
window.

Optionally, select the Remove All Linux Partitions on This System button if you're installing Linux over an old Linux installation.

Optionally, if you want to completely erase any existing operating system and start fresh with Red Hat Linux, select the Remove All Partitions on This System button along with all programs and data on the disk.

Optionally, click the option labeled Review (and modify if needed) the partitions created. Using this option forces the installation process (see Step 5) to display the partitions that will be created.

4. **The Warning dialog box opens.**

   Click the Yes button to continue with the installation. Click the No button to return to the Automatic Partitioning window in Step 3.

5. **(Optional) The Partitioning window, as shown in Figure 3-3, appears if you selected in Step 3 the option labeled Review (and modify if needed) the partitions created.**

6. **Review the three partitions and modify them if needed.**

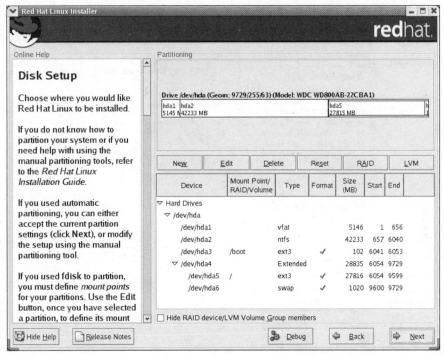

Figure 3-3:
The Disk
Setup
window
displays the
partitions to
be created.

The Partitioning window shows you how the Red Hat installation process will divide the available space on your hard drive into three partitions. (The available space is determined by the option you selected in Step 2.) The partitions created are root (/), boot (/boot), and swap. (swap is used internally by Red Hat Linux and, unlike the other partitions, isn't accessible by you.)

At this point, you can click the Edit, Delete, and Add options if you want to modify the default disk partitions. You should modify the default partitions only if you're an experienced Unix or Linux user and understand the concept of using multiple partitions. We recommend that unless you feel really lucky or are very experienced, you let Red Hat do the work here.

7. **Click the Next button.**

The Boot Loader Configuration window, as shown in Figure 3-4, appears. The boot loader helps start your operating system when you start your computer; if you create a dual boot computer, the boot loader allows you to select one operating system or another. The standard Red Hat Linux boot loader is GRUB, a powerful system that can do more than just load an operating system. However, the GRUB default options should be all you need (and its advanced features are beyond the scope of this book to describe), so click the Next button.

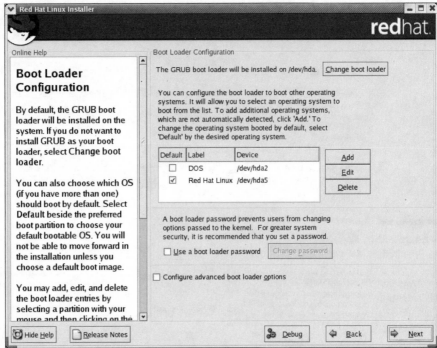

Figure 3-4:
The Boot
Loader
Configura-
tion
window.

If your computer has an NIC (network interface card), Red Hat detects it and the Network Configuration window appears, as shown in Figure 3-5. You should proceed to Step 1 in the next section and configure your network. However, if you don't have an Ethernet NIC, or are using a wireless device that Red Hat doesn't detect, the installation process skips the network configuration and continues at Step 7 in the following section, "Installation Stage 3: Configuring your Network."

Confidential for Windows users

If you're installing Red Hat Linux in a dual boot configuration with Windows NT, Windows 2000, or Windows XP, your NT boot record is temporarily overwritten, meaning that you can't boot Windows NT. Don't panic: Your NT partition isn't erased — it has just been rendered unbootable. (An NT *boot record* is what enables a Windows NT system to start automatically when you start your computer.)

You can install Red Hat Linux without overwriting the NT boot partition if you select the Configure Advanced Boot Loader Options button (refer to Figure 3-4). When you click the Next button, the Advanced Boot Loader Configuration window opens. Select the First Sector of Boot Partition option and then click the Next button. Your Windows boot configuration continues to operate as before.

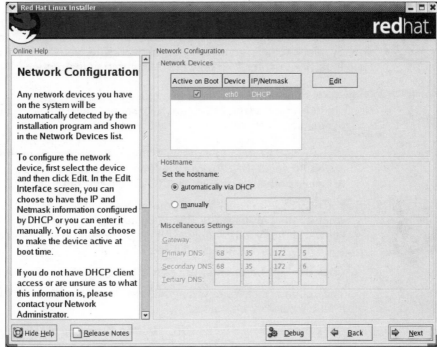

Figure 3-5:
The
Network
Configura-
tion
window.

In the following section, we show you how to configure your network for Red Hat Linux use. If you don't have a network or just don't want to haggle with it right now, you may want to read the following section anyway because it makes your life easier if your decide to create a network sometime in the future. If you're still not interested, click Next and skip to the section after that, "Installation Stage 4: Configuring Your System."

Installation Stage 3: Configuring Your Network

If you're ready to configure your network and your computer has an Ethernet or Wi-Fi (a wireless network interface using the 802-11b standard) adapter, enter the appropriate information, as described in the following steps. If you have a network adapter but don't have a network to connect to, you should still enter a host name in Step 3. Entering a host name makes life easier down the line if and when you eventually connect to a network.

Sometimes the installation process doesn't detect a network device and skips the steps described in this section. If that happens, continue with the installation as described in the following section, "Installation Stage 4: Configuring your System." You can configure your network after you finish installing Red Hat Linux. See Chapter 7 for network configuration instructions.

If you pick up from the end of the preceding section, the Network Configuration window appears (refer to Figure 3-5). Follow these steps to configure your system for a network:

1. **If you're connecting to a network that uses the Dynamic Host Configuration Protocol (DHCP), you don't have to do anything more to configure your network connection. Click the Next button and skip to Step 8.**

   You may need to consult with your LAN's administrator to find out whether the LAN uses DHCP. If you constructed your own LAN and don't know whether you're running DHCP, you're not. Go to Chapter 15 to learn how to install and configure a DHCP server.

2. **Click the Edit button and the Edit Interface eth0 window opens.**

   The Edit Interface window may refer to eth1 rather than eth0 if you have multiple network interfaces.

3. **Click the Configure Using DHCP button (to toggle off DHCP) and enter your IP address and netmask in the subwindow.**

   Click the OK button.

   The following list briefly explains IP addresses and netmasks:

   • **IP address:** This address is the numeric network address of your Red Hat Linux computer and is the address by which your computer is known on your local network and — in many cases — the Internet. If you haven't registered your private network's address space with InterNIC (the organization in charge of distributing IP addresses), you can use the public address space that goes from 192.168.1.1 to 192.168.254.254.

   If you're connecting to an existing LAN, consult the administrator to get an IP address that isn't already being used. You have to keep track of unused IP addresses if you're running your own LAN.

   • **Netmask:** Private networks based on the Internet Protocol (IP) are divided into subnetworks. The netmask determines how the network is divided. For IP addresses, such as the example in the preceding bullet (192.168.1.1), the most common netmask is 255.255.255.0.

4. **Click the Manual button under the Hostname section of the window. Type your computer's host name, including the network (domain) name in the Hostname text box.**

   For example, if you want to name your computer cancun and your network name is paunchy.net, you type **cancun.paunchy.net**.

TIP

If you don't give your computer a name and domain name during the network configuration process, it's referred to as `localhost.local domain`. Otherwise, the Welcome screen refers to whatever name you gave it. For example, in the preceding example, you would see `Welcome to cancun.paunchy.net`.

5. **Enter your gateway and primary DNS (and, optionally, the secondary and tertiary DNS) IP addresses in the appropriate text boxes in the Miscellaneous section at the bottom of the screen.**

   This list describes what these parameters do:

   - **Gateway:** This is the numeric IP address of the computer that connects your private network to the Internet (or another private network). Red Hat Linux uses the address of `192.168.1.254` by default. You can accept this address, but leaving it blank is a better option, unless that address is really your gateway. Chapters 5, 6 and 7 describe how to configure your Linux computer to connect to the Internet via a telephone, broadband (DSL, cable) and existing LAN connections respectively. If you do that, setting a default route now can interfere with your connection.

   - **Primary DNS:** The Internet Protocol uses the Domain Name Service (DNS) system to convert names such as `www.redhat.com` into numeric IPs. A computer that acts as a DNS server is a *name server*. We suggest leaving this box blank, however, unless you're on a private network with a name server or will be connected to the Internet (your ISP supplies a DNS). When you designate a nonexistent name server, many networking programs work very slowly as they wait in vain for the absent server.

   - **Secondary and tertiary DNS:** The secondary and tertiary DNS backup the primary DNS server. If your computer can't find the primary DNS server, it might find the secondary. If not, it should find the tertiary. Best of luck!

6. **If you're connecting to the Internet directly using a modem (regular dialup, DSL, or cable), leave the Gateway address blank. Otherwise, if your computer is connected to a LAN with Internet access, enter the Internet gateway's address in the Gateway text box.**

   If you're connecting to someone else's LAN — if you're building a Red Hat Linux computer at work, for example — you should obtain this address from your system administrator. If you're connecting to your own LAN at home, consult yourself because you're probably the administrator.

7. **When you complete the Network Configuration form, click the Next button to continue.**

8. **Select the Medium Firewall option (the default) and click the Next button.**

Red Hat creates for your computer a firewall designed for use by a workstation. The firewall is adequate and provides a reasonable amount of protection.

However, we show you how to construct a better — safer and simpler — firewall in Chapter 8.

The next section shows you how to finish the configuration of your Red Hat Linux workstation.

Installation Stage 4: Configuring Your Options

This section covers basic configuration for your Red Hat Linux computer. We describe how to set your time zone and the root user password. You also can choose to install extra software in addition to the default packages. These steps describe how to perform these basic tasks:

1. **The Additional Language Support window opens. This window gives you extra linguistic options. Make your selection (although almost anyone in the United States won't have to make a selection) and click the Next button.**

   The Time Zone Selection window appears.

2. **To select your time zone, click the dot representing a city closest to where you live.**

   You can use the map to point and click your way to your time zone bliss. When you click one of the thousand points of light, the represented city and its time zone appear in the subwindow below the map. You can also click the slider bar at the bottom of the screen to locate the name of your city or time zone. After you find it, click the text to select your time zone.

3. **Click Next.**

   The Set Root Password window appears.

4. **Type your root password in both the Root Password and Confirm text boxes.**

   The password is for the root user, also known as the *superuser,* who has access to the entire system and can do almost anything — good and bad.

   The root user is the only user who can access all the resources on your computer. All files, processes, and devices are controlled by root. You should log in as the root user only to perform system maintenance or administrative tasks. To avoid making unwanted changes or deletions to these important files, you should normally log in as a regular (non-root) user. Go to Step 2 in the section "Post Installation: Using the Setup Agent," later in this chapter, to learn how to add a user.

   You have to type the password two times to make sure that you typed it correctly. The password appears onscreen as asterisks as you type it.

"Holy breach of security, Batman!" You wouldn't want someone to be able to look over your shoulder and get your password, would you?

5. Click Next.

The Workstation Defaults window opens and displays a summary of the important software that will be installed. (A summary for whatever installation type you're using is displayed if you're not using the Workstation type.) You're given the choice of selecting either the Accept the current package list (the default) or the Customize the set of packages to be installed buttons.

We use in this book the default package list for the Workstation installation type.

If you select the Customize the Set of Packages to be Installed button, the Package Group Selection window opens. You can select additional packages to be installed individually or by group. For example, if you want to install the KDE environment, simply click the radio button next to the KDE Desktop Environment menu and all the necessary packages will be selected. Select individual packages by clicking the Select individual packages radio button. After you make you selection, click the Next button and proceed to Step 6.

6. Make your selection and click the Next button.

The About to Install Window appears.

Introducing password etiquette

Your password must be at least six characters long, but you should use at least eight characters: The more characters you use, the harder the password is to break. If you're concerned about security, we recommend that you use a combination of uppercase and lowercase letters, symbols, and numbers to make your password as difficult as possible to compromise. In addition, don't choose anything you can find in a dictionary or names or items that are easy to associate with you. In other words, your name, your name spelled backward, your birthday, your dog's name, or any word in any language are all poor choices. Beer, for example, is a poor selection for Jon's password, even though it has both uppercase and lowercase letters, because Jon and beer are usually seen in close proximity with each other.

A good way to come up with a good password is to select a phrase and destroy it. For example, make "I am not a number" into something like imNOtun#. Even though the result doesn't spell out the phrase in any real way, it gives you all the cues to remember the essentially random characters ("I am" = im, "not" = NOt, "a" = un, and number = #). Other common substitutions are 3 for e, 4 for a, 9 for g, 1 for l, 8 for b, and 5 for s. In this way, you can create passwords like sOuthb4y (southbay) and 14mnOt4g33k (iamnotageek).

Also, be sure to write down your password where it won't get lost and can't be easily found or stolen. For example, save your work passwords at home or store them in a locked desk or safe. And please don't write your password on a sticky note and attach it to your computer monitor!

GNOME is the default Red Hat graphical environment for Red Hat and is what we use throughout this book. However, many people prefer the KDE environment. The choice is yours; you can use either environment or both if you like. (If you install both GNOME and KDE on your computer, you can select one or the other as your desktop environment when you log in.) To install KDE, click the Customize the Set of Packages to be Installed radio button, as described in Step 5. Click the check box next to the KDE package group and then click the Next button.

Installation Stage 5: The Point of No Return!

If you have been following the steps in this chapter, you haven't made any permanent changes to your computer. The partitions you selected earlier haven't been written in stone, so to speak. No Red Hat Linux packages have been written to your hard drive either. You can stop the installation process and go back to your good old computer by clicking the Back button.

Otherwise, take a deep breath and follow these instructions to install Red Hat Linux on your computer:

1. **After you suck in your breath and decide to take the plunge, click Next in the About to Install window.**

Customizing the software to install

If you select the Customize the Set of Packages to be Installed option and click the Next button in Step 5, the Package Group Selection window appears.

Red Hat organizes individual software packages into package groups. (Packages are described in Appendix D.) For example, individual packages used by the GNOME graphical system are grouped into the GNOME package group. The Red Hat installation process selects certain package groups for each of its installation types. Both the Workstation and Personal Desktop types use the same package groups except that the Workstation adds the software development package group. The Server installation type uses a different set of package groups.

Generally, you don't need to modify the default Red Hat package groups when using the Workstation or Personal Desktop installation types. You can certainly do so if you want, but the default creates a computer that serves most of your needs.

Your disk partitions are created and formatted, and then the Red Hat Linux distribution is written to it. Yikes! The Installing Packages window (see Figure 3-6) tells you which package is being installed in addition to how many have been installed, how many remain to be installed, and the estimated time remaining.

The process takes several minutes if you have the latest, greatest high-speed computer and CD-ROM drive and takes quite a bit longer with older equipment.

The installer then asks whether you want to create a boot disk. This option is a good one, just in case something happens to the boot partition on your disk. Microsoft products, for example, have a bad habit of overwriting the Master Boot Record (MBR) — and therefore your Red Hat Linux booting system — when they're installed or even updated. Hard drive boot failures can also happen for any number of reasons — aliens and gremlins are well known for wreaking havoc. The boot disk is a great tool for foiling these dastardly mischief-makers.

This boot disk is different from the one you use to start the Red Hat Linux installation. This boot disk can start your Red Hat Linux computer in case the Red Hat Linux boot information stored on your hard drive ever becomes corrupted.

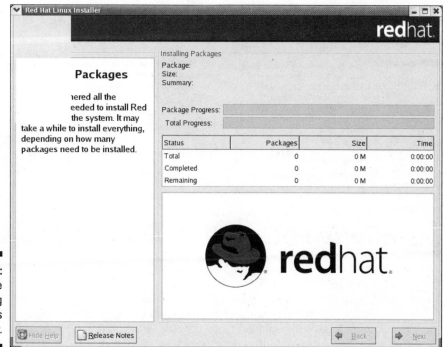

Figure 3-6:
The Installing Packages window.

2. **(Optional) Insert a blank disk into your main floppy drive, select the Create Boot Floppy option, and click Next to create a boot disk.**

Before the system reboots, remove the CD and any floppy disks in your drives. Otherwise, you have to go through the entire installation process again. If this happens, don't groan — you can always remove the pesky critters and then reboot.

The boot disk is created and the Graphical Interface (X) Configuration window appears, as shown in Figure 3-7.

Move on to the next section to finish the installation.

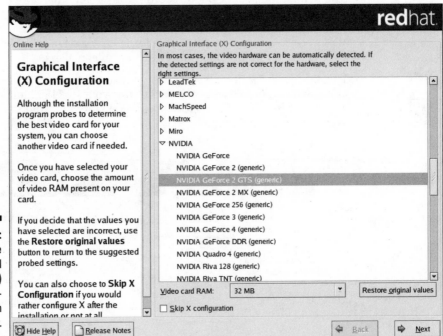

Figure 3-7:
The
Graphical
Interface (X)
Configura-
tion
window.

Installation Stage 6: X Marks the Spot

Phew. You're almost at the finish line. Really!

One of the last things you need to do is install and configure the X Server, which gives you a graphical environment to use with Red Hat Linux. To configure X Server, you need to specify the video card and monitor for your system and give information about how much video memory is contained on the video card, the speed at which it runs, and a series of other items.

Picking up from the end of the last section with the Graphical Interface (X) Configuration window (refer to Figure 3-7), follow these steps to configure your graphical system:

1. **Select your computer's video card and memory and click the Next key.**

   The Red Hat installation process usually detects the video driver and configures the parameters for you.

   Video memory is different from computer memory. Video memory is used exclusively to display graphics on your monitor, but computer memory — called Random Access Memory (RAM) — is used by the operating system for every other task. Most modern video cards have 16MB to 128MB of video memory.

   If you don't know how much video memory your card contains, try 1MB (the 1 Meg option). Although this setting limits the resolution of your screen, you probably can get the X Window System going. Later, you can experiment with the Xconfigurator program (which we describe in Chapter 20) to figure out the best values for how much video memory you have, if the probe didn't work properly.

2. **Select a monitor from the Monitor Configuration window and click the Next key.**

   Red Hat again does a good job of automatically detecting monitors, so there's a good chance that your monitor will be displayed.

   If your monitor isn't included on the list, you can select from within the Unlisted or Generic Monitor choices.

   Older monitors can't handle resolution rates and scan frequencies higher than what they were designed for. A monitor designed for a 640 x 480 resolution (and a low scan frequency) can't display a 2,048 x 1,024 resolution (and a high scan frequency). If you try to make the monitor display a higher frequency than it's capable of displaying, the monitor may burst into flames. (We didn't believe this either until we saw a monitor smoking. Hey, at least you get a new monitor out of it. Welcome to the 21st century.)

   Modern monitors, called *multiscanning monitors,* can automatically match themselves to a series of scan frequencies and resolutions. Some of these monitors are even smart enough to turn themselves off rather than burst into flames if the frequencies become too high. Finding the documentation and matching your vertical and horizontal frequencies properly is the best way to go (particularly with older monitors). Lacking this information, try a lower resolution first, just to get X Window System running.

   The Customize Graphical Configuration window opens.

3. **Click the Test Setting button.**

   If you configured X correctly, the following message appears: Can you see this message?.

4. **You have ten seconds to either click the Yes button with your mouse or press the Enter key.**

   If you click Yes, Red Hat uses this configuration as its default and the Custom Graphical Configuration window opens.

   If you click No, or wait for the time to expire, no configuration is saved. You can try new configurations until you find the right combination.

5. **Click the Next button.**

   Red Hat configures your system to start in graphical mode.

We assume that you select Graphical mode during the X configuration steps. Selecting the Graphical mode tells your Red Hat Linux computer to start X and the GNOME graphical environment (alternatively, KDE) every time you boot. If you choose the Text option, whenever Red Hat Linux boots you're faced with the unexciting command prompt where, after logging in, you have to enter the startx command at the prompt to start X and your GUI.

If you select Text, your system always starts in Text mode (also known as Character Cell mode). You can always manually start X with the aptly named startx command or modify /etc/inittab to automatically start X. To do that, change the line id:3:initdefault to id:5:init default in the inittab file.

After you make your choice, a screen appears and informs you where you can find the configuration file. You're also pointed to the X README.Config file for more information.

The Installation Complete window appears. You're prompted to remove media such as boot floppies and the Red Hat CD.

6. **Remove all removable items and click Next.**

   Your computer reboots.

If you have a problem with your X configuration, you see an onscreen message that regretfully informs you about the situation. You can quit or go back and start over. If you're game, go back and try, try again.

Post Installation: Using the Setup Agent

After your computer reboots, the Red Hat Setup Agent starts. The Setup Agent simplifies the installation process by pushing some configuration work to the post-installation phase. Your new Red Hat Linux computer works just fine whether or not you run the Setup Agent. The Setup Agent helps you to fine-tune your computer. The fine-tuning need not occur during the installation, which makes that entire process a bit easier.

The Setup Agent automatically runs the first time you boot your computer after installing Red Hat Linux. The Setup Agent helps you add or configure user accounts. It also helps you configure your computer's date/time and sound system.

The Setup Agent also helps you perform these functions:

- ✔ Register with the Red Hat Network.
- ✔ Set up the Red Hat Update agent.
- ✔ Install additional applications. The Linux operating system provided with this book doesn't include extra applications, so you can't use this function.

The process of configuring these systems is described throughout this book. The following steps describe how to use the setup system immediately after completing the Red Hat Linux installation:

1. **When the Red Hat Setup System starts, you see the Welcome screen, as shown in Figure 3-8. Click the Forward button to start the post-installation configuration process.**

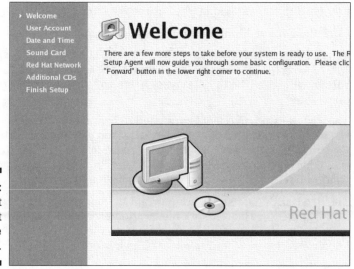

Figure 3-8:
The Red Hat
Setup Agent
welcome
screen.

The Create a User window opens. Only the root user was created during the installation process, but you have the chance here to create one or more user accounts.

2. **Enter an account name, the name of the account owner, and its password. Click the Forward button to continue.**

3. **After the Date and Time Configuration window appears. Change the date and time if you need to.**

   You can also let your computer automatically and continuously update your clock. If you're going to be connected to the Internet, either through a LAN (Local Area Network) or a broadband modem (DSL or cable), click the Enable Network Time Protocol (NTP) radio button. You can choose from a drop-down menu full of time NTP servers. The default choice, `time.nist.gov`, works well, but you may enter any one you want. Alternatively, you can have access to an NTP server not on the list and can enter it manually. Click the Forward button to continue to the Sound Configuration screen.

   We recommend that you use the NTP option, if possible. PC clocks tend to drift from seconds to minutes per day. It's better to be up to date than not.

4. **Red Hat does a good job of detecting hardware such as sound cards and should detect yours — click the Play test sound button to test your system.**

   Consult the section about setting up your sound system, in Chapter 11, for help if the sound test fails. Click the Forward button to continue.

5. **Click the Forward button and the Update Agent window opens.**

   Red Hat strives to provide extra value to the Linux operating system. One of its excellent services is the Red Hat Network, which provides various services. The Update Agent helps you keep your computer up-to-date.

   The Red Hat Update Agent is designed to continually connect to the Red Hat network and check for new software. You can register with the service by leaving the Yes, I would like to register with Red Hat Network radio button enabled and click the Forward button. A registration window opens, where you enter the required information.

   The Red Hat Update Agent is important to your computer security. We're skipping the Red Hat Network registration process because we discuss it more in Chapter 16, which concentrates on security issues. Click the No, I don't want to register my system radio button.

6. **Click the Forward button.**

   The Install Additional Software screen opens. The Red Hat Linux Publisher's Edition CDs that are bundled with this book don't include any additional software, so there's nothing to do here.

7. **Click the Forward button.**

   The Finished Setup window opens. You're done!

8. **Click the Forward button and the Setup Agent exits.**

You can run Setup Agent whenever you want. The Setup Agent is a script named firstboot. You can run the Setup Agent by running the firstboot script with the Reconfig option. Just run the following commands as root from a GNOME Terminal window:

```
rm /etc/sysconfig/firstboot
/usr/sbin/firstboot --reconfig
```

That's it! You have built yourself a Red Hat Linux computer. After your computer reboots itself, you can then use it as your personal workstation.

Chapter 4

Getting Red Hat Linux

● ●

In This Chapter

▶ Checking out the Red Hat Linux file system

▶ Booting Red Hat Linux

▶ Comprehending logins and the root user

▶ Configuring the graphical display

▶ Adding users with a graphical tool

▶ Adding users without a graphical tool

▶ Stopping Red Hat Linux

● ●

*Y*ou should learn a few basics before you start to use your new Red Hat Linux computer. This chapter covers enough of the Linux fundamentals to get you started, including topics such as starting and stopping Red Hat Linux and understanding the difference between graphical and nongraphical applications.

We start by introducing the system Linux uses to store information on a disk. Linux, like Windows, uses files and directories to store and organize information and applications. The following section describes the Linux file system.

Introducing the Linux File System Tree

Linux, like Unix, refers to everything as a file, giving each device, file, and directory a *file address* to identify it. Linux refers to drives and drive partitions by using a system of letters and numbers; for example, /dev/hda could be the name of the first IDE hard drive, and /dev/sdb could be the name of the second SCSI hard drive.

You can compare the Linux file system to a tree, as shown in Figure 4-1, which shows three *subdirectories* of root (more than a dozen subdirectories are in the root directory); a *subdirectory* is a directory within a directory. The top of the upside-down tree, represented by a / (slash), is the *root directory*. A series of limbs, branches, and leaves extends below the root: Limbs are mount points, the branches that extend from the limbs are directories, and the leaves on those branches are your files.

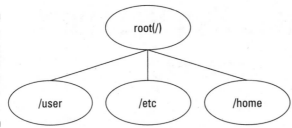

Each *mount point* is a drive partition or remote file system (such as your CD-ROM drive) that is *mounted,* or made visible to, a directory of the limb above it. When a disk partition or remote file system is mounted on the directory branch, it turns that branch into another limb, allowing even more branches to be positioned and attached below the mount point.

Red Hat Linux needs at least a root partition in your directory structure and a swap space partition. The root partition is used to store all your personal and system files and directories, and Linux uses *swap space,* the Hamburger Helper of the computer world, to extend your memory beyond the limit of your random access memory (RAM). If you have 512MB of RAM and 512MB of swap space, for example, you can run programs that use 1GB of memory.

This configuration isn't much different from Windows and MS-DOS file systems. Windows uses the concept of a hierarchical directory tree. However, the syntax is somewhat different. The top-level directory in Red Hat Linux, root, is designated with a forward slash (/). Every subsequent subdirectory name follows that initial slash. For example, the home directory is a subdirectory of root and is shown as /home. In the Windows world, the root directory is designated with an initial backslash (\). The famous C: is synonymous with C:\. The theme for both operating systems is carried forward when dividing subdirectories: Linux uses forward slashes, and Windows uses backslashes. Your home directory is then shown as /home/me in Linux and as \user directories\me in Windows.

Another primary difference between Linux and Windows file systems is that Linux requires you to explicitly mount file systems. Windows does so automatically. Explicitly mounting the file system isn't as onerous as it sounds. Red Hat Linux installs utilities that automatically sense and mount file systems when necessary. For example, the default Red Hat Linux configuration mounts a CD-ROM automatically whenever you insert it in the drive.

The Workstation installation type we use in Chapter 3 automatically sets up your root and swap partitions in addition to an additional boot partition used for storing the Red Hat Linux kernel and other files used for booting your computer. (The Personal Desktop installation type uses the same partitioning scheme as the Workstation installation type.)

The next section describes how to start and stop Linux.

Giving Red Hat Linux the Boot

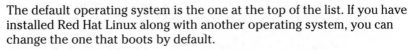

To *boot* a computer means simply to start it (and to *reboot* means to restart it). Follow these steps to boot your Red Hat Linux system for the first time:

1. **Make sure that your computer is turned off.**

2. **Turn on the power to the monitor and then turn on the computer's main power switch.**

   After a short time, the Red Hat boot menu appears on your screen. If you have only Red Hat Linux installed on your computer, you are given only one choice of operating systems to boot: `Linux`.

   The default operating system is the one at the top of the list. If you have installed Red Hat Linux along with another operating system, you can change the one that boots by default.

   Linux runs in three different states: 1, 3, and 5 (referred to as *run levels*). Each run level is used to perform different functions. At Level 1 (also called single-user mode), Linux operates with a minimum of processes so that you can make configuration changes and debug problems. Level 3 is essentially the same as Level 5 except that Level 3 doesn't run the X server — it's nongraphical. You typically run servers that don't need to run graphical applications, such as word processors, at Level 3. Level 5 is the default for personal workstations. You can use GRUB (Grand Unified Bootloader) to select a different Linux run level. When GRUB appears, press **e** for edit. Three lines appear. Press the down-arrow key to select the line that begins with *kernel*. Press the **e** key again, append either **1**, **3**, or **5**, at the end of the line and press the Enter key. Next, press the **b** key and your computer boots into the specified state.

3. **Press the up- and down-arrow keys to highlight the word** *Linux* **(if it's not highlighted already) and press Enter.**

   If you don't press anything, the default operating system (Linux sets itself as the default when you install it) starts automatically after a five-second delay.

   If you're running more than one operating system (for example, Red Hat Linux and Windows), you can select any of the listed operating systems to boot; we assume here that you choose Linux.

After you press Enter, Red Hat Linux boots. During this process, lots of information is displayed on your screen. Red Hat Linux gleans this information as it probes your computer in order to determine what hardware (disk drives and printers, for example) are present.

Because Red Hat Linux is a multiuser system, one or more users can use it at the same time; for example, you can be logged in at the computer console (the attached keyboard and monitor) while someone else is logged in via a network connection). Therefore, you and every other user need a user account in order to use the computer. Each account requires an individual account name and password to protect your information and keep your tasks separate from other people's tasks.

Logging In

When you use Red Hat Linux, you must log in as a particular user with a distinct login name. Why? Because Red Hat Linux is a multiuser system and therefore uses different accounts to keep people from looking at other people's secret files, erasing necessary files from the system, and otherwise (intentionally or unintentionally) doing bad things.

The use of unique identities helps to keep the actions of one person from affecting the actions of another because many people may be using the same computer system at the same time (for example, over a network). A benefit of this strategy is that Red Hat Linux systems are essentially invulnerable to viruses simply because each user's files and directories can't be used to corrupt the system as a whole. (Not that we're keeping score or anything, but viruses can destroy or just make life miserable for Windows 9x systems because they don't have this capability.)

As Red Hat Linux boots, you see all sorts of messages scrolling by on the screen. After the scrolling stops, the login screen appears.

If you chose during installation not to have X start automatically whenever you boot your system, you see the `login:` prompt.

If you make a mistake while typing the password or your login, the system asks you to retype it.

We strongly recommend that you do most of your experimentation with Red Hat Linux as a nonprivileged user and log in as the root user only when necessary. By operating as root, you run the risk of corrupting your system, having to reinstall again, or losing data because you can delete or change anything and everything. When you are logged in as a regular user, you can accidentally erase your own files and data, but you can't erase someone else's files or system files.

Fortunately, Red Hat Linux provides many graphical administration utilities you can start as a nonprivileged user. Each Red Hat administrative utility prompts you to enter the root password as it starts and then performs its specific function, but only that function, with root privileges. You're prevented, therefore, from doing unintended damage to other systems. (See Appendix C for information about how file permissions work and how you can modify them.)

The Command-Line Interface (CLI) versus the Graphical User Interface (GUI)

Red Hat Linux installs the X Window System by default. You can perform most administrative tasks with the GUI-based tools (GUI stands for *graphical user interface*) that Red Hat provides. Most of the how-to instructions in this book use the X-based applications and utilities. We do that because they're generally easier to use and because this book wasn't written for systems administrators.

Occasionally, a utility or program doesn't run graphically; at other times, using nongraphical methods and systems is just more interesting or convenient. Believe it or not, some geekier Linux users *prefer* to use a text-based, command-line interface (CLI). If you're not familiar with doing some basic administrative tasks with a CLI, we don't recommend using one just to prove that you can. It's okay to be less of a geek. We still like and respect you. On the other hand, it makes good sense to know some basics, just in case a need arises for you to have to wing it with the text-based interface.

Command-line interfaces are generally run from a *shell,* which acts as a text-based interface between the Red Hat Linux operating system and you. The `bash` shell, which Red Hat Linux uses by default, displays a prompt like `[lidia@cancun lidia]$`. You enter commands at the shell prompt. That's where the term command-line interface (or CLI) comes from.

You can start a shell from within the GNOME interface by starting a GNOME Terminal (also known as a terminal emulator). Click the GNOME Menu and then choose System Tools⇨Terminal (you can also right-click anywhere on the GNOME Desktop and choose New Terminal) to start a terminal session, as shown in Figure 4-2. (You can find out more about the GNOME interface in Chapter 9.)

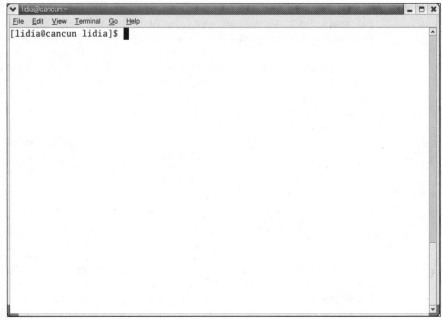

Figure 4-2:
A GNOME
Terminal
session.

You can run individual programs without starting an interactive shell by using the GNOME Run Program menu. Click the GNOME Menu button — the red hat in the lower-left corner of the screen — and choose Run Program. The Run Program window opens; type the name of any program in the text box. The program then runs — if it's graphically oriented. You don't see the output if the program is designed to interact with the terminal screen (the technical term is *standard output*). Entering **xclock**, for example, displays a graphical clock on your screen.

The GNOME Menu button looks like a red hat and is on the toolbar in the lower-left corner of your desktop. The button works in a manner similar to the Windows Start button.

The GNOME Terminal is similar to the MS-DOS window in Windows. Opening an MS-DOS window provides a CLI in which to enter DOS commands. The underlying technology of a Windows CLI is different from that of a Linux CLI. However, the capabilities are more or less the same.

Configuring Your Graphical Display

The Red Hat installation process is good at automatically configuring itself to use your video hardware and display — Linux uses the X Window System (X, for short) to display graphics. However, occasionally the X configuration process fails or you may want to reconfigure it. Red Hat gives you access to the same configuration tool it uses during the installation process.

The Red Hat X configuration utility is `redhat-config-xfree86`. We refer to it as simply the *Display Configurator*. Generally, the Display Configurator automatically detects your display (monitor) and graphics card. After they have been detected, you can set your display's resolution and color depth.

X was invented at the Massachusetts Institute of Technology (MIT). MIT designed X to display graphical applications across a wide range of machines. It was originally built to run on Unix platforms, but it has been adapted to Linux, Windows, and other platforms.

If you're already running X and want to, for example, reconfigure it, click the GNOME Main Menu button and then choose System Settings⇨Display. Figure 4-3 shows that the Display Configurator has detected the computer's display and video adapter hardware.

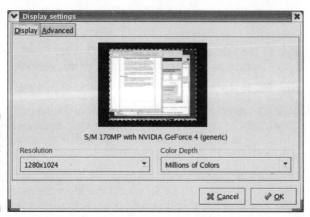

Figure 4-3:
The Red Hat
Display
settings
dialog box.

Old monitors that aren't multiscanning can be damaged if you try to use them at a higher resolution than VGA, which is 640 x 480 and 60Hz (a multiscanning monitor can switch to the same signal frequency that a video card is generating). Most newer monitors have built-in protection mechanisms to keep them from burning up in what is known as *overdriving,* but older monitors don't have this type of protection. Older monitors can literally catch on fire. If you hear weird noises from your monitor or smell burning components, turn off your computer immediately!

You can manually change your display settings if the Display Configurator doesn't automatically detect them. These steps describe how to access and use the advanced Display Configurator features:

1. **Start the Display Configurator and click the Advanced tab at the top of the window.**

   Figure 4-4 shows that you can configure both the monitor and video adapter.

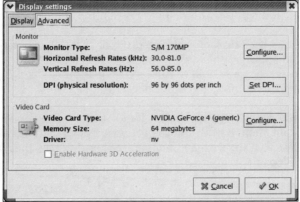

2. **After you're in the advanced section of the Display Configurator, click the Configure button in the Monitor section of the window.**

   The Monitor Settings window opens, as shown in Figure 4-5.

   Try to locate and select your particular monitor. You have dozens and dozens of monitors to choose from, so you have at least as good a chance of finding yours as winning the PowerBall. If not, your best bet is to rummage around in the Generic section.

   Generic monitors include several laptop configurations and old-fashioned heavy ones. If you don't know what type fits your monitor, take a guess and try one. Keep trying different generic monitors if your first choice doesn't work.

   Click the OK button and return to the Advanced Settings window.

   You can configure your mouse's behavior by clicking the GNOME Menu button and choosing System SettingsÍMouse. The Mouse Configurator functions essentially like the Display Configurator.

3. **Click the Video Card Configure button. Control is sent to the Video card settings window (as shown in Figure 4-6). Select your video card from the long list of choices.**

   You can tell the Display Configurator to probe and locate your video card for you by clicking the Probe Videocard button. Your card is most likely detected and highlighted for you.

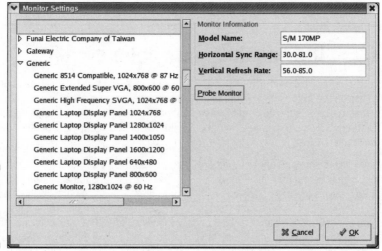

Figure 4-5:
The Monitor
Settings
dialog box.

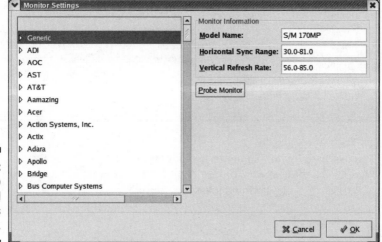

Figure 4-6:
The Video
card
settings
dialog box.

The lowest (8-bit) option allows only 256 colors on the window at one time. The 16-bit option allows for 65,535 colors, and 24-bit allows for more than 16 million colors (also known as *true color*).

4. **Click the OK button to return to the Advanced Display Settings window.**

5. **Click the OK button and the Display Settings window closes.**

   An Information window opens, informing you that you need to log out and log back in to make the changes take effect.

   Log out and log back in to make the changes take effect.

Delving deep into color depth

Color depth, the number of colors your system can have active on the window at any one time, is loosely a function of both the amount of video memory contained by your system and the window resolution.

If your system has a small amount of memory (such as 1MB), your screen can have a resolution of 1024 x 768 pixels (dots) with 256 colors (8 bits) on the screen at one time. If your system has 2MB, you can have 64K colors (16 bits) on the screen at the same time at the same resolution. If you have an older video board with a small amount of video memory but some additional video memory sockets, you may be able to upgrade the amount of video memory on the video card.

If you have only 1MB and want to see 64K colors on the screen at one time, you can reduce your resolution from 1,024 x 768 to 800 x 600 pixels. If you want true color (24 bits), you can set your resolution to 640 x 480 pixels. The picture you're viewing takes up more of the screen, but color depth versus resolution is a trade-off you can make by choosing the right options.

When you want to display an image and the color depth isn't correct, nothing drastic happens. The picture may look lackluster or not quite normal. X has an interesting capability to have virtual color maps, which allow the active window to utilize all the colors of the bits of color depth, even if other windows are using different colors. When this option is turned on (as it is with the Red Hat distribution on this book's companion CDs), the various windows turn odd colors as your mouse moves from window to window, but the window that your mouse activates is shown in the best color available. With newer video cards and larger video memories, which allow for true color at high resolutions in every window, this option is less useful.

 You can also restart X in emergencies (for example, if it freaks out) by pressing Ctrl+Alt+Backspace. Your current X session is stopped and eventually restarted. You can then log back in.

Creating User Accounts with the Red Hat User Manager

If you have cause to add new users (if you have a home network, for example) or you forgot to create a nonroot user during installation, this section shows you how. Red Hat offers several systems administration tools for your convenience. The Red Hat User Manager is an excellent administration tool that can make your life easier.

The following instructions assume that you're using the GNOME window system, which is the Red Hat default. But the User Manager works the same under the KDE window system as with GNOME. KDE comes bundled with Red Hat Linux and can be selected rather than GNOME during the installation process. (We discuss GNOME in Chapter 9.)

You can use the Red Hat User Manager to modify an existing user account. Click the user name and then the Properties button, and a window similar to the Create New User window opens. You can then modify any aspect of the account.

Use the User Manager to create a new account by following these steps:

1. **Open the User Manager by clicking the GNOME Menu button and then choosing System Settings⇨Users & Groups.**

   If you're not logged in as the root user, you're prompted to enter the root password.

   The Red Hat User Manager window appears, as shown in Figure 4-7.

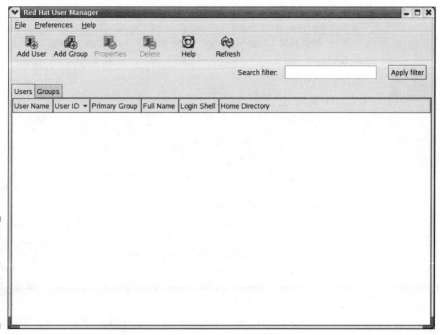

Figure 4-7:
The Red
Hat User
Manager
administra-
tion tool.

2. **Click the Add User button in the upper-left corner of the screen.**

   The Create New User window appears, as shown in Figure 4-8.

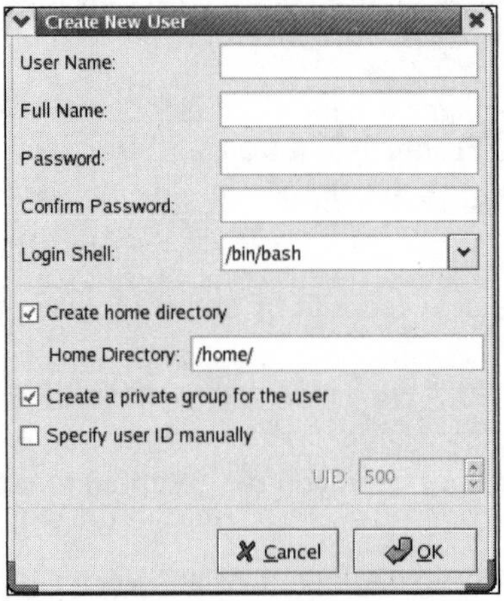

Create New User

Create New User

User Name:

Full Name:

Password:

Confirm Password:

Login Shell: /bin/bash

☑ Create home directory

Home Directory: /home/

☑ Create a private group for the user

☐ Specify user ID manually

UID: 500

✗ Cancel   ✐ OK

Figure 4-8:
The Create
New User
dialog box.

3. **Enter your user name, real-life name (full name), and password twice (to confirm its correctness); accept the Login Shell default of** bash. **The Red Hat User Manager also creates a home directory by default.**

   Most of these items are self explanatory, but here's some additional information:

   • Your user name (also known as a login name) is the name you use to log in to your computer. Make your login name easy to remember and use all lowercase letters. Cute names may not seem appropriate later. And avoid choosing a name that is too long because you may have to type it several times a day. You may also end up using your login name as your e-mail address and have to give it over the telephone, so a login name such as phool results in missent messages, leaving you feeling phoolish.

   • You can enter your full name if you want. That information is saved in the /etc/passwd file, which anyone with an account on your system can read. This information is generally useful to system administrators because it allows them to connect a person with each account. It's probably superfluous if you're configuring your personal system.

   • The new password should be different from the one you use for root.

     As you type the password, little asterisks, rather than the actual password, appear onscreen in case someone is looking over your shoulder as you type. (Red Hat Linux is showing its paranoid side here.) In text mode, you don't get any feedback (asterisks or other characters).

- Among your many choices for a default shell, /bin/bash is a good choice (bash is a popular shell that is the default for Red Hat Linux).

4. **Click OK.**

Your account is created.

Red Hat Linux uses the Pluggable Authentication Module (PAM) that prevents you from entering trivial or otherwise dangerous passwords; don't use that as assurance, however, that your new password is a good one. A good password can't be found in any dictionary because password crackers have programs that automatically try all dictionary words to crack your password. Avoid birthdays and anniversaries — or anything someone could associate with you. For ideas about good passwords, check out Chapter 3. Just don't forget it, and *don't* write it on a sticky note and put it on your monitor!

You can also use the Red Hat User Manager to delete an existing user account. Click the user name and then the Delete button, and the account is immediately removed. Be careful because you're not asked to confirm the account deletion. However, because the account home directory is left intact (not deleted) you can go back and re-create the account if necessary.

Creating an Account without X

If X isn't working or you want to work from a terminal emulator, you can still add user accounts. To do so, follow these steps:

1. **Open a GNOME Terminal window by clicking the GNOME Menu button and choosing System Tools⇨Terminal.**

2. **Log in as root by entering this command:**

```
su -
```

3. **Enter the root password when prompted.**

4. **Type useradd *name* at the command prompt, where *name* is the login name for the new login account.**

5. **Type passwd *name* at the command prompt and press Enter.**

This step changes the password of the new account, which had a default password assigned to it by the useradd command in Step 1. What good is a password if you use the default one?

As you type the password, little asterisks, rather than the actual password, appear onscreen in case someone is looking over your shoulder.

6. **Type your password again.**

Red Hat Linux asks you to retype your new password to ensure that the password you typed is the one you thought you typed. If you don't retype the password exactly as you did the first time (which is easy to do because it doesn't appear onscreen), you have to repeat the process.

Red Hat Linux updates the password for the new login.

Ending Your First Session

Logging off the system and restarting the login process is simplicity itself. To do so, click the GNOME Menu button and choose Log Out. The Are You Sure You Want to Log Out? window appears and you're asked to confirm that you want to log out. If you do (do you really?), click the OK button and you're outta there. Click No if you change your mind and want to play around with your new operating system a little while longer.

You can also choose to reboot or halt your computer from this window by clicking either the Shutdown or Reboot button and then clicking OK to confirm your decision. Depending on which you choose, your system proceeds to stop completely or reboot. You can also press the Ctrl+Alt+Backspace keys to shut down your current session. This method is less graceful but still effective, especially in case some renegade process freezes your X session.

Part II
Got Net?

The 5th Wave   By Rich Tennant

"When we started the company, we weren't going to call it Red Hat. But eventually we decided it sounded better than Beard of Bees Linux."

In this part . . .

After you have created your Red Hat Linux workstation, it's time to get to work. The chapters in this part shows three different ways to connect to the Internet: via the traditional, slow dial-up (analog) modem; with a fast broadband DSL or cable modem; or by connecting your Red Hat computer to an existing Local Area Network (LAN) that itself is connected to the Internet.

Chapter 5 concentrates on telephone-based modems. Modems are much like an old, reliable pickup truck that may not be the fastest way of getting somewhere but still gets you there. In fact, these modems provide the simplest, most economical and effective Internet connection available.

Chapter 6 introduces broadband Internet connections. Telephone, cable, and independent companies now provide broadband service to many communities. For not altogether unreasonable prices, you can get high-speed, always-on service.

Many people have access to existing computer local networks (called LANs) at work, school, and home. Chapter 7 shows how to connect your computer to a LAN, and, if your LAN has an Internet connection, you can find out how to configure your workstation to use it.

Your computer becomes vulnerable after you connect to the Internet, especially if you use a service, such as DSL, that is constantly connected. It's like the difference between living on a quiet versus a busy street: You're more vulnerable on the busy street. That's why we show you in Chapter 8 how to build a firewall.

Chapter 5

Dial-Up Modems Still Get the Job Done

. . . .

In This Chapter

▶ Finding an Internet Service Provider (ISP)

▶ Configuring your modem

▶ Configuring your Internet connection

▶ Connecting to your ISP

. . . .

Surfing the Internet is lots of fun and a surprisingly useful activity. Come on, admit it: You know you want to tie up your phone line for hours in order to annoy your family or roommates, browse sites with ridiculous addresses such as `www.theonion.com`, and chat chummily with people you would never dream of speaking to in person. The catch is that before you join the fray of the new online universe, you've gotta have access to the Internet.

This chapter describes how to use a modem to connect to an Internet Service Provider (or ISP) and create your bridge to the Internet. After you're hooked up to the Internet, you too can go to a party and drop this casual phrase: "I found this while surfing the Net this afternoon . . . on my Red Hat Linux system." If you have never been the life of the party, this statement will certainly make you more popular.

This chapter assumes that you're connecting to the Internet using a standard dial-up modem. We describe how to configure your Red Hat Linux computer to use faster connection technologies, referred to as *broadband connections,* in Chapter 6.

Many people have access to Internet-connected networks at work and school. (Or maybe your 5-year-old has constructed an Internet-connected home network.) Chapter 7 describes how to connect your Red Hat Linux computer to an existing private network and gain access to the Internet through its connection. You can then surf at light speed until the cows come home.

Desperately Seeking an ISP

To get connected using a dial-up modem, you have to successfully hook up a modem to your computer and then find a good Internet Service Provider (ISP) to dial up to. Odds are that you have an internal modem that came installed with your computer. If you don't, you may want to consider upgrading. Check out *Upgrading & Fixing PCs For Dummies,* 6th Edition, by Andy Rathbone (published by Wiley Publishing, Inc.).

The best way to find a good ISP is by word of mouth. Getting personal recommendations is a good way to find out both the good and bad points of an ISP that you can't find from reading advertisements. Before you sign on with an ISP, make sure that the company supports Linux.

If you don't have any friends and your acquaintances won't speak to you, try finding a local Linux User Group (LUG) to ask. You can look up LUGs at the Red Hat community Web page at `www.redhat.com/apps/community`.

Table 5-1 shows a sample of national and worldwide ISPs that support Linux.

Table 5-1	ISPs That Support Linux	
ISP	*Toll-free Phone Number (U.S. Only)*	*Web Address*
AT&T WorldNet	800-967-5363	`www.att.net`
CompuServe	800-336-6823	`www.compuserve.com`
Earthlink	800-EARTHLINK	`www.earthlink.net`
Prism Access	888-930-1030	`www.prism.net`
SprintLink	800-473-7983	`www.sprint.net`
CompuGlobalMega-HyperNet Network	867-555-5309	`www.compuglobalmegahyper.net`

Whoever you want to use, make sure to ask your potential new ISP whether it offers a dial-up PPP service. PPP (which stands for *point-to-point protocol*) is what Linux uses to connect to the Internet. If the person you talk to gives you the verbal equivalent of a blank stare, you may have troubles. If there appears to be some kind of a hitch, be forewarned. The ISP's tech staff probably can't walk you through the procedures. You're on your own.

If you're buying a modem

Dial-up modems are an old technology but still the most common method for making personal or small-business Internet connections. This statement may not be true much longer because the number of users with broadband connections is rising fast, and most large businesses also use broadband services.

An *internal modem* plugs into a PCI or ISA slot on your computer's motherboard and receives its power from the computer. An *external modem* comes in its own case, requires its own power supply, and connects to the computer via a serial (RS232) connection. Both types of modems use your phone jack to connect to the Internet.

Internal modems are generally less expensive than external ones, but external modems have

several advantages. You can easily turn them on and off, you can connect them to a computer without opening the computer case, and if your telephone line is struck by lightning, the charge passing through the modem doesn't damage your computer. On the other hand, internal modems need only a telephone line cable, whereas external modems require a telephone line, a serial connection, and power-supply cables.

A third type of serial line modem is a *PCMCIA card* (sometimes called a PC card). These cards are used most often with laptop computers. Most laptops come with internal modems already installed.

Now is a good time to verify that your own telephone service is billed at a flat rate and not metered; you should make sure that the dial-up number you use isn't a long-distance call either. If you have metered service or end up making a long-distance toll call, you run up huge phone bills while you're spending hours chatting about lone gunmen and reading about interdimensional space travelers.

After you choose your Internet Service Provider and arrange payment, the ISP provides you with certain pieces of information, including

✔ Telephone access numbers

✔ A username (usually the one you want)

✔ A password (usually the one you supply)

✔ An e-mail address, typically your username added to the ISP's domain name

✔ A primary Domain Name Server (DNS) number, which is a large number separated by periods into four groups of digits

✔ A secondary Domain Name Server (DNS) number, which is another large number separated by periods into four groups of digits

✔ An SMTP (mail) server name

✔ An NNTP (news) server name

✔ A POP3 or IMAP4 server name, used to download e-mail from the ISP's server to your machine

When you're shopping for a new modem, avoid WinModems like a dot.com IPO because these modems are designed for Windows computers only. They're cheaper than regular modems because they're lazy (or smart, depending on how you look at it) and depend on the Windows operating system to do much of their work for them. Linux drivers are only now beginning to appear for these types of modems. See the nearby sidebar, "If you're buying a modem," for more information on purchasing a modem for your Red Hat Linux computer.

Configuring Your Internet Connection

You need to configure your modem so that Red Hat Linux can use it to connect to your ISP. The Red Hat Dialup Configuration utility does a good job of detecting, and then configuring, your modem. It also sets up a dial-up account to connect your computer to your ISP and thus to the Internet.

Get started by following these steps:

1. **Click the GNOME Menu button and choose System Tools⇨Internet Configuration Wizard.**

   The GNOME Menu button is the icon that looks like a red fedora in the lower-left corner of your screen.

   If you're not logged in as root, you are prompted to enter the root password in the Input dialog box.

2. **The Select Device Type window opens, as shown in Figure 5-1. You use this window to configure any type of communications device, such as a modem or network interface. Click the Modem Connection option from the menu and then click the Forward button.**

   The Searching for Modems dialog box appears if no modem is found immediately. The Dialup Configuration Tool scans your computer for modems. If no modem is found, a window pops up warning that no modem was found. Click the OK button.

3. **The Select Modem window, as shown in Figure 5-2, appears (the information displayed may differ on your computer).**

   If the Internet Configuration Wizard doesn't find a modem, it guesses that a modem is attached to your first serial port — /dev/ttyS0.

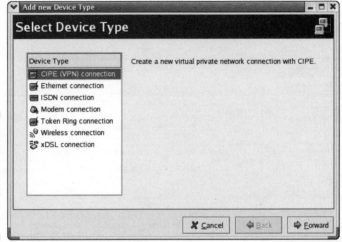

Figure 5-1:
The general-purpose Select Device Type dialog box.

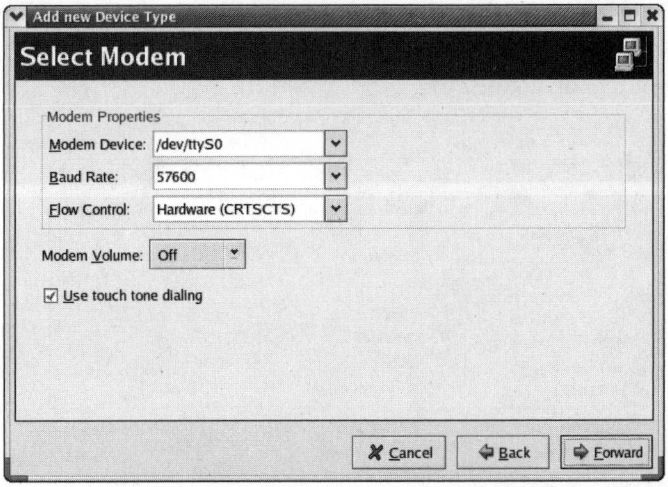

Figure 5-2:
The Select Modem dialog box.

You can modify the modem settings, if you want, in the Select Modem window. (Please see the following sections — "Locating Your Modem with Linux" and "Locating Your Modem with Windows" — for instructions on how to get information about your modem.)

4. Click Forward again.

The Select Provider window appears, as shown in Figure 5-3.

5. Enter your phone number, the name of your Internet Service Provider (ISP), and your login name and password in the appropriate boxes.

You should also enter your ISP's prefix and area or country code, if necessary, in the appropriate text boxes.

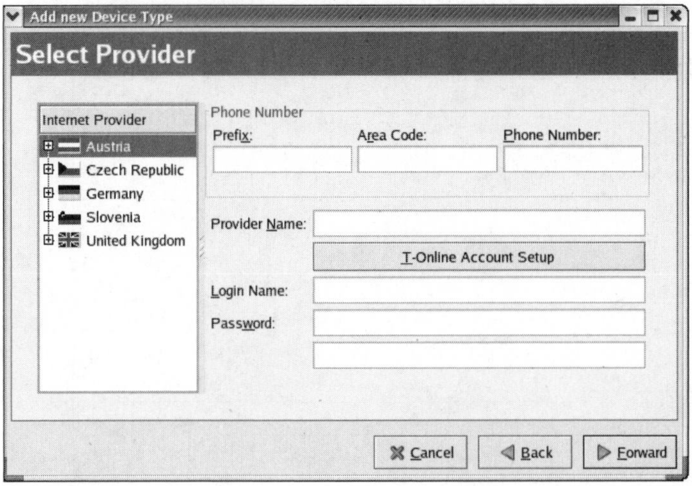

Add new Device Type

Select Provider

Internet Provider
- Austria
- Czech Republic
- Germany
- Slovenia
- United Kingdom

Phone Number
Prefix: Area Code: Phone Number:

Provider Name:

T-Online Account Setup

Login Name:

Password:

✗ Cancel   ◀ Back   ▷ Forward

Figure 5-3:
Enter your
ISP account
information
in the Select
Provider
dialog box.

6. **Click Forward when you're finished filling in the info.**

The next window, as shown in Figure 5-4, allows you to further configure
your dial-up connection.

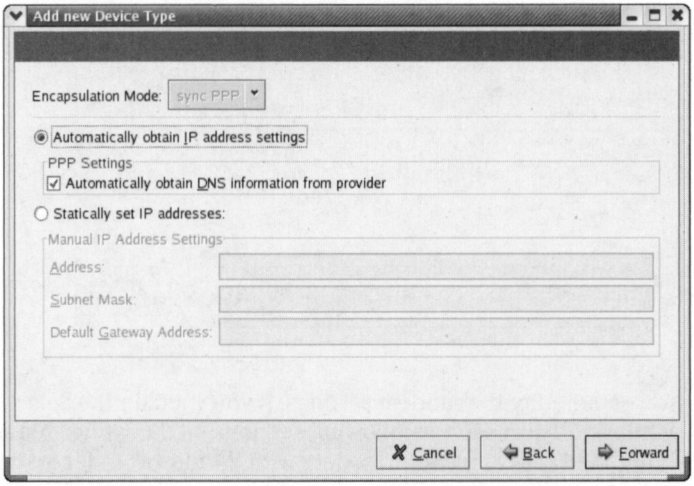

Add new Device Type

Encapsulation Mode: sync PPP ▼

◉ Automatically obtain IP address settings
  PPP Settings
  ☑ Automatically obtain DNS information from provider
○ Statically set IP addresses:
  Manual IP Address Settings
  Address:
  Subnet Mask:
  Default Gateway Address:

✗ Cancel   ◀ Back   ▷ Forward

Figure 5-4:
Configuring
your dial-up
IP selection
method.

The default is Automatically obtain IP address settings and
Automatically obtain DNS information from provider options.

Using the default options permits your ISP to automatically assign an
IP address and DNS server address to your computer every time you
connect.

7. **Click the Forward button.**

   The Create Dialup Connection appears, showing a summary of the information that you just entered.

8. **Click Apply.**

   The Network Configuration window, as shown in Figure 5-5, opens. You see your new modem and any other network device, such as an Ethernet interface, included in the window.

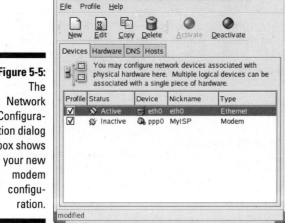

Figure 5-5: The Network Configuration dialog box shows your new modem configuration.

9. **Choose the File⇨Save menu options to save your modem configuration.**

10. **Click the Activate button to connect to your ISP.**

You now have configured your modem to connect to the Internet. The next two sections help you if you have problems using the Internet Connection wizard to configure your modem.

Locating Your Modem with Linux

Linux uses device files to communicate with peripherals. Device files occupy the /dev directory and are somewhat equivalent to Windows drivers — you need them so that your hardware works.

Your modem can connect to one of four serial ports available on your PC. A *serial port* is the mechanism your computer uses to communicate with a device, such as a modem. An external modem is generally connected to port /dev/ttyS0 or /dev/ttyS1, although configuring it as /dev/ttyS2 or /dev/ttyS3 is possible. If you have an internal modem, it can be any one of the tty devices.

During the boot process, Red Hat Linux provides the kudzu utility, which automatically tries to locate new devices on your system. The kudzu utility is good at detecting equipment like modems (both internal and external). When kudzu detects a new device, it prompts you to configure the device, and you should let it do so.

If kudzu cannot find your modem, finding it by process of elimination is a crude but effective method. The following two numbered lists describe how to find your modem. The first method, for an external modem, involves sending a string of characters to the modem and watching for the light-emitting diodes (LEDs) to light up. The second method is for internal modems, which don't have LEDs, so you have to use the hideous screeching sound of your modem to track it down.

To use kudzu to find an external modem, follow these steps:

1. **Run this command from a command prompt:**

   ```
   echo "anything" > /dev/ttyS0
   ```

   Honestly, it doesn't matter what you put between the quote marks in the preceding commands. It just has to be some text — *any* text.

   If your modem is connected to the target serial port, you see the send/receive LEDs (sometimes marked as RX/TX) light up in a short burst.

2. **In the unlikely situation that your modem isn't found, try sending the string to /dev/ttyS1, /dev/ttyS2, and, finally, /dev/ttyS3 by altering the number at the end of the command in Step 1 to match the port you're targeting.**

Life is a bit harder if you have an internal modem because you don't have a visual response. You can, however, listen to the modem's speaker to find out what's going on. Follow these steps:

1. **Enter this command at a command prompt:**

   ```
   echo "atdt5555309" > /dev/ttyS0
   ```

If you hear the modem pick up and dial, you have won the game of hide-and-seek and know which device the modem is connected to. You can then skip to Step 4.

2. **If you don't hear anything, make sure that you have the speaker turned on by entering the following command and then retry Step 1:**

   ```
   echo "atv" > /dev/ttyS0
   ```

   If you hear the modem pick up and dial, skip to Step 4.

3. **If you still can't hear anything, try using the other serial ports by trying again, substituting ttyS1, ttyS2, and ttyS3 in the command.**

4. **After your modem is found, send the following command to the modem to kill the connection:**

   ```
   echo "atz" > /dev/ttyS0
   ```

Locating Your Modem with Windows

If you're running a Windows 9x, Windows Me, Windows NT, or Windows 2000 computer, you can see which port your modem is connected to by following these steps:

1. **Send e-mail to Bill Gates and ask him for your configuration.**

   If he's tied up in court or is otherwise too busy to respond, see Step 2.

2. **Choose Start⇨Settings⇨Control Panel.**

   The Control Panel window appears.

3. **Double-click the Modem (or Phone and Modem Control on Windows NT and 2000 systems) icon.**

   The Modems Properties dialog box appears.

4. **Select the Diagnostics tab.**

   You see your modem listed with a COM line number beside it. That is the Windows designation for your modem's serial communications line. If the number 1 appears, it means that Windows knows it as COM1; if the number is a 2, it's on COM2; and so on. These number designations translate directly to the matching number of ttyS0, ttyS1, ttyS2, and ttyS3 in Red Hat Linux.

If you're running Windows XP, follow these steps to see which port your modem is connected to instead:

1. **Click the Start button and then click the Control Panel icon.**

   The Control Panel appears.

2. **Double-click the System icon.**

   The System Properties window appears.

3. **Select the Hardware tab and click the Device Manager button.**

   The Device Manager appears.

4. **Click the little plus sign next to the Modems menu item.**

   Your modem should be listed under the Modems menu item.

Firing Up Your Internet Connection

Red Hat Linux provides the Red Hat PPP dialer utility to help you establish a PPP connection. You establish this connection by using the PPP configuration you set up with the Dialup Configuration Tool (which we describe earlier in this chapter, in the "Configuring Your Internet Connection" section).

To connect to the Internet with the Red Hat PPP dialer, follow these steps:

1. **Log in to Linux as any user.**

2. **Click the GNOME Menu button and choose System Tools⇨Network Device Control.**

   The Network Device Control window appears, displaying all the network interfaces you have, as shown in Figure 5-6.

Figure 5-6: Choosing your connection in the Network Device Control dialog box.

3. **Click the name of your modem (for example, Myconnection) and then click Activate.**

If you have an Ethernet (network) adapter, it shows up as eth0 or eth1. You generally can ignore the NIC because it probably won't interfere with your modem. However, if a network device appears to cause interference with your modem, you should deactivate it in the same way you deactivate a modem. Step 4 describes how to deactivate a device.

The Network Device Control utility dials and connects to your ISP.

4. **When you're finished using the Internet, click the Deactivate button in the Network Device Control window.**

Your connection comes to an end.

The firewall Red Hat installs is quite good. However, we describe an even more secure firewall in Chapter 8.

Linux is a multiuser and multitasking operating system, meaning that more than one task can be run at one time; more than one person can be logged in at one time. This technological advancement offers an attractive launching point for black hats (hackers). If someone can gain access to your Linux computer while it's on the Internet, that person can use your machine to launch attacks against other machines — and you become the proxy that helps the hacker hide his or her identity — not a good thing.

Chapter 6

Broadband Rocks!

· ·

· ·

*Y*ou're probably familiar with the ubiquitous dial-up Internet connection: You log on to the Internet, hear that fax-like connection sound and a little static, and then — presto! whammo! — you're online. If you're lucky, the entire dial-up process takes about five minutes, but it can take longer. And then there's the fact that Web pages take just a *little* while to build onscreen with a dial-up modem — especially when you compare dial-ups with high-speed connections (also called *broadband* connections).

The *broad* in broadband means that wires and cables that connect a modem to the Internet have a wide *bandwidth;* they can handle more data at faster speeds and with greater reliability. Plain old telephone service (POTS) was created for transferring analog voice data. Needless to say, POTS just doesn't do as well as broadband media when it comes to the Internet.

The two most popular broadband connections you can use to access the Internet are cable modems (which use your existing cable television lines to transfer data) and DSL (which use fancy-schmancy digital phone lines). Broadband connections work from roughly 500 kilobits per second (Kbps) up to several million bits per second (Mbps). That's enough to transfer graphics-rich Web pages in a few seconds; it's also enough to listen to several audio streams or to watch a low-resolution video stream.

If you're ready to make the switch to a DSL or cable Internet connection, believe us when we tell you that you'll never go back to a dial-up modem. This chapter describes how to obtain and configure a broadband connection.

We recommend avoiding ISDN, satellite, and mental telepathy Internet connections. ISDN is an old technology that is rapidly being replaced by DSL. ISDN is also difficult to configure and isn't much faster than a dial-up modem connection. Satellite Internet connections are just being introduced and suffer from problems, such as transmission delays (latency), that wreak havoc with your communications. Some people say that mental telepathy works great, but we don't think that Intel makes a chip yet. Perhaps satellite systems will improve quickly, but until that happens, we recommend using a plain-old dial-up modem or, if you can, DSL or cable modem connections.

Introducing DSL and Cable Connections: The Proof Is in the Wiring

Although today's telephone network system is modern in many ways, its underpinnings haven't fundamentally changed since the early 20th century. The telephone network consists of pairs of copper wire that connect homes and businesses with a telephone company's central offices (CO). The phone company use switches in its COs to connect you to your destination when you make a call. The switches are designed to limit the range of frequencies — called *bandwidth* — that a phone call can use. The bandwidth is roughly 3,000 cycles per second (Hz), enough to recognize a voice but not a whole lot more. Those limits prevent today's analog modems from pushing more than approximately 56,000 bits per second, or 56 Kbps, through the telephone network. (That 56 Kbps speed varies, mostly downward, depending on the condition of the copper wires you're connected to.)

What does all this mean to you? Improve your modem and the wiring, and you get faster Internet access. Two of the most commonly used broadband alternatives are

- **Cable Television (CATV):** Although CATV companies don't provide service to as many residences and businesses as the telephone companies do, their fiber and coaxial cable networks can carry much more bandwidth than telephone wires can. CATV networks don't have the 3- to 4-mile limits that DSL has. Typically, you can get Internet cable through your CATV company if the company offers it and if the company serves your neighborhood.

- **Digital Subscriber Lines (DSL):** Designed to skip the restrictions of the traditional telephone system by making an end run around the voice switches, DSL rewires your existing telephone setup. Your local telephone company can connect your computer to new equipment that provides more than ten times the speed a dial-up modem can.

  The main limitation of DSL is that traditional copper wire can carry a high-speed connection for only a few miles. Your telephone company can tell you whether it can provide you with service.

The Cable Modem Option

Cable companies have invested lots of capital (much more than telephone companies) to upgrade their networks in order to gain Internet market share. Their effort has paid off for you the consumer, and many places in the United States now have access to high-speed Internet connections.

However, you have to consider some downsides:

- ✔ Unfortunately, not all cable companies have caught up with 21st century technology. Many companies may provide you with TV but not Internet service.

- ✔ Many people don't live in an area served by cable TV. Internet cable is also not a good medium to provide services such as Web page hosting.

- ✔ Most cable companies require you to connect to their ISP. Many people like to use a different ISP because it provides better service. Using your own ISP also makes it easier to set up your computer (or network) to provide services going out to the Internet. Cable companies can't prevent you from using a different local ISP, but they don't charge you less — so you end up paying for two services, one of which you're not using.

- ✔ Few cable companies support Linux. You may get a connection, but you're on your own if you need to troubleshoot problems, even problems that have nothing to do with Red Hat Linux but affect your machine.

If you decide that cable access is the right choice for your Internet access needs, here's an overview of the process for connecting your Red Hat Linux computer to the Internet via a cable modem:

1. **Do some research and subscribe to an ICP service.**

   Locate an Internet cable provider (ICP) — usually your existing cable TV company — and subscribe to the ICP service.

2. **Make a hardware commitment.**

   Obtain an Internet cable modem through your ICP. Many ICPs provide cable modems as part of their service. Otherwise, you can purchase the modem from the ICP or a consumer electronics store.

3. **Get registered.**

   Register the cable modem with your ICP.

4. **Set up the cable modem.**

   Cable modems have two connectors: a 75-ohm coaxial port and a twisted-pair (RJ-45) connector. (The coaxial connector is the same type that's used for cable TV. The RJ-45 connector looks like a large telephone plug.)

- Connect a coaxial cable from the cable modem's coaxial port to the cable jack on your wall just like you would a TV set.

- Connect a network cable from the RJ-45 modem port to your Red Hat Linux computer. Normal network cables (referred to as category 5 cables) don't work if they're connected directly from the modem to your computer. You need to use a *crossover* cable if you want to directly connect a computer to a cable modem. You can use normal category 5 cables if you connect the cable modem and your computer to an Ethernet hub or switch.

5. **Set up your Internet protocols.**

   Configure your computer to use DHCP on the network interface that connects to the modem. Restart your computer's network interface, and you should be good to go.

The following sections take you through the process of finding a cable provider and setting up your access.

Finding an Internet cable provider

Finding an Internet cable provider (ICP) is as simple as calling your cable television company. Not all cable TV systems carry Internet traffic, but many do.

Locating a cable television company that provides broadband Internet connections is unfortunately quite easy. It's unfortunate because little competition exists within the cable industry. Federal law effectively restricts competition within municipalities and creates the environment for monopoly-like companies. The result, of course, is that prices remain higher than necessary. Oh, well, at least many cable companies are offering Internet connections.

Your ICP is your default Internet Service Provider (ISP). Most cable companies give you one or more e-mail addresses. However, cable companies don't generally provide login accounts like other ISPs do.

Login accounts are used for launching applications and storing information. They aren't essential, but they're useful. However, nothing stops you from maintaining a regular ISP and using its login account. You then have a high-speed Internet connection you can use to log in to any account you have.

We don't run you through the process of signing up for cable Internet service; we think that the process is simple enough. A good portion of the sign-up process involves waiting on hold and listening to Muzak. One suggestion, though: Make sure that you have pertinent information about your system and that the cable company knows you're using Red Hat Linux 9.

Dealing with the hardware

One great thing about Internet cable is that you can buy the cable modems from your local electronics store or an Internet distributor. DSL equipment is less readily available. Cable modems are generally priced the same whether you purchase through your provider, the Internet, or a bricks-and-mortar store. But the convenience of running to a local store is great, especially if your cable modem breaks on a Saturday night and you just *have* to download the latest game patch.

Before you purchase a cable modem, make sure that you

> ✔ Ask whether you have to buy your modem through the cable provider. If not, you can shop around for the best price.
>
> ✔ Make sure that the modem you buy is compatible with your service provider. The cable industry is converging on using the Data Over Cable Service Interface Specification (DOCSIS) as its Internet hookup standard. DOCSIS modems are quite easy to configure, so keep your fingers crossed that your service provider uses them.
>
> If your provider doesn't use DOCSIS, you likely have to purchase your modem through your provider.

The instructions we provide later in this chapter are designed for DOCSIS modems.

Setting up your cable modem is usually a straightforward process. Modern DOCSIS cable modems act as *network bridges.* A network bridge simply rebroadcasts network packets in both directions — incoming and outgoing. One side of the bridge connects to the cable TV company. The other side connects to your computer through your Ethernet NIC through a Cat 5 crossover cable; you can also connect through a network switch or hub (LAN). If your modem is the bridge type — we believe that the cable industry in the United States mostly uses that system — it doesn't require any configuration.

Setting up Internet protocols

You don't have to configure your cable modem for it to work. What you *do* need to do, however, is tell your Red Hat Linux computer how to connect to the modem. This task requires configuring the Ethernet adapter that connects to your cable modem to use the Dynamic Host Configuration Protocol (DHCP); you, of course, need an Ethernet adapter installed on your computer. Your cable modem sets the IP address of your Ethernet NIC by using DHCP. These instructions show how to do that:

1. **Log in.**

2. **Click the GNOME Menu button.**

   The button is in the lower-left corner of your screen and looks like a red fedora.

3. **Choose System Settings⇨Network.**

   The Network menu pops up, prompting you to enter the root password if you're not logged in as the root user.

4. **Enter the root password and click OK.**

   The Red Hat Network Configuration window opens, as shown in Figure 6-1.

5. **The Devices tab is active by default, and you see the device — eth0 — that the Ethernet device is.**

   You may see a different device number, such as eth1, if you have multiple network devices configured. For example, you may have both an Ethernet and a wireless network adapter.

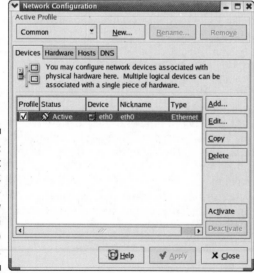

Figure 6-1:
The Red Hat Network Configuration window with the Devices tab active.

6. **Click the `eth0` device and then the Edit button.**

   The Ethernet (or wireless, if you're configuring one) Device window opens.

7. **Click the Activate Device When Computer Starts check box so that your network connection automatically starts up when you turn on your computer.**

   You must see a check mark in the check box.

8. **Click the Automatically Obtain IP Address Settings With radio button.**

   Make sure that the dhcp option is selected.

9. **Enter your host name in the Hostname (optional) text box.**

   The Configure Wireless Connection window looks similar to the one shown in Figure 6-2.

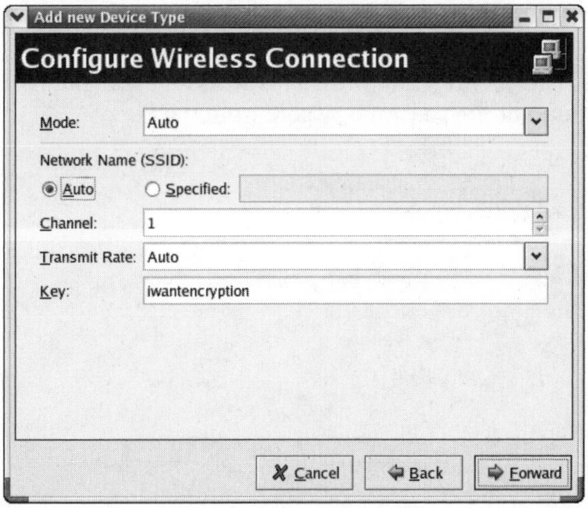

Figure 6-2:
The
Configure
Wireless
Connection
window.

10. **Click the OK button.**

    You still need to save the your changes before exiting the configuration system.

    You return to the Red Hat Network Configuration window.

11. **Click the Apply button.**

12. **Click the Close button and you exit the Red Hat Network Configuration window.**

You have saved the configuration necessary to use your cable modem. However, the settings don't activate until you reboot your computer or restart your computer's network interfaces.

You can restart your network as follows:

1. **Click the GNOME Menu button.**

2. **Select Server Settings➪Services.**

   Scroll down until you see the network option, as shown in Figure 6-3.

3. **Click Network to highlight it.**

4. **Click the Restart button in the upper-right corner of the window.**

   Your network restarts and a window pops up, confirming the process.

5. **Check to be sure that you're connected to the Internet.**

   When you're satisfied, turn off your network connection by clicking the Stop button.

We strongly advise against leaving your Internet connection permanently active until you protect yourself with a firewall. Turn off your Internet connection — turn off the modem, for example. If you're not using the default firewall that comes with Red Hat Linux, of if you're looking for a more secure firewall, go to Chapter 8. After the firewall is working, you can restart your Internet connection and be reasonably safe from hackers.

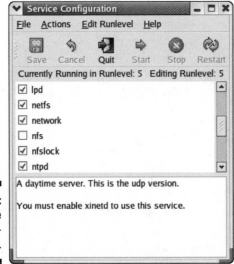

Figure 6-3: The Service Configuration window.

Registering your modem with your ICP

You do have to register your modem with your ICP. During the registration process, your computer is assigned a network address to connect to the ICP. Network addresses are called Internet Protocol (IP) addresses.

How cable modems work

Modern cable modems do more than just transmit network packets. They transmit data packets by modulating and demodulating electrical signals over the cable TV wires — thus, the name modem (*mo*dulate/*dem*odulate). Cable modems now use the industry standard Data Over Cable Service Interface Specification (DOCSIS) protocol to deliver the electrical signals across the cable network. The electrical signal carries the actual bits and bytes that comprise the network packets. A good analogy is an AM/FM radio system. The DOCSIS-based electrical signals carry data packets just like radio waves transmit speech or music.

You register your modem by giving your ICP the modem's Media Access Control (MAC) address. The ICP generates an IP address by using the MAC address as its reference. You don't need to do anything to your cable modem. The registration process is all done by your ICP, and your modem automatically is assigned an IP address. You're ready to use your Internet cable modem to connect to the Internet. Woo-hoo! Blazing speed is yours now!

The DSL Option

The world is wired — wired for telephones, that is. DSL modems take advantage of this old, but common, technology to provide a high-speed Internet connection to the consumer. The DSL option uses special equipment to pump much more data through the POTS lines than the traditional analog modem does.

The telephone system is referred to as plain old telephone service (POTS) in the telecommunication industry.

DSL provides high-speed Internet connections by electronically converting your computer's digital information into a form that can be transmitted from your home or business to the telephone company. When your data finds its way to the telephone company, it's converted into another form and sent to your ISP.

DSL uses frequencies in the millions of cycles per second — the megahertz (MHz) range — compared to traditional analog modems, which work with signals in the thousands of cycles per second (kHz). You get much higher connection speeds when you use higher frequencies. The problem is, however, that the telephone system wasn't designed to work with higher frequencies.

Fortunately, the brainiacs of the world have figured out how to get high-speed DSL connections out of old, slow POTS wiring. They have designed new digital signal processing chips to overcome the POTS architecture. The result is that if you live close enough — roughly three to four miles — to your DSL provider's equipment, you can use DSL to get connected to the Net.

Facing DSL configuration woes head-on

This section describes the basic DSL modem-configuration issues. We take the time to give you an overview because it's easy to get confused if you concentrate on just the details. Please check out the following list and get familiar with it. Getting your DSL modem working is easier after you do so.

Most consumer DSL providers now use the asymmetrical DSL (ADSL) type of connection. The following list describes the process for getting an ADSL connection working. (Please note that we use the generic acronym DSL interchangeably with ADSL. Most consumer DSL connections are really ADSL, and that is the type of connection we describe in this chapter.) Follow these steps to set up DSL service:

1. **Find a DSL provider.**

   You need to find out whether you live or work close enough to the DSL provider's equipment to get a connection. DSL providers check your address and tell you whether they can take your business.

2. **Connect your DSL modem to your telephone jack and your computer.**

   Your DSL modem acts as the intermediary between your computer and your DSL service provider. You must connect one side to the phone jack and the other to your computer's Ethernet NIC.

3. **Configure your Red Hat Linux computer to communicate with the DSL modem.**

   Your Red Hat Linux computer connects to the DSL modem via an Ethernet NIC. You must configure your Ethernet NIC to work with the modem.

4. **Set up the DSL modem user and administrative passwords.**

   DSL modems provide a reasonable level of security. You should take advantage of this security by assigning your own password to the modem. That prevents hackers from breaking into your modem and causing you problems.

5. **Set up your ISP PPP account name and password.**

   You must authenticate your DSL modem to your ISP. DSL connections get logged on to your ISP just like traditional analog modems do. You configure your DSL modem with your ISP username and password.

6. **Configure the DSL modem's internal (private) network interface.**

   Your DSL modem must be able to communicate with a Red Hat Linux computer over an Ethernet connection. You must configure the DSL modem so that it uses the same network parameters as your computer.

7. **Configure the modem's network address translation (NAT) settings.**

   The Internet was designed to send — route — information as quickly as possible to its destination. Internet Protocol (IP) addresses are used to designate where the information is coming from and where it's going. IP addresses can be routable or nonroutable. Nonroutable addresses can be reused; you can use the same nonroutable addresses that your neighbor uses without interfering with one another.

   NAT is used to convert nonroutable IP addresses into routable ones, which is useful when connecting your private network to the Internet by translating your internal IP addresses into one of your ISP's routable IP addresses. You need to configure your DSL modem to convert your computer's private (for example, `192.168.1.1`) and nonroutable address into an address assigned to your DSL connection by your ISP.

8. **Save the settings to nonvolatile memory and reboot.**

   You need to save your DSL modem's settings after you have them working. You don't want to enter the configuration every time you turn on the modem.

Finding a DSL provider

You must obtain both DSL and ISP services to make your broadband connection. Some companies — notably, the regional Bell telephone companies — can provide both services. However, in our case, we preferred our ISP to the ISP that was aligned with the DSL provider. We were fortunate enough to retain our existing ISP when we purchased our DSL service.

The DSL provider market is fluid. Analyze the DSL service providers in your area carefully before choosing one, and remember that longevity is as important as a low price. Regional Bells are more likely to provide long-term service than many of their competitors.

One advantage of DSL service is that you often don't have to sign a service contract; you can reasonably switch providers if you're not satisfied with the service.

Usually, you have to select an ISP after you choose a DSL provider. DSL providers either provide their own ISP or allow you to select from several independent ones (the DSL provider makes the arrangements and works directly with the third-party ISP).

The many faces of DSL

DSL comes in a variety of flavors. Most consumers end up using ADSL because it offers inexpensive Internet connections at reasonably high speeds. ADSL serves an individual computer user's Internet needs very well; it even provides a small business with adequate service. ADSL is, not surprisingly, the most available of all DSL flavors.

The other types are more suited for business use. Most locales probably have access to only two or three of these services. This list describes the DSL variations:

✔ **ADSL (Asymmetrical DSL):** The ADSL download (*downstream*) speed isn't the same as its upload (*upstream*) speed. (That's why it's asymmetrical.) The maximum ADSL speed is 8 Mbps, but it's usually limited to less because of the POTS infrastructure limitations.

✔ **G.Lite:** Also known as Universal DSL or splitterless ADSL, G.Lite is a low-speed version of ADSL that doesn't require filtering out the POTS signal. It provides as much as 1.5 Mbps downstream and 512 Kbps upstream.

✔ **HDSL (high bit-rate DSL):** HDSL is a symmetrical protocol with equal upstream and downstream speeds. You can use HDSL as a substitute for T1 connections because it provides the same data rates of 1.544 Mbps.

✔ **HDSL2 (high bit-rate DSL 2):** HDSL2 provides the same specifications as HDSL but works over a single twisted-pair connection.

✔ **IDSL (ISDN Digital Subscriber Loop):** IDSL, the successor to the current ISDN technology, uses the same line encoding (2B1Q) as ISDN and SDSL. IDSL is used mostly to provide DSL service in areas where the more popular forms, such as ADSL and SDSL, aren't available. IDSL is capable of providing upstream and downstream rates of 144 Kbps.

✔ **SDSL (Single-line DSL):** SDSL is commonly called *Symmetric DSL* because SDSL upstream and downstream speeds are the same.

✔ **VDSL (Very high bit rate DSL):** VDSL provides as much as 50 Mbps over distances up to 1,500 meters on short loops. VDSL is particularly useful for campus environments — universities and business parks. VDSL is now being introduced in market trials to deliver video services over existing phone lines. You can also configure VDSL in symmetric mode.

✔ **xDSL:** xDSL is a generic term for all the DSL flavors.

Connecting your Cisco modem to your Red Hat Linux computer

Writing explicit configuration examples is always difficult. The DSL world is still young, and we're not convinced that any standards have emerged. Chances are that our instructions don't match your equipment.

This section shows you how to use one of the more common DSL modems. Qwest, which is a "baby Bell" and one of the larger DSL providers, uses this equipment. Our Cisco 675 or 678 DSL modem/router is the Qwest-recommended equipment.

Even if you're using different equipment, our instructions should still be useful in outlining the general process of configuring a DSL connection.

Cisco and other manufacturers' DSL modems can be configured four different ways:

✔ **By using the proprietary, Windows-based Cisco application.** This system works well, but you need to run it on a Windows computer.

✔ **By using the Cisco Web-based (HTML) configuration system.** This system also works well and is independent of any operating system because it works with any Web browser, including Mozilla. However, you first need to configure the DSL modem's administrative password before you can use the browser to configure the modem.

✔ **By using Telnet and running the Cisco configuration commands.** Cisco provides a command-line interface for entering configuration commands. Unfortunately, you need to communicate with the DSL modem over its network connection to use Telnet.

✔ **By connecting to the modem with a serial cable and running the Cisco configuration commands.** This connection method uses the Cisco command-line interface, just as Telnet does. However, no network is used, and thus, no prior configuration must take place before using this method.

The first three methods require that you can communicate with the Cisco modem over a network connection. Getting the modem's network connection to work with your Red Hat Linux computer (or your LAN, if you're using one) can be tricky, so we recommend (and explain) the one sure method that uses a serial cable and terminal-emulation-based connection:

1. **Connect the blue cable that comes with the Cisco modem (the blue cable is a RS232 serial cable with a 9 pin DB9 female connector) between the computer and the Cisco 675 or 678 DSL modem.**

   You must be able to communicate with your DSL modem from your Red Hat Linux computer. Unfortunately, your modem isn't configured to speak to Red Hat Linux over its network connection until you configure it to do so. Therefore, you must use the serial cable to get its network connection running.

2. **Log in as root.**

3. **Open a GNOME Terminal window.**

   Refer to Chapter 4 for information about the GNOME Terminal.

4. **Run the minicom program.**

```
minicom
```

Don't worry about the warning you see about running `minicom` as root. You don't do anything dangerous if you follow these steps.

The initial minicom screen is displayed:

```
Welcome to minicom 2.00.2

OPTIONS: History Buffer, F-key Macros, Search History
        Buffer, I18n
Compiled on Jun 23 2002, 16:41:20.

Press CTRL-A Z for help on special keys
```

5. **Press Ctrl+A and then Z to display the configuration menu.**

Change the communication device from `/dev/modem` to `/dev/ttyS0` or whatever serial device is appropriate to your system (`/dev/ttyS1`, `/dev/ttyS2`, or `/dev/ttyS3`).

6. **Change the communication parameters to a speed of 9600, 8 bits, and no parity.**

Turn off hardware and software flow control too.

7. **Connect to the Cisco DSL modem by pressing the Enter key.**

The first time you connect to the modem, you should see this prompt:

```
User Access Verification
Password:
```

8. **Set the DSL modem's password by pressing Enter.**

You then see the Cisco Broadband Operating System (`cbos`) prompt:

```
cbos>
```

You have successfully configured the serial connection to the Cisco DSL modem.

Configuring the Cisco DSL modem

The steps in this section describe how to configure a Cisco 675 or 678 DSL modem. We use a DSL modem here because it's the most common DSL device now available.

The following process involves setting up your authentication, routing, and NAT. You must first configure the DSL modem with its own passwords and other information. (See the preceding section, "Connecting your Cisco modem to your Red Hat Linux computer.")

To configure your DSL modem so that it works with Red Hat Linux, follow these steps:

1. **Only the** `enable` **account can be used to configure the modem, so type** enable.

   You need to set the Cisco modem passwords. Cisco 675 or 678 modems use two passwords. One password is for the regular (nonprivileged) password, named `exec`, and the other works for the administrative account, named `enable`.

2. **No** `enable` **password is set, so press the Enter key when prompted for the password.**

   The `cbos>` prompt changes to `cbos#` with the pound sign (#) indicating that you're in enable mode.

3. **Enter the nonadministrative** `exec` **password:**

   ```
   set password exec dslrocks!
   ```

   You should use your own password — not `dslrocks!` — of course.

4. **Set the administrative enable password:**

   ```
   set password enable dslisablast!
   ```

   Our sample password is printed in millions of copies of this book. Well, probably just three or four copies, but we can be optimistic. Make sure that you use a different password.

   Your DSL modem is mellow because it uses *nonvolatile memory*. It's good at remembering things like the passwords you just set, but only if you tell it to remember these items.

5. **Save your changes by running this command:**

   ```
   write
   ```

   The `show nvram` command shows what's in the DSL modem's memory. Run the command, and you see something like this:

   ```
   [[ CBOS = Section Start ]]
   NSOS Root Password = a_lsbgegr
   NSOS Enable Password = a_lsbgegr
   ```

6. **Set up the DSL modem so that your computer can connect to the Ethernet interface:**

   ```
   set interface eth0 address 192.168.1.1 netmask
           255.255.255.0
   ```

7. **Configure the DSL modem's** `wan0-0` **interface to authenticate with your ISP:**

   ```
   set ppp wan0-0 login iwantdsl@myisp.com
   set ppp wan0-0 password dslrocks!
   ```

   Use the values your ISP gives to you in place of our fictitious examples (in *italics*).

8. **Set the DSL modem's default route:**

```
set ppp wan0-0 ipcp 0.0.0.0
```

9. **Set up the DSL modem's DNS:**

```
set ppp wan0-0 dns 0.0.0.0
set dhcp server disable
```

10. **You don't ever allow Telnet connections to be established from the Internet, so just turn off all connections:**

```
set telnet disabled
```

11. **Finally, enable NAT:**

```
set nat enabled
```

The Cisco 675 or 678 DSL modem now automatically converts the source addresses and ports of outgoing connections to its external (wan0-0) interface.

12. **Save the changes to** nvram **again:**

```
write
```

13. **Reboot your DSL modem by entering this command:**

```
reboot
```

The Wide Area Network (WAN) LED indicator on the modem starts blinking after several seconds. The blinking LED indicates that the device is attempting to connect to your ISP. When the connection is established and authenticated, the light turns to a constant On state.

14. **To see what you have done, run the command** show nvram **to examine your modem's configuration.**

15. **Turn off your DSL modem and set up your firewall.**

Whew, that was easy! Wasn't it? Maybe not, but you're connected to the Internet with a fat DSL pipe, aren't you? Unfortunately, the great features that DSL gives you — high speed and a continuous connection — can also work against you. Hackers now have a fast and continuous connection to your computer. Oh, no, Mister Bill!

Don't worry. If you selected the default medium, or optional high-level firewall, during the installation we describe in Chapter 3, you have reasonable protection from the Internet. However, if you haven't installed a firewall, you should turn off your DSL modem until you create one! In either case, go to Chapter 8 and build the harder firewall we describe there.

Chapter 7

Connect Locally, Communicate Globally: Connecting to a LAN

In This Chapter

▶ Networking with an Ethernet or wireless NIC

▶ Using the Red Hat Network Utility

▶ Starting and stopping your local network connection

*T*his chapter shows how to connect your Red Hat Linux computer to an existing Local Area Network (LAN), also referred to as a private network. It's different from connecting directly to the Internet with a dial-up modem or broadband connection, as we describe in Chapters 5 and 6; those chapters describe how to connect a single stand-alone Red Hat Linux computer directly to the Internet. In this case, you connect your Red Hat Linux computer to a LAN.

You may be building your Red Hat Linux computer to use at work or at school. It doesn't matter what the venue is; you can use the information in this chapter to connect your computer to an existing LAN. You can access the Internet if that LAN is connected to it.

Don't get discouraged if you don't have access to a LAN. You can make your own! Chapter 14 describes how to put one together.

In this book, the terms LAN and private network are used interchangeably.

If you configured your Ethernet card during the installation process we describe in Chapter 3, that's great! You can skip this chapter or just browse through it if you need to later. Otherwise, if you have a wireless adapter or didn't configure your Ethernet adapter during the installation, use this chapter to do just that.

Although forming a private network isn't exactly rocket science, describing in detail how to network two or more computers is beyond the scope of this book because so many network configurations are possible. Many good books are available that explain how to do that, and the best place to start is at the Wiley Web site: www.wiley.com.

Introducing Local Area Networks

The invention of Linux revolutionized computer networking. Creating a LAN before Linux existed was complicated and expensive. LANs were the nearly exclusive domain of big corporations, universities, and other monstrous organizations.

But the TCP/IP networking protocols were built into Linux from the beginning. In the mid-1990s, if you could afford a couple of PCs, a cheap piece of coaxial cable, and a few 10 Mbps (megabits per second) or faster Ethernet adapters, a LAN was born. The Ethernet adapters, also commonly known as *network interface cards* (NICs), cost about $150 at the time. Prices, fortunately, have crashed since then, falling to earth like Ziggy Stardust: A 100 Mbps NIC now costs as little as $15, and you can buy an 11 Mbps wireless NIC for less than $100.

To get your Red Hat computer on a network, you have to configure only a handful of networking subsystems. Here are the tasks that need to be performed in order for your networking to work:

- ✔ Load your wireless or Ethernet NIC kernel module. Red Hat Linux generally detects your hardware and loads the correct kernel modules.

- ✔ Configure your network interface card (NIC).

- ✔ Configure your domain name service (DNS), which converts Internet names into Internet Protocol (IP) addresses.

Wireless networking suffers from some security vulnerabilities. Consult the "Wireless network warning" sidebar, later in this chapter.

Performing these steps is pretty heavy lifting. The load is eased somewhat by using the graphical Network Configuration Utility system administration tool provided by Red Hat. Have fun!

Configuring Your NIC with the Red Hat Network Utility

To use your Red Hat Linux computer with an existing Local Area Network (LAN), you need a wireless or Ethernet NIC installed on your computer and a network hub, or switch, to which to connect the NIC. After you set up the hardware, you need to configure your Red Hat Linux network settings.

If your LAN also has an Internet connection, you can set up that connection, too. A high-speed Internet connection is best, but in terms of the network configuration, the type of connection doesn't matter.

Preparing to configure your wireless NIC

Before you can configure your wireless NIC, you need to figure out two things:

- ✔ Which type of wireless NIC you have (or need)
- ✔ How your wireless NIC will connect to your network

Two main types of wireless electronics (or *chip sets*) are now in use: Wavelan, built by Lucent Technologies, and Prism2, designed by Intersil. Both types are supported by Red Hat. The following list shows the manufacturers of each type. You can use the list to help figure out what kind of chip set your device uses:

- ✔ **Wavelan:** Orinoco, Apple Airport Enterasys RoamAbout 802, Elsa AirLancer 11, and Melco/Buffalo 802.11b.

- ✔ **Prism2:** D-Link DWL-650, LinkSys WPC11, and Compaq WL110. Other, less popular models include Addtron AWP-100, Bromax Freeport, GemTek WL-211, Intalk/Nokia, SMC 2632W, YDI, Z-COM X1300, and Zoom Telephonics ZoomAir 4100.

IEEE and wireless networks

The dominant wireless standard is based on the IEEE 802-11b (and the older 802-11a and the about-to-be-released 802-11g) standard; 802-11b is also referred to as *Wi-Fi* (which is short for the wireless industry's trade term *wireless fidelity*). If you hear people talking about a Wi-Fi NIC, they're just talking about wireless NICs.

IEEE (pronounced "eye-triple-e") stands for the Institute of Electrical and Electronic Engineers, a worldwide professional society of nerds. (Is it necessary to use words like nerds or geeks to convey some technical meaning?) The IEEE, the "triclops" of wireless networking, concerns itself with issues like what frequency wireless networking devices should use. Fortunately, this group has devised this wonderful standard that now enables everyone who's interested to communicate without stringing wires between machines.

You need to figure out how your wireless NIC (or network adapter) will connect to your network. Wireless NICs can connect to a LAN in two ways:

- **Adapter-to-adapter:** This type, referred to as an *ad hoc* connection, is useful if you have two or more computers that you want to talk and form their own, exclusive private network.

- **Adapter-to-wireless hub:** This type, called *infrastructure,* provides a single entrance (an access point) into a LAN. An *access point* allows one or more computers to be connected to a network. However, unlike an ad hoc network, the individual computers can connect to any access point that allows them to.

The wireless-configuration instructions we provide work with either the infrastructure or ad hoc connection methods. Your wireless NIC can connect to either the access point or other computers (Linux and Windows) as long as you correctly configure your Network ID (ESSID) and encryption key.

Choosing between ad hoc and infrastructure

Using Ad Hoc mode provides two advantages:

- **Lower costs:** You don't have to purchase an access point; an access point starts at around $70. Computers using wireless NICs running in Ad Hoc mode communicate directly with each other.

- **Simpler configuration for Linux users:** Older access point devices could be configured using only Windows-based software — the simple network management protocol (SNMP), to be exact. You had to physically connect a Windows computer to the access point via a wired Ethernet network and then use the software supplied with the device. That was difficult if you didn't have any Windows-based computers. Newer access points are beginning to use HTML-based configuration systems, so you can use Mozilla to configure these newer devices.

  Ad hoc networks eliminate the need to configure any access point. You only need to configure the wireless NIC in each computer on your network. You can use the Red Hat Network Configuration Utility to configure a wireless NIC, which simplifies the process. Each NIC must have the same Network ID and encryption key.

Ad hoc networks can also provide a bit more security because they connect to other networks — and the Internet — through a network router. Access points work as network bridges. Routers examine IP addresses and then decide where to direct network traffic from one network to another. Bridges automatically pass on all traffic. Ad hoc networks can be configured to more

---

Wireless network warning

Wi-Fi, the standard for wireless technology, uses an encryption system called wireless equivalent privacy (WEP) to provide security. WEP encrypts communication between wireless devices to prevent someone with the right equipment from listening to and using your wireless network. But WEP is flawed and can be broken using tools available on the Internet (that's a big surprise). If a hacker breaks in to your Wi-Fi network, he can read your communications. But your problems don't end there. Hackers can use your wireless network to connect to both your private network and the Internet; you give the bad guys a launch pad to the Internet.

On the other hand, wireless networking is so useful that many people make accommodations

for the risk. The logic? If you assume that your wireless network has already been hacked, you don't have to worry about *when* it might be hacked in the future.

You should use Open Secure Shell (open SSH) and Secure Sockets Layer (SSL) — both bundled with Red Hat Linux — to conduct all your internal and external communication. Keep in mind that using SSH and SSL protects your information, but doesn't prevent someone from connecting to your network. The next generation of Wi-Fi, 802.11g, is supposed to fix the WEP weakness. Until the WEP problems are solved, be aware of the risks.

---

tightly control network traffic than access-point-based ones. You can configure ad hoc networks with a firewall more easily than a network using an access point. (Many of the current crop of access points now provide NAT and firewall support, however.)

Configuring your Ethernet or wireless NIC

To get your Red Hat Linux computer working on a LAN, you must first configure its NIC. The NIC is the device that electrically connects your computer to your LAN. To work with the other computers on your network, your Ethernet or wireless adapter must be given a network address and a few other pieces of information.

We have divided the configuration instructions between Ethernet and wireless (or Wi-Fi) NICs. The instructions start by explaining how to start the Red Hat Network Configuration Utility. We then devote a subsection apiece to describing the particulars of configuring Ethernet and wireless devices. After we cover the device specifics, we discuss general configuration issues. The overall configuration process is outlined in these steps:

1. Start the Network Configuration Utility.

2. Configure your Ethernet or wireless device.

3. Configure your computer's host name.

4. Configure your computer's domain name service.

5. Restart your network.

Starting the Network Configuration Utility

Follow these steps to start the Network Configuration Utility:

1. **Click the GNOME Menu button and choose System Settings⇨Network.**

   Alternatively, you can click the GNOME Menu button and choose System Tools⇨Network Device Control. When the Network Device Control window opens, select the Ethernet or Wireless device and click the Configure button. The Network Configuration utility starts.

2. **Enter the root password if you're prompted to do so.**

   Figure 7-1 shows the initial configuration window. A NIC may or may not be displayed in the window. The NIC is displayed only if you configured your networking during the Red Hat installation.

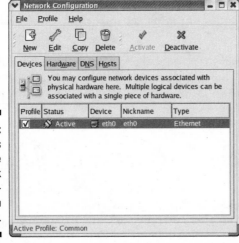

Figure 7-1:
The Devices
tab in the
Network
Configura-
tion
window.

3. **Click the New button if no NIC is displayed in the devices window or if you want to configure an additional one.**

   Otherwise, skip to Step 3 in the following section when you're working with an Ethernet device; skip to Step 1 in the section "Configuring a wireless NIC," later in this chapter, if you're working with a Wi-Fi NIC.

   The Select Device Type window appears, as shown in Figure 7-2.

Figure 7-2:
The Select
Device Type
window.

4. **Select the appropriate NIC from the list of devices.**

   For example, select Ethernet if you're using that type of interface.
   (Ethernet NICs are by far the most common network adapters now in
   use.) If you're using an IEEE 802.11b (also referred to as Wi-Fi) device,
   select Wireless Connection.

5. **Click the Forward button.**

What you do next depends on whether you're configuring an Ethernet NIC or
a wireless NIC. The following two sections are devoted to the Ethernet and
wireless NICs, respectively.

Configuring an Ethernet NIC

If you're using an Ethernet NIC, follow the steps in this section to configure
its parameters. (If you're using a wireless NIC, go to the next section,
"Configuring a wireless NIC.")

1. **Follow the steps in the preceding section, "Starting the Network
   Configuration Utility."**

   When you choose Ethernet from the drop-down list in Step 4 of the preceding list, the Select Ethernet Device window, as shown in Figure 7-3,
   appears.

2. **Select the appropriate Ethernet device and click the Forward button.**

   The Network Configuration utility detects all the Ethernet devices
   attached to your computer. Most PCs have only one Ethernet device, so
   you don't have to make a decision about which one to select.

   The Configure Network Settings window opens, as shown in Figure 7-4.

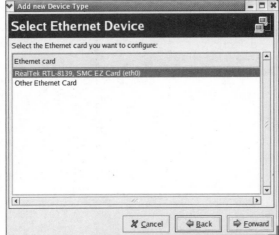

Figure 7-3:
The Select
Ethernet
Device
window.

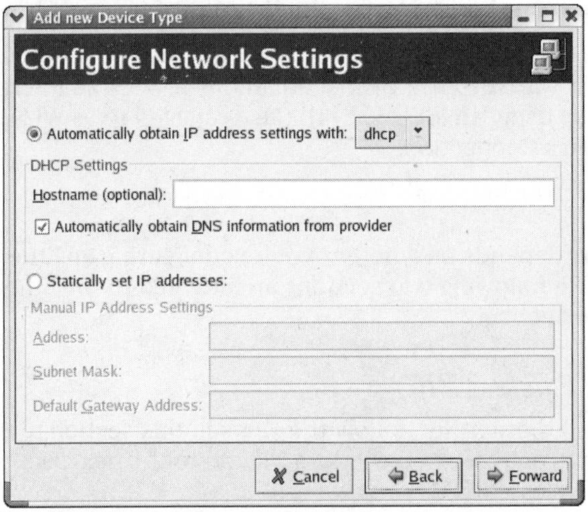

Figure 7-4:
The
Configure
Network
Settings
window.

3. Configure your TCP/IP address settings.

The Red Hat Network Configuration Utility selects DHCP (Dynamic Host Configuration Protocol) as the default method for determining your machine's IP address. (DHCP dynamically assigns an IP address to your Ethernet NIC, and you're finished configuring your NIC.) If you're connecting to a network that provides DHCP service, type your computer name in the Hostname (optional) field (for example, Cancun) and click the Forward button.

If your network doesn't use DHCP, you need to manually configure your IP address.

4. **Click the Statically Set IP Addresses radio button.**

   You should ask your friendly local system administrator (unless you're the administrator, in which case you might want to avoid talking to your-self) which system your network uses.

   Life is a bit more complicated if you have both a wireless and an Ethernet NIC on your computer. You can run both devices at one time, but the configuration is much more difficult. You can solve the problem by clicking the Automatically Obtain IP Address Settings With radio button so that the dot disappears. This simple mouse click prevents the Ethernet NIC from starting automatically.

5. **Assign an IP address to your computer by typing it in the Address text box.**

   IP addresses are analogous to street addresses: They provide a number that uniquely distinguishes your machine from all others. Private IP addresses don't require any registration with the powers that be — the InterNIC organization that distributes IP addresses. Public IP addresses aren't routed on the Internet and can be used on LANs for your own use.

   If you're on a network with registered IP addresses, be sure to get an IP address from your system administrator. Otherwise, go ahead and use a private IP address. (Use any Class C address between 192.168.1.1 and 192.168.254.254; for example, 192.168.128.5 or 192.168.1.20.) Private IP addresses in this range are designated for use by private net-works. By design, private IP addresses don't get *routed* (sent from one machine to another) through the Internet, and anyone can use them. Private IP addresses would wreak havoc on the Internet if they were routed.

6. **Type** 255.255.255.0 **or the netmask for your IP address in the Subnet Mask text box.**

   The Internet Protocol (IP) defines only three network address classes: A, B, and C. Only Class C addresses are assigned by the InterNIC. Use the 255.255.255.0 netmask for Class C networks, 255.255.0.0 for Class B, and 255.0.0.0 for Class A.

   Class C netmasks are used almost universally now, and we use only Class C addresses here. If you're not using a Class C address, you're probably experienced in the ways of TCP/IP and know which netmask to use. Godspeed. Otherwise, don't fool with Mother Nature: Use a Class C address.

7. **In the Default Gateway Address text box type the IP address of the Internet gateway for your LAN.**

   The Internet gateway is the device (router or computer) that connects your network to your ISP and the Internet. Obtain the address from your system administrator if you're at work and have one. If you're a home user, a typical convention is to assign the highest address — 254 — of a Class C subnetwork as the gateway. For example, type **192.168.1.254**.

Your TCP/IP Settings look similar to the window shown in Figure 7-5.

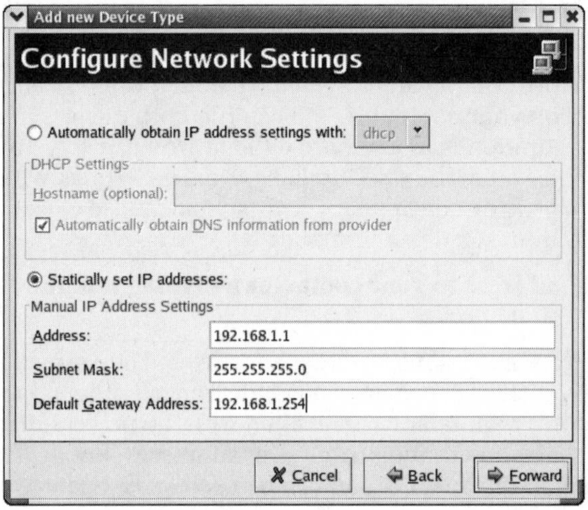
Add new Device Type
Configure Network Settings
Automatically obtain IP address settings with:
dhcp
DHCP Settings
Hostname (optional):
Automatically obtain DNS information from provider
Statically set IP addresses:
Manual IP Address Settings
Address:
192.168.1.1
Subnet Mask:
255.255.255.0
Default Gateway Address:
192.168.1.254
Cancel
Back
Forward

Figure 7-5: Entering your static (non-DHCP) IP address settings.

The Create Ethernet Device window opens, indicating that you have finished the configuration process. The window shows a summary of the information you entered in the preceding steps.

8. **Review the summary and click the Apply button.**

   The Network Configuration window displays the newly configured Ethernet NIC.

9. **Start the NIC by clicking the Activate button.**

   This step completes your Ethernet NIC configuration.

You still need to configure your domain name service (DNS) if you aren't using DHCP. Proceed to the section "Configuring DNS service," a little later in this chapter.

TIP

You don't have to enter information into the Kernel Module, IO Port (opt), or IRQ (opt) text boxes because Red Hat Linux is good at detecting this information directly from the device.

TECHNICAL STUFF

Kernel modules are the Linux equivalent to Microsoft Windows device drivers. Usually, Red Hat Linux can detect your Ethernet adapter and automatically load the correct module. However, if Red Hat Linux can't find your Ethernet adapter, you probably won't find the correct one from the supplied list. You can still go ahead and try; there's no harm in that.

Configuring a wireless NIC

This section describes how to configure the parameters for a wireless NIC, also called a Wi-Fi NIC. (Skip this section if you don't have a wireless NIC.)

If you haven't already done so, read the earlier section "Preparing to configure your wireless NIC," to make sure that your NIC is a Wavelan and that you want to set up your network for Infrastructure mode.

Then follow these steps:

1. **Follow the steps in the section "Starting the Network Configuration Utility," earlier in this chapter.**

   When you choose Wireless from the drop-down list in Step 4 of the earlier list (in the section "Starting the Network Configuration Utility"), the Select Wireless Device window appears.

2. **Select the appropriate wireless device.**

3. **Click the Forward button.**

   The Configure Wireless Connection window opens, as shown in Figure 7-6.

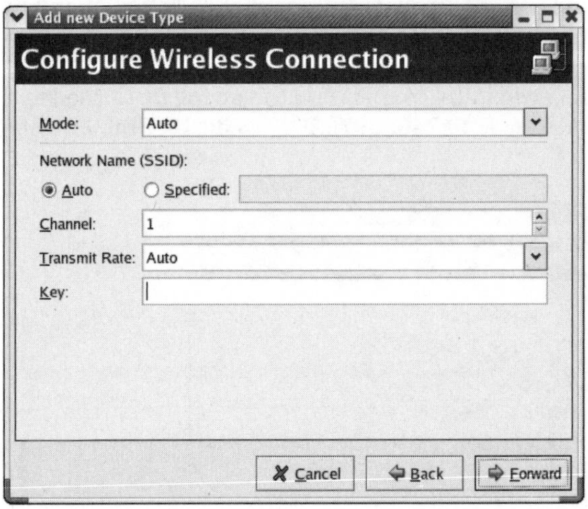

Figure 7-6:
The
Configure
Wireless
Connection
window.

4. **Select either Managed or Ad-Hoc from the Mode drop-down list.**

   You use Managed mode when using an access point. Use Ad-Hoc mode if you configured a wireless network without an access point.

5. **Type** ANY **in the ESSID (Network ID) text box if you use an access point. Type the specific ESSID name for an ad hoc network.**

All machines connected to an ad hoc wireless network must share the same ESSID. For example, you may choose the string mynetwork as your ESSID. In that case, you must enter **mynetwork** as the ESSID for all machines connected to your ad hoc network.

6. **Enter the encryption key in the Key text box and then click the Forward button.**

You should obtain the encryption key from your network administrator. If you have set up your own wireless home network, you can generate the key yourself. An *encryption key* is similar to a password and protects your wireless network from casual eavesdropping. Enter in the text box a key that is 13 characters or fewer — for example, **this_is_a_key**; using all 13 characters maximizes the encryption key's effectiveness. Figure 7-7 shows an example of the Configure Wireless Connection window.

Encryption keys are 40- or 128-bit binary numbers. They can be represented as text strings, as described in Step 6, or as a string of hexadecimal — hex — numbers. Hex numbers are commonly used in computer science to represent binary numbers. For your purposes, it's sufficient to know that a hex number is represented by 16 characters: 0 through 9 and A through F. For example, hex 0 is represented as decimal 0; hex 3 as decimal 3; hex 9 as decimal 9. But decimal 10 is hex A, and decimal 16's hexadecimal value is F. The hexadecimal value of the sample key — *this_is_a_key* — is *746869735F69735F615F6B6579*. You can enter the hex value in the Key field by prepending the string *0x* to the key. In the example, you would enter **0x746869735F69735F615F6B6579**.

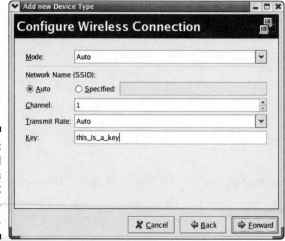

Figure 7-7:
A typical wireless NIC configuration.

After you enter your encryption key and click the Forward button, the Configure Network Settings window opens. The processes of assigning a host name, IP address, netmask, and gateway to your computer are the same as for an Ethernet interface. Please consult Steps 3 through 9 in the preceding section, "Configuring an Ethernet NIC," for instructions on how to configure your wireless NIC TCP/IP parameters.

Your Wireless NIC configuration is complete. You still need to configure your domain name service (DNS) if you aren't using DHCP. Proceed to the section "Configuring DNS service," if that is the case.

Configuring DNS service

You need to configure your computer to use one to three DNS servers. You can use your LAN's DNS servers if available. You can also use external DNS servers whether or not any exist on your LAN. To configure your Red Hat Linux computer to use DNS, follow these steps:

1. **Click on the DNS tab in the Network Configuration window, which is where you leave off in the preceding step list.**

2. **Type the host name of your computer in the Hostname text box.**

   The host name is any name (for example, Cancun) that you want to use.

   If you're connecting to a network controlled by someone else (for example, at work), check with the system administrator before selecting a host name.

3. **Type the IP address of your DNS server in the Primary DNS text box.**

   IP addresses are made up of four sets of numbers separated by periods (192.168.1.254, for example).

   If your LAN provides a DNS server, you can use it as your primary name server (DNS).

4. **If you have one, type the IP address of your secondary name server in the Secondary DNS text box.**

   Most ISPs provide a backup DNS server address. If your LAN has its own DNS server, you can specify your ISP server as your secondary DNS server if you want.

5. **Type the domain name of your network in the Search Domain text box and then click the Add button.**

   Figure 7-8 shows a sample DNS configuration screen.

   The DNS Search Path value is the domain name of your network. For example, paunchy.net is a domain name, which is the domain name of the sample LAN used in this book. You should, of course, replace the paunchy.net domain name with the name of your LAN.

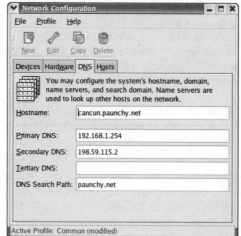

Figure 7-8:
A sample
DNS con-
figuration.

6. **Click the Apply button.**

7. **Click Close.**

   The Network Configuration Utility closes. Your settings are saved and are activated the next time you reboot your computer. Proceed to the following section to activate your settings immediately.

Manually Starting and Stopping Your Network

Sometimes the Network Configuration Utility configures your network stuff but cannot activate it. Why does that happen? Who knows? It may be because the Network Configuration Utility is still relatively young and will become better with age. In the meantime, you can start your networking systems another way by following these steps:

1. **Click the Gnome Menu button and choose System Settings⇨Services.**

2. **Enter your root password if prompted.**

   The Service Configuration Utility appears, as shown in Figure 7-9. Scroll down until you find the Network option.

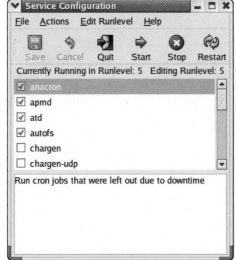

Figure 7-9:
The Service
Configura-
tion
window.

3. **Select the Network option and then click the Restart button.**

   The Information window opens and confirms that your network has been restarted. Your new network settings take effect.

4. **If you're using a wireless NIC that doesn't communicate, you may have to restart your PCMCIA system. Here's how:**

   a. Locate and click the PCMCIA service in the Service Configuration Utility.

   b. Click the Restart button.

   c. Repeat Step 3 to restart your network.

You can use the /etc/rc.d/init.d/network script to start and stop your networking system. To start your network modules, NIC, and routes, log in as root and run this command: /etc/rc.d/init.d/network restart.

All networking components are stopped and then started again. Alternatively, you can use /etc/rc.d/init.d/network start to simply start and config-ure your Ethernet NIC and routes. The /etc/rc.d/init.d/network stop command turns off all networking on your system.

Chapter 8

Fire, Fire! Heh-Heh, Firewalls Are Cool!

*A*fter connecting to the Internet, you run the very real risk that the bad guys will try to break into your computer. The bad guys wear black hats, just like in the movies (as opposed to red hats, which are a bit odd but still cool). You may also have heard them called hackers, crackers, the Joker, and whatever. Whatever their names and whatever their intentions, the Internet is getting more dangerous every day, so ya gotta protect yourself.

A *firewall* is a device that enables you to use the Internet while minimizing the possibility that the Internet will use you. Firewalls basically allow your network communications to go out but prevent anyone from opening unwanted connections into your computer or private network.

Not surprisingly, this chapter describes how to build a firewall to help protect your Red Hat Linux computer from the bad guys. First, in case you doubt that you truly need a firewall, we explain why firewalls are important. Then we introduce you to `iptables`, the Linux firewall system, and describe how to set up your firewall-filtering rules. After you set up your firewall filters, you need to know how to run the firewall automatically. You do that by setting up a script — something else we explain in this chapter. And, of course, what good would your firewall be if it didn't work? So we show you how to do a simple test to make sure that your firewall is burning brightly.

Understanding Why You Need a Firewall in the First Place

You may think that there's safety in numbers. After all, literally millions of people, businesses, and organizations are connected to each other through networks and the Internet at any given time. What do you — a simple person with a simple computer connected to the Internet — have to be concerned about? The bad guys are usually interested in big money or big publicity, right?

Well, that's all mostly true, and chances are that you will never get hacked. In technical jargon, you're relying on security by obscurity.

However, many hackers have tools that automatically scan and attack entire networks. The happy hacker doesn't have to work hard to find and exploit unprotected computers. Don't risk getting *owned* — your computer broken into and controlled — by a hacker, especially when Linux provides effective tools for protecting yourself.

Using a firewall is a simple but quite effective method for protecting yourself when you connect to the Internet. A firewall allows you to connect to the Internet while blocking unnecessary and unwanted connections from coming in.

Firewalls provide good bang-for-the-buck protection. However, they're not the only security measure you should take. For example, locking your doors certainly helps to protect against burglars but is not 100 percent effective. You must add layers of security by locking your windows, using alarms, and keeping tabs on neighborhood activities. Chapter 16 describes how to add security layers to your computer.

Linux is a *multiuser* and *multitasking* operating system — more than one person can be logged in, and more than one task can be run at the same time. This flexibility comes at a price: It offers an attractive launching point for hackers. If someone can gain access to your Linux computer while it's on the Internet, that person can use your machine to launch attacks against other machines, and you become the proxy that helps the hacker hide her identity.

Building an Effective Firewall the iptables Way

Linux comes bundled with a simple but extremely effective firewall system named `Netfilter/iptables`. The `Netfilter` part refers to the firewall system that's built into the Linux operating system — the kernel, to be exact —

and `iptables` is the interface that controls it. We refer to the overall system as `iptables` because that is the part that you work with.

The `iptables` system filters IP packets, which are the backbone of the Internet (IP stands for Internet Protocol, in fact). When you're connected to the Internet, all the information (graphics and text) that you send and receive is sent in the form of IP packets. All the information that enters and leaves your computer via the Internet is packaged in the form of IP packets. You can use `iptables` to accept or deny IP packets based on their destinations, source addresses, and ports.

`iptables` is effective because it uses *stateful filtering*, which means that the firewall can keep track of the state of each network connection. It's a technical way of saying that `iptables` knows which IP packages are valid and which are not. For example, if you're browsing `www.dummies.com`, `iptables` keeps track of all the packets that belong to that connection. The `iptables` utility can deny packets that are trying to reach your computer but don't belong to your connection, thus preventing any hackers from sneaking packets through your firewall.

Red Hat Linux installs an `iptables`-based firewall by default. The installation system configures a medium level of protection during the installation process. You may recall from Chapter 3 that we advise you to use the default firewall configuration. However, the default firewall isn't as secure as we would prefer for connecting to the Internet. Therefore, we describe in this chapter how to construct a more comprehensive and secure firewall.

The concept of ports is an essential part of the Internet Protocol. *Ports* are used to organize the communication between clients and servers. For example, when you click on a Web page, your browser communicates with the Web server by using a port. That's a gross simplification, of course, but it describes the basic idea. Suffice it to say that ports are used to control the internal workings of the Internet for such tasks as Web browsing.

LAN-ho: Adding firewall protection to a network

Firewalls are especially important if you're connecting to the Internet via a Local Area Network (LAN). Most Internet-connected LANs have a firewall that protects your computer from the worst aspects of the Internet. But a LAN's overall firewall technology may not protect your computer; the danger of the insider threat always exists — no, not from evil tobacco companies but rather from your fellow LAN users. Running a personal firewall gives you an added layer of protection. For example, if you want to connect your computer to a university network, you definitely want to use a firewall because those environments are dangerous.

Designing filtering rules: Permissive and restrictive methods

Firewall-filtering rules are like the bricks (or asbestos, if you prefer) that build your firewall. Basically, filtering rules determine what network communication can go out of and come into your computer.

When designing firewall-filtering rules, you can choose between two philosophies:

- Allow all connections by default and then deny specific access.

- Deny all connections by default and then allow specific access.

Allowing all connections takes the view that it's best to start by allowing all communication with your computer and then denying connections one by one. (This method is used by the Red Hat firewall, which you create during the installation process.) The danger with this method is that you unintentionally allow dangerous traffic to reach your machine. The alternative method is to start by denying *all* communication and then selectively allowing certain traffic. This more

restrictive method is, from a security standpoint, the best way to create a firewall because you know exactly what access you're allowing. However, the restrictive method can also create problems because you may unintentionally prevent needed or wanted network traffic from reaching your computer.

We explain in this chapter how to use the restrictive method, for two reasons:

- **It's the safest method.** The restrictive method is safer because it nearly completely prevents port scanning and other hacker attacks from accessing your computer.

- **It's much easier to configure.** Because iptables provides stateful filtering, you need to configure only two rules to create a safe firewall. However, you need to configure numerous individual rules when using the permissive model. Extra, unnecessary complexity makes for less security.

Setting Up a Firewall

So you know that you need a firewall and want to create one. What's next? The following sections explain how to set up an iptables-based firewall by using the restrictive model. This section describes how to manually create the firewall-filtering rules. When you're done setting up your rules, see the section "Saving your filtering rules to a script," later in this chapter, so that you don't have to enter these rules every time you turn on your computer.

In this section, you design an iptables-based firewall that turns off all incoming connections on your modem but still enables you to establish an outgoing connection to the Internet. You must follow all the steps in this list or else the firewall is likely to prevent you from using the Internet:

1. **Log in to your computer as root.**

2. **Open a GNOME Terminal window by right-clicking on any empty portion of the desktop and choosing New Terminal from the menu.**

3. **Make sure that you're not already running a firewall by entering these rules at the command prompt in the terminal window:**

   ```
   iptables --flush
   iptables --flush -t nat
   ```

   The `iptables` entries remove any existing filtering or Network Address Translation (NAT) rules. *NAT rules* masquerade your network address as another address, making your computer appear to be used by someone else. NAT is frequently used to make your computer appear to be coming from your ISP so that you don't have to register your computer for an official Internet Protocol (IP) address.

4. **Filter out all network communication to, from, and through your computer by entering these rules:**

   ```
   iptables --policy INPUT   DROP
   iptables --policy OUTPUT  DROP
   iptables --policy FORWARD DROP
   ```

   These commands set the default policy of your firewall not to allow any network traffic into (the INPUT rule) or out of (the OUTPUT rule) any network interface; nor is any traffic allowed to pass between multiple network interfaces (the FORWARD rule) if you have them. At this point, you have an extremely safe firewall. However, your computer is useless in terms of using it for any network-related tasks. The next step opens the firewall a little bit so that you can access the Internet (or any network you're attached to) in a safe way.

5. **Enter these rules to allow network traffic to pass through the loopback device:**

   ```
   iptables -A OUTPUT -j ACCEPT -o lo
   iptables -A INPUT -j ACCEPT -i lo
   ```

   Linux computers use an internal network called a *loopback interface (lo)*. The loopback is not a physical device, but rather a virtual one. Linux uses *lo* for internal communications. (A great deal goes on behind the scenes on a Linux computer.)

6. **Turn on all outgoing communication from your computer:**

   ```
   iptables -A OUTPUT -m state --state NEW,RELATED,
        ESTABLISHED -j ACCEPT
   iptables -A INPUT -m state --state RELATED,ESTABLISHED -j
        ACCEPT
   ```

These rules don't specify any particular network interface. However, because the filter is stateful, these rules effectively work on your Ethernet, wireless, or a dial-up Point-to-Point (PPP) interface.

The first filter rule permits all outgoing communication. The —state NEW, RELATED, ESTABLISHED option tells the firewall to allow packets of both new and already established connections to pass. (Packets are the basic part of all network communication.) Packets that are related to existing connections but use a different port, such as FTP data transfers, are also permitted.

The second filter rule controls the packets coming back from outgoing connections. When you connect to a Web site, for example, your browser sends out packets, and the Web server responds to them. You may click a button on the Web site, and a new display pops up. Clicking a button sends a packet out, and the Web server sends packets back. You have previously blocked packets from the Internet. This rule creates an exception that allows packets that belong to an existing connection — such as the connection that represents you clicking a button — to return to your computer through the firewall. Note that we don't allow new incoming connections (—state NEW) to be established because that would defeat the purpose of this firewall.

7. **(Optional) Use the following rule to allow SSH connections to your Linux computer:**

```
iptables -A INPUT -p tcp -m state --state NEW,ESTABLISHED
        -j ACCEPT --dport 22
```

This rule permits SSH connections on Port 22 to enter into your computer.

Start the OpenSSH server by running this command:

```
/etc/init.d/sshd start
```

You can modify this rule to allow other types of incoming connections to your computer. For example, add a new rule using -dport 80 and the firewall allows incoming HTTP packets. All you need to do is install the Apache Web server (included on the companion CD and described in Chapter 16) and your workstation morphs into a Web server.

You have just created a simple, effective firewall that protects your computer from the werewolves of Netdom. ("They'll rip your heart out, Jim!") Your firewall remains active until you turn the rules off or reboot your computer. The next section shows how to display your new firewall rules.

Displaying Your Firewall Rules

After you configure your firewall, you naturally want to verify that the filtering rules are set up correctly. To display the firewall rules, follow these steps:

1. **Open a GNOME Terminal emulator window by right-clicking on any empty portion of the desktop and selecting the New Terminal menu.**

2. **If you're not already the root user, enter the su - command in the GNOME Terminal window.**

3. **Enter the root password.**

4. **Type this command to display the firewall rules:**

```
iptables -L
```

You see the firewall-filtering rules displayed in the terminal window as follows (use the verbose *-v* option in the preceding command to display extra information, including the network interfaces — for the sake of brevity, we don't use the option in this example):

```
Chain INPUT (policy DROP)
target  prot opt  source     destination
ACCEPT  all  --   anywhere   anywhere
ACCEPT  all  --   anywhere   anywhere    state
        RELATED,ESTABLISHED
ACCEPT  tcp  --   anywhere   anywhere    state
        NEW,ESTABLISHED

Chain FORWARD (policy DROP)
target  prot opt  source     destination

Chain OUTPUT (policy DROP)
target  prot opt  source     destination
ACCEPT  all  --   anywhere   anywhere
ACCEPT  all  --   anywhere   anywhere    state
        NEW,RELATED,ESTABLISHED
```

The first *chain*, INPUT, is for incoming packets. You can see that the default policy is to deny all packets. The first rules in the INPUT chain direct iptables to allow all internal packets on the logical loopback (lo); many programs use the internal (lo) network to communicate with each other. The second rule allows the return packets, RELATED and ESTABLISHED, from outgoing connections to come back in. The last rule is optional and allows the incoming Secure Shell connections to your computer.

The next chain, FORWARD, denies all packets from being forwarded through your Linux computer. Forwarding is necessary only if you use your computer for routing or other advanced networking functions.

The last chain, OUTPUT, defines which IP packets are allowed out of your computer. Again, the first rule allows unlimited traffic through the loopback (`lo`) interface. The second and last rule allows any and all packets to leave your firewall.

The next section describes how to save the rules you just created and displayed so that they can be started automatically.

Firing Up Your Firewall (And Dousing the Flames)

The preceding section describes how to display your firewall-filtering rules. However, you certainly don't want to manually enter these rules every time you reboot your computer. This section shows you how to automate your firewall. We show you how to make use of the Red Hat utilities that save the rules you just created and start up the firewall whenever you boot your computer.

These instructions assume that you have configured the firewall as described in the preceding section and that the configuration is still in effect.

Saving your filtering rules to a script

You need to save your rule-set after you've created your firewall. Red Hat provides a utility for doing just that. The `iptables-save` utility reads your current firewall rules and converts them into script-compatible form. Red Hat also provides a script to start up your firewall whenever you start your computer. The `/etc/init.d/iptables` script is run whenever you start your computer and, thus, your firewall is started too. Follow these steps:

1. **Log in as root, if necessary.**

2. **Open a GNOME Terminal window (refer to Chapter 4), if necessary.**

3. **Run this command, and your firewall rules are saved to a script:**

   ```
   iptables-save > /etc/sysconfig/iptables
   ```

Turning your firewall off and on

Red Hat uses the `/etc/sysconfig/iptables` script to start Netfilter/ `iptables` firewalls. The `/etc/init.d/iptables` script uses the filtering rules stored in the `/etc/sysconfig/iptables` file to implement the filtering rules.

You can start the `Netfilter/iptables` firewall by running this `iptables` script:

```
/etc/init.d/iptables start
```

You must be logged in as root, of course. Note that you can turn off your firewall by replacing `start` with `stop`.

You can also use the graphical Red Hat Service Configuration utility. These instructions show you how to use the utility to start or stop your firewall:

1. **Click the GNOME Menu button and choose Server Settings⇨Services.**

2. **If you're not logged in as root, the Input window pops up and you're asked to enter the root password.**

   Enter the root password you set during the Red Hat installation process.

   The Service Configuration window appears. This window controls all the Linux *daemons* (processes that provide services).

3. **Scroll down the Service Configuration window until you find the `iptables` service.**

   The check mark should be set in the check box. Figure 8-1 shows `iptables` in the Service Configuration window.

Figure 8-1: Finding `iptables` in the Service Configuration window.

4. **Click the Restart button in the upper-left corner of the window.**

   You could click the Start button, but we advise you to use the Restart function. The Start and Restart buttons give you the same result, but restarting works if the service is already running. Using the Start function doesn't work if the service is already running.

Click on the Stop button to turn off your firewall.

After the service restarts, you see a confirmation message.

5. Click OK.

Your firewall is restarted, and you can exit from the Service Configuration window.

You can also prevent the `iptables` script from being automatically started when you boot the system. Click in the box immediately to the left of the service name to remove the check mark. Click the Save button, and the pointer (`/etc/rc.d/rc5.d/S08iptables`) to the startup script (`/etc/init.d/ iptables`) is removed. You can restore the pointer by clicking in the box so that the check mark reappears.

Testing Your Firewall

Your new firewall is no silver bullet against Internet wolves, but it does provide a great deal more protection than if you didn't have one. Treat it for what it is: a good, sturdy lock. A firewall is the beginning of your Internet security, but not the end. Don't trust your firewall, however, without first making sure that it works.

To test your firewall, follow these steps:

1. Pour some gasoline in a circle around your computer and light a — no, no, just kidding. Don't do that, especially if you plan to sue.

2. Use Open Secure Shell (OpenSSH) to connect to your ISP or university account; any computer account that's external to your own computer will do.

For example, from a GNOME Terminal window, enter the following command: **ssh *ssh.myisp.com***, where you substitute the address of your ISP for *ssh.myisp.com*.

The SSH program encrypts all communication to securely connect to a remote computer and interactively enter commands.

3. If you don't know your temporary (dynamic) IP address already, find out what it is by entering this command at the command prompt:

```
who | grep login
```

where *login* is your, well, login name. This command shows an IP address in numeric form, similar to

```
iamme (192.168.1.254) ...
```

4. **Run a port scan against your Red Hat Linux computer by typing the address you received in Step 3 in place of *IP_address* in this command:**

```
nmap IP_address
```

For example, if your IP address is 192.168.1.254, run the nmap command:

```
nmap -P0 192.168.1.254
```

The preceding IP address has been changed to protect the innocent. The address is what is known as a private address and will (should) never exist on the Internet, anyway.

If your firewall is set up correctly, nmap shouldn't be able to detect anything of interest about your computer. The wolves have been held at bay!

Congratulations! You have successfully set up your firewall. Your job as a security professional, however, has only just begun. In reality, there's no silver bullet where security is concerned. Education is your one true defense. For more information on firewalls and security, search the Internet for security-related topics. The SANS (www.sans.org), USENIX (www.usenix.org), Red Hat (www.redhat.com), and CERT (www.cert.org) Web sites are all good places to start. Consult Chapter 19 for the top ten Linux security vulnerabilities.

Part III
Linux, Huh! What Is It Good For? Absolutely Everything!

The 5th Wave   By Rich Tennant

"Think of our relationship as a version of Red Hat Linux — I will not share a directory on the love-branch of your life."

In this part . . .

You have finished your initial journey. Red Hat Linux is up and running, and you have mastered the basics of connecting to the Internet and private networks. You have looked at the map enough to know where you are. Now, the big question is "What do I do with it?"

One thing you can do with the computer is to put up your feet and wait for the screen saver to kick in. You can also confide to all your friends at the next party you go to that you have a "Red Hat Linux box." Wow — that will make you popular as they clamor to know when your stock options mature. Or, you can *use* your new Red Hat Linux workstation to get things done.

To that end, Chapter 9 introduces you to the wonderful world of the GNOME windows environment. GNOME is a friendly li'l guy who likes to put a friendly face on Linux. With GNOME, you can set up the "look and feel" of Linux so that you feel comfortable and at home. Chapter 10 takes you a bit further and introduces some of the many cool things you can do with GNOME applications.

In Chapter 11, the fun really starts. Can you say "Par–*tay*?" (Sorry.) Find out how you can listen to audio CDs and Ogg or MP3 files. We also show you how to record the music from CDs. And we show you how to become your own recording studio by recording audio — and data, if you're a nerd — to CD.

Chapter 12 takes the audio thing one step further. It shows how to use the Open Source multimedia players XMMS and MPlayer to listen to flowing streams. No, they're not water streams, but rather audio and video streams flowing from the Internet. You can listen to radio and audio clips and watch video too. With this knowledge, you never have to leave your couch again. Now, that's living!

We finish Part III with lucky Chapter 13, which describes how to get work done with OpenOffice. Sorry, but reality bites and personal productivity suites — word processor and spreadsheet, for example — are a necessary evil. Gotta make the doughnuts.

Chapter 9

Gnowing GNOME

· ·

· ·

*T*he Red Hat Linux operating system provides two interfaces to work from: the text-based command-line interface (CLI) and the graphical X Window System. The command-line interface is similar to the old Microsoft Disk Operating System (MS-DOS) environment, which requires you to feed individual commands to the operating system. The X Window System, also known simply as *X,* provides a graphical "point-and-click" environment from which most people prefer to work. X provides the foundation that GNOME runs on. GNOME provides a desktop environment that makes using Red Hat Linux as your workstation not only possible but also easy and pleasurable.

GNOME is the default desktop environment for Red Hat Linux. Red Hat also provides the option of installing the K Desktop Environment (KDE). KDE is an excellent environment that many people prefer. However, because of limited space, we describe only how to use GNOME because it's the Red Hat default environment.

In this chapter, you find out a little bit about X and the basics for working with GNOME. You also get to mess around with the GNOME Panel and desktop (the Panel is similar to the taskbar on a Windows computer). We show you some simple but effective maneuvers to manage your desktop plus some applications.

Separation anxiety? Not with Linux

The version of X that comes with Red Hat Linux is both sophisticated and simple to use. This wasn't always the case; in fact, it took lots of natural — dare we say Darwinian? — selection to arrive at the current arrangement of X, and the result works well.

Introducing the X Window System

Red Hat gives you the option of using the GNOME and KDE desktop environments. GNOME and KDE, however, run on top of X, and X runs on Linux. X is the software that provides the low-level graphical tools that systems like GNOME use. X is the middleware that makes it possible to build complex systems like GNOME.

X is composed of three main parts:

- The X server
- A set of graphics libraries
- A set of graphics applications that usually use the graphics libraries

The *X server* is a program that talks to a bunch of important hardware — such as the video card, keyboard, and mouse — on your system and runs interference between this hardware and the other graphics software.

The X server commands from the set of graphics libraries that are associated by default with specified programs. Sometimes these programs are executed directly on the same system where the graphics device resides; at other times, these programs talk across a network to a graphics device on another system. Using X, you can run your program in one part of the world, and someone can see the output in another part of the world over the Internet.

Suppose that you're logged into a computer in Australia and you want to see what time it is there. You could run the date command (from a command line) to see the date and time, but that would be boring. Instead, you could run the xclock program on the remote machine and see a graphical clock displayed on your local computer. You can then verify that the Aussies use clocks that run clockwise and have 24-hour days.

The X server program, often called simply *X,* isn't part of the operating system, as it is in some other operating systems. Instead, the X server is a *user-level* program — although it's special and complex.

The X Window System provides the foundation for these graphical-based systems:

- ✔ **Desktop environment:** GNOME and KDE provide a desktop environment that makes using your computer easy. Desktop environments provide high-level functions like menu systems, icons, and backgrounds. A desktop environment is equivalent to a house where X is the foundation.

- ✔ **Graphical applications:** Red Hat installs numerous applications, such as games, system administration utilities, Mozilla, and Ximian Evolution to provide the functionality that helps you use your computer and the Internet. Graphical applications are equivalent to the appliances found in a house.

Exploring the GNOME Desktop Environment

GNOME, pronounced "guh-nome," stands for GNU Network Object Model Environment. (GNU itself stands for GNU's Not UNIX, a recursive acronym designed by guys who never went to their prom but went on to change the world.) If you have trouble remembering acronyms, just think of GNOME as great graphics for *no money*. However you remember it, GNOME is an Open Source graphical desktop environment. It provides a platform for doing your everyday tasks, such as word processing and Internet browsing, on your Red Hat Linux computer.

Log in to your Red Hat Linux computer and check out the GNOME interface. It should look something like Figure 9-1 and consists of these three major elements:

- ✔ **The desktop:** Quite simply, the desktop is the space where you do your work. It's equivalent to — ta-da! — the top of a desk. The desktop comes preconfigured with a background and several icons that include links to places such as your home directory and the trash bin. Icons are equivalent to the junk you pile on your desk.

 When you click the home directory, a Nautilus window opens and displays the contents of those directories. *Nautilus* is a graphical system for working with not only files and directories but also administration utilities and Web pages. See Chapter 10 for more information about Nautilus.

- ✔ **The Panel:** The menu bar that runs across the bottom edge of your GNOME screen is the Panel. You can access every GNOME function and Red Hat or third-party application from the Panel. The Panel represents the drawers in a desk.

✔ **Applications:** These elements include user system and GNOME-level applications. User programs include applications such as Mozilla, Evolution, XMMS, and Xine. System applications include the Red Hat Linux system administration utilities, such as the network configuration and user management utilities; GNOME utilities, such as the Help browser; and Control Center. Applications are equivalent to the toys on and in your desk.

Figure 9-1:
The GNOME
desktop.

Mucking about the Desktop

GNOME performs all the basic graphical functions you expect from a desktop environment. You can set the background, create icons, and so on. This section shows you how to do some basic GNOME desktop maneuvers and configurations. After you master the basics, you can continue to explore on your own.

The default GNOME desktop — as installed by the Red Hat Linux installation — comes with several elements preinstalled. We take a quick trip around the desktop.

Introducing the default desktop icons

In the upper-left corner of the desktop are three icons: your home directory, Start Here, and Trash (refer to Figure 9-1). They perform these tasks:

- **Home directory:** This icon, which looks like a folder, represents your home directory. For example, if you create a user account named lidia, a directory /home/lidia is created. When you log in as lidia, the home directory icon is linked to that directory. Double-click the home directory (or right-click and choose Open) and a Nautilus window opens, displaying the contents of the home directory.

- **Start Here:** GNOME configures a Preferences window that provides links to the major GNOME and Red Hat configuration utilities and applications. Double-click the Start Here icon, and the Start Here window opens. Double-clicking any of the icons — Applications, Preferences, Server Settings, and System Settings — opens another Nautilus window that provides access to utilities and applications.

  The Start Here window provides connections to these applications and utilities:

- **Trash icon:** GNOME provides a method to dispose of files and directories in the form of the Trash directory. Click any icon, file, or directory and drag it to the Trash icon. Although Jesse James's Monster Garage automated trash minivan doesn't come for your file, it's placed in the Trash directory; the Trash directory is in your home directory.

  Trashed items aren't really deleted until you right-click the Trash icon and choose Empty trash. You can undelete items by opening the Trash (double-clicking the icon) and then clicking the item and dragging it out onto the desktop or an open Preferences window.

- **Applications icon:** Clicking the Applications icon is equivalent to selecting from the GNOME menu. You see a window of icons that mirrors the GNOME menu.

- **Preferences:** Clicking the Desktop Properties icon is equivalent to choosing GNOME Menu⇨Preferences. You get to choose from a number of GNOME configuration options. The GNOME Preferences window is described later in this chapter, in the "Tinkering with GNOME" section.

- **System Settings:** Double-clicking the System Settings icon opens the System Settings window, which allows you to start various administrative utilities. You find icons such as the Red Hat Network Configuration and the Printing utilities here.

Changing themes and backgrounds

GNOME provides the ability to change the look and feel of the various parts that comprise your desktop; the desktop is made up of applets, windows, and panels. The look and feel of the desktop is referred to as a theme. *Themes* control the size, shape, texture, and color of the buttons, slides, menus, borders, and other pieces of your window.

You can change your theme more easily and quickly than a politician during an election by choosing GNOME Menu➪Preferences➪Theme; alternatively, you can open the Start Here icon and select Preferences in the window that opens. Double-click the Theme icon when the Preferences window opens.

The Theme Preferences window opens. You see several preinstalled themes, such as Blue Curve, which Red Hat uses by default. Clicking a theme switches the desktop to that theme. Try using different themes until you find one you like. There's no penalty for experimenting because you can always return to the default. Click the Close button to finalize your selection.

You can select themes for just the window borders and icons too. Click the Details button. When the Theme Details window opens, click the Window Border tab. Select any of the menu items and your window borders change to the theme you select. Alternatively, click the Icon tab and select the theme to use for your icons.

You can keep selecting different themes until you're satisfied. Click the Close button when you're finished. You return to the Theme Preference window and can save your selections as a custom theme.

Right-clicking anywhere on a blank section of the desktop and then choosing Use Default Background resets the background. The default background gets reactivated.

Toiling in your workplace

After using GNOME for a while, you find that as you start more and more applications, you create lots and lots of windows on the screen. You may even lose windows behind other windows. Perhaps you wish that you could strap several monitors together so that you can display all the windows at one time.

Monitors are expensive and bulky, so you're probably stuck using a single monitor. But you don't have to be stuck with one *screen.* GNOME lets you spread your work across multiple virtual monitors.

Imagine that you have a huge GNOME desktop that is spread equally across four monitors. Life would be good if you could open windows on any of the monitors. You would have lots of real estate to spread out on.

However, because you don't have four monitors, GNOME simulates four virtual monitors, called *workspaces*. Each workspace is equivalent to a real monitor, and you can spread out your work across it. The only limitation is that you can view only one workspace at a time.

Trading places on your workspace switcher

Switching between workspaces is easy. GNOME provides a utility, the Workspace Switcher, to select any workspace. The Workspace Switcher is on the GNOME Panel.

You use the GNOME Workspace Switcher to access each workspace. The Workspace Switcher is divided into four quadrants. Clicking any of the quadrants places you in the corresponding desktop. Click the lower-right one and you enter that workspace.

You can force a window into any or all workspaces. Click the downward-facing arrow in the upper-left corner of a window. The menu that opens provides all the expected functions that close, minimize, maximize, and resize the window. However, toward the bottom of the menu are options for placing the window in any of the remaining three workspaces; or, you can put the window in all the workspaces. You may, for example, want to put an application like Mozilla in all workspaces in order to use it no matter what you're doing.

Messing Around with Windows

Before you can do anything to a window, you have to get its attention. When you have a window's attention, it has *focus*. Depending on how you have set up GNOME, you can give a window focus with GNOME in several ways, including

- ✔ Click the window's name in the Panel.
- ✔ Click the window's title bar, at the top of the window.
- ✔ Click a part of the window itself, which typically also makes the window the topmost one.
- ✔ If you're working in an office with lots of people, you can shout, "Hey, you — wake up!" Although this tactic isn't likely to wake up your window, it sure is fun.

In this book, we stick with the Red Hat/GNOME default of clicking a window to focus it.

Moving windows

To move a window, click anywhere on the window's title bar and hold down the left mouse button. As long as you continue to hold the left mouse button down, the window moves anywhere you move your mouse. Release the button and the window stays there.

Resizing windows

Sometimes a window is a little too big or a little too small, and you know that life would be much easier if you could just nudge that window into shape. To do just that, position the mouse cursor on any border of the window. Click and drag the window's outline to the size you want. Release the mouse button and the window takes the new size.

Minimizing windows

Now that you have put lots of windows on the screen, how can you get rid of a few or all of them? You can *minimize* (or *iconify*) a window by clicking the bold, underscored button toward the upper-right corner, which removes the window from the desktop and places it in a storage area of the Panel. If you're in a particularly devilish mood, you can be more drastic and *close* a window. Figure 9-2 shows an open Mozilla window minimized — you can see its icon in the GNOME Panel along the lower, central edge of the screen.

Figure 9-2:
Mozilla
minimized
inside
GNOME.

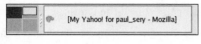

Here are a few ways to get rid of a window, starting with the least drastic and escalating to outright window death:

✔ Take advantage of any exit buttons or menu options that the window or application in the window gives you. For example, many applications allow you to choose File↪Exit to close the application.

✔ Click the X button in the upper-right corner of the window's title bar to close the window.

✔ Click the upper-left corner of the window (or right-click the title bar) and choose the Close option from the menu that appears.

You can return a minimized window to the desktop by clicking the icon that corresponds to the window on the Panel.

Maximizing windows

To make a window fill the entire screen, click the Maximize button in the upper-right corner of the window. Check out the buttons to the right of the title bar in a typical window. The Maximize button is the one in the middle; it looks like a square and is similar in action to the Cascade button in Windows.

The Making of a Desktop Icon

You can create an icon on your desktop for any application on the GNOME menu. Just click the GNOME Menu button, find the menu item for the application you want an icon for, and then left-click the application's icon and hold the mouse button down. While continuing to hold down the button, drag the mouse cursor to any open area on the GNOME desktop (or the GNOME Panel). Release the mouse button, and an icon for that application is placed on the desktop. You can then start the application by double-clicking the icon on the desktop (or just clicking the icon on the GNOME Panel).

With GNOME, you can enhance icons with emblems. *Emblems* provide additional information about what an icon is meant for or to do. You can assign an Emblem by right-clicking an icon and choosing Properties. The Properties window opens. Click the Emblems tab and select one of the emblems. For example, if you select the Cool emblem, a pair of Wayfarers is displayed with the icon on the desktop — cool. You can see the cool icon dude in the margin.

Another cool GNOME icon feature is the ability to stretch an icon's boundaries. Right-click an icon and choose Stretch Icon. A dashed line and four square buttons bracket the icon. Click any of the buttons, and you can stretch the icon image as much as you want.

Playing with the GNOME Panel

The GNOME *Panel* is the menu bar along the bottom of the desktop. The Panel, similar to the taskbar in Windows, provides a location to place common menus and applets for easy starting or viewing. The Panel also gives you a view of the virtual desktop and enables you to keep track of minimized windows.

By default, Red Hat Linux places icons on the Panel for accessing the GNOME menu, Mozilla, Evolution, OpenOffice (Writer, Impress, and Calc), and the GNOME Workspace Switcher. You can start any of these programs or use the switcher by clicking its icon.

 The most important element on the Panel is the GNOME Menu button, on the far left side, which you use to access all the standard GNOME applications and configuration tools. The GNOME Menu button, which looks amazingly similar to a red hat, is in the lower-left corner of the screen. You can choose from any of the menus that are displayed when you click the GNOME Menu button. For example, the System Settings and System Tools menus contain many of the Red Hat utilities you can use to administer your Red Hat Linux computer. The Sound & Video menu provides access to a CD player, and the Graphics menu provides access to graphical applications. You get the idea.

You can use the Add to Panel submenu to modify the configuration and behavior of the Panel. For example, if you right-click any unused portion of the GNOME Panel and choose Add to Panel➪Amusements➪Geyes, you get the nifty pair of eyes applet added to the Panel. The eyes follow your mouse around the screen — ooh, scary. Geyes demonstrates the tremendous extra dimension of functionality that enters your life when you use Red Hat Linux. (You can remove the eyes by right-clicking its icon and choosing the Remove from Panel option.)

 One other interesting function of the Panel menu is the Add New Launcher function. Click any unused section of the GNOME Panel and choose Add to Panel➪Launcher Buttons. The Create Launcher Applet window appears. By entering the pathname of an application, you can add a new applet to the Panel that *launches,* or starts, that application.

 GNOME provides a file searching utility called Search Tool. Click the GNOME Menu button and choose Search for Files, and the Search Tool starts. Enter the name of a file you want to find and click the Find button. Click the Advanced tab and you can conduct a more finely tuned file search.

Give it a try. For example, if you frequently use the X MultiMedia System (XMMS) to listen to audio streams (described further in Chapter 12), you can add an applet for it to your Panel so that you don't have to haggle with menus to launch XMMS. From the Create Launcher Applet window, add the name, generic name, comments, and the command — /usr/bin/xmms — to launch the program. If you click the No Icon button, you see a few pages of standard icons you can use to distinguish your new applet from others on the Panel; in this case, we chose the xmms.xpm as our icon mascot. Figure 9-3 shows the finished applet launcher window.

Figure 9-3:
The XMMS launcher applet is born.

After you finish editing the Create Launcher Applet window, click OK. The icon is added to your Panel, as shown in Figure 9-4. You can create in the same way a launcher for any application on your Red Hat Linux computer.

Figure 9-4:
The XMMS launcher applet icon on the Panel.

Adding and Deleting Panels

You're not limited to the default GNOME Panel. You can create additional panels at will. Click anywhere on an unused portion of the GNOME Panel and select New Panel. Next, click any of the Panel options. For example, selecting Edge Panel places a blank panel along the top of the screen.

The new panel is blank and doesn't contain any icons like the default GNOME Panel. It does have a basic menu you can use to populate it with icons and other menus. Right-click the new Panel and the Add to Panel submenu appears. You can use the Add to Panel menu to build up the new Panel. For example, choose Accessories⇨Clock and a digital clock is added to the Panel, as shown in Figure 9-5. Or click Amusements⇨Geyes. Keep adding icons until you're satisfied with the new system.

Figure 9-5:
A new
Panel with a
clock and
kooky eyes.

You can, of course, remove any Panel you created, but you can't remove the default GNOME Panel. The process is simple: Right-click any unused section of the Panel and choose Delete This Panel. Click the Delete button in the Delete Panel window that opens, and the Panel is de-Paneled.

Any Panel can be made to hide when it's not in use. Right-click any unused section of the Panel and choose Properties from the pop-up menu, and the Panel Properties window then opens. Click the Autohide radio button and then the Close button. The Panel disappears off the edge of the screen until you move the mouse cursor back to that edge. The Panel then reappears.

Every new Panel contains arrows at each end, called Hide Buttons; the original default Panel does not. Clicking either of the arrows forces the Panel to slide off to one side or the other. The Panel is hidden except for those same arrows. Clicking the arrow uncovers the hidden Panel.

Leaving GNOME and X

If you want to leave your computer on but don't want to leave it open to anyone just walking along, you can save the time spent logging out of your GNOME desktop by using the screen lock. To do so, click the GNOME Menu button and choose Lock Screen; the screensaver is displayed. To return to productive life and your desktop, press any key or wiggle your mouse and enter your password in the X Screensaver window that appears.

Securing your computer while you step out for a moment

Locking your screen is one of the best security features you can use. To lock your screen, click the GNOME Menu button and choose Lock Screen. Your screen locks up and you must enter your password to get back in. Locking your screen is a good idea when you're going to be away from it for even a minute or two.

Going home for the night

After you have finished for the day and want to go home (or just upstairs), you need to log out. Click the GNOME Menu button and choose Log Out. The Are You Sure You Want to Log Out? window appears. Click Logout to log out. You also have the options to shut down or reboot your computer.

GNOME configures a random screensaver by default. You can select a single screensaver by clicking the GNOME Menu button and choosing Preferences⇨ Screensaver. The Screensaver Preferences window opens. For example, you can switch from the default random screensaver to the Xjack (we all know that all work and no play makes Jack a dull boy) screensaver. it's not a bad selection for those long winters spent at peaceful resorts with plenty of time to write Linux books!

eXterminating X

When you can't get your applications to respond to you, you can simply stop X, which kills all the programs running under it. To do so, press the Ctrl+Alt+Backspace keys all at one time. If you started X manually, you can then log out of the account. If X is started automatically at boot time (as we assume in this book), you get the X login screen and you can log back in.

Tinkering with GNOME

You can modify the look and feel of your desktop by using an assortment of GNOME configuration utilities. Double-click the Start Here icon on the desktop. When the window opens, double-click the Preferences icon. (You can access the same functions by clicking the GNOME Menu button and then selecting the Preference menu. A submenu opens, showing the same options as in the Preferences window.)

Figure 9-6 shows the Preferences window, where you can modify GNOME properties. For example, double-click the File Types and Programs option, and you can associate applications with MIME types.

Double-click the Files Types and Programs icon and the File Types and Programs window appears. GNOME recognizes MIME types by the information stored by this utility. For example, choose Audio⇨OGG and then click Edit. The Edit File Type window, as shown in Figure 9-7, opens.

The Edit File Type window shows that Ogg audio files belong to the application/x-ogg MIME type. The window also shows that Ogg audio files use .ogg file suffixes. The default action is to use XMMS to play Ogg audio files and streams.

You can click the Default action pull-down menu and then choose Custom if you want to use another application to play your Ogg files. In that case, enter the name of a program manually in the Program to run subwindow. Whatever program you select is used to play Ogg files whenever you click them in any Nautilus or other file manager window.

The Preferences window also lets you configure things other than screensavers with maniacal rantings. We leave it to you to explore the wonderful world of setting your keyboard bell and other items. This system gives you lots of flexibility.

Figure 9-6:
The
Preferences
window.

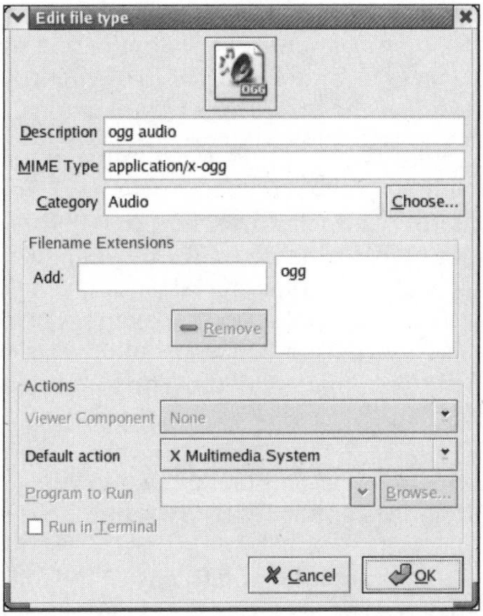

Figure 9-7:
The Edit
File Type
window.

Accessing GNOME Applications

The last GNOME element consists of the applications that come packaged with GNOME. GNOME provides numerous applications intended for work and fun. Red Hat also provides a wide range of applications, some of which are accessible via GNOME. (You can also add your own applications from the Open Source community and third parties.)

Nautilus provides another way of accessing many of the applications on your Red Hat Linux computer. Applications that don't have links to GNOME aren't accessible via the GNOME menu system; you can generally correct that situation by manually adding links provided by the GNOME Add to Panel option.

This list describes the methods used to access applications:

- ✔ **Start Here:** From the GNOME Start Here window, opening the Applications icon provides access to most of the applications installed on your computer.

- ✔ **Nautilus:** Clicking your Home directory icon opens a Nautilus window. You can then start any executable application stored in your home directory by double-clicking its icon. You can also change to any other directory — that you have access permission to — in order to run an application.

✔ **GNOME Menu:** Selecting the GNOME menu provides access to every application that GNOME "knows" about (every application that GNOME has been configured to access). Using the GNOME menu provides access to the same set of programs as the Start Here➪Applications windows.

✔ **Old School:** GNOME provides two methods for running programs from a CLI (a bash shell running in a terminal emulator window). You can start a GNOME Terminal emulator window or use the GNOME Run Program function. The former opens a Bash shell in a Terminal emulator window from which you can launch applications; the latter opens a window in which you can enter the name of a program to execute. The primary difference between the two systems is that you can interact with an application when using the Terminal emulator. The Run Program system allows you to interact with an application only if it creates a GUI.

The following list illustrates the rich application landscape you get with Red Hat and GNOME. The list categorizes applications by type:

✔ **Accessories:** Applications that don't belong to any of the following groups in this list are labeled as accessories. Applications such as the GNOME Calculator, gedit, and a dictionary are placed in this category; the dictionary is quite useful — enter a word and its definition is displayed.

✔ **Games:** Because Linux was initially oriented toward running services, you may not think of it as being oriented toward game players. But Red Hat Linux has lots of games. Open the Games icon and you see many of them. You can waste your life with Linux just as easily as with Windows! Ha!

✔ **Graphics:** You can view and manipulate images with these graphical utilities; ImageMagick and The GIMP are excellent tools for working with pixels. You can use the Scanning tool to scan images on a scanner. DVI, Adobe Acrobat Reader, and general-purpose image viewers are included, as is a digital camera tool. You can access some utilities by choosing Graphics from the GNOME menu. More graphics applications are accessible via the GNOME menu and choosing Extras➪Graphics.

✔ **Help:** Clicking the Help menu opens the GNOME Help browser. It provides information about many GNOME topics.

✔ **Internet:** The new Red Hat default e-mail client Evolution is in this folder. You also find a graphical chat application, Instant Messenger.

✔ **Network Servers:** You can view Samba servers on your network. Network Servers provides the same function that Microsoft Network Neighborhood provides.

✔ **Office:** The Open Source OpenOffice applications are stored in this folder. OpenOffice provides a word processor, spreadsheet, presentation manager, and drawing tool, all of which are accessed here. You can also find the OpenOffice repair and printer configuration utilities here. (Icons are automatically placed in the GNOME Panel as well.)

- ✔ **Programming:** Linux provides a good programming environment. Red Hat Linux provides links, via this menu, to several programming utilities, such as Emacs, that many people use for editing source code.

- ✔ **Search for files:** This application helps you search for files and directories on your hard disk. It's easy to use and quite useful.

- ✔ **Sound and Video:** Lots of fun stuff is stored here. The Red Hat Linux CD player, XMMS, is found here, for example. You also find in this folder more mundane items, such as the volume control and volume monitor utilities.

- ✔ **System Settings:** Red Hat places many of its fabulous configuration utilities here. For example, the Red Hat Network Configuration, X configuration, and Soundcard Detection utilities are here. You access the Server Settings menu from here; this menu provides access to the Services utility, which allows you to start and stop Red Hat Linux services.

- ✔ **System Tools:** You can access more of the Red Hat system administration utilities from this folder.

Going Old School with the Terminal Emulators

One important — almost essential — GNOME application is the *GNOME Terminal,* as shown in Figure 9-8, a program that emulates the old-style terminal from within the GUI. Back in the good old days, you could type only text commands and see the results in text — and you did that on a terminal. You may be wondering why you would want to simulate a dumb, inexpensive terminal when you paid lots of money for a neat graphics monitor.

Well, in the early days of X, few graphical programs were available. Most programs were written to run on nongraphical interfaces and didn't include the libraries that create graphical programs on an X server. In other words, in order to run both graphical and nongraphical programs, the dumb terminal had to be emulated through software.

When you start a terminal emulator, the emulator usually executes a shell and gives you a command-line prompt. You type commands at this command prompt, and the results are printed to the terminal emulator window. GNOME provides a terminal emulator named the *GNOME Terminal.* You can start it by choosing GNOME Menu⇨System Tools⇨Terminal.

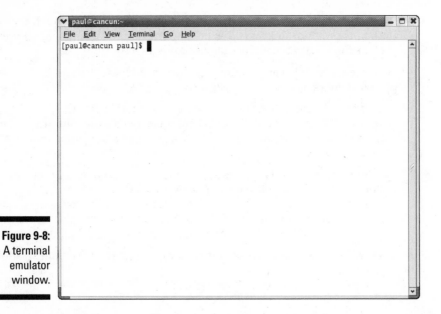

Figure 9-8:
A terminal emulator window.

You can also run command-line programs by using the GNOME Run Program menu. Click the GNOME Main Menu button and choose Run Program. The Run Program window, as shown in Figure 9-9, opens. You can enter any command you want. For example, enter **xclock** in the text box, and the graphical clock window opens on the desktop.

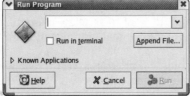

Figure 9-9:
The Run Program window.

Suspending Your Computer

One useful Linux application is the Advanced Power Manager (APM). APM performs two functions: monitoring a laptop computer's battery and placing your computers — both desktops and laptops — into a suspended animation power-saving mode.

An APM system consists of both a client and a server. The server daemon, apmd, is installed during the Red Hat Linux installation process and is started automatically by default. You use the APM client to both monitor your laptop's battery and place your computer into power-saving mode.

You can install the APM client in the GNOME Panel to monitor your laptop's battery:

1. **Log in to your computer as any user.**

2. **Right- click the GNOME Panel and choose Add to Panel⇨Utilities⇨ Battery Charge Monitor.**

3. **An icon that looks like — you guessed it — a battery is added to the Panel.**

The Battery Charge Monitor icon displays that state of your battery. APM starts beeping frantically when your power level goes below 10 percent.

You can use APM to place your computer into one of two power modes:

✔ **Suspend:** Saves your computer's current state on disk and turns the power off. When you turn the power back on, your computer's last state is recovered from disk and your computer starts in where you left it. Suspend mode turns off power to your computer and saves the maximum amount of energy; it also makes your computer quiet.

✔ **Standby:** Places the state in memory and reduces power. You only need to press any keyboard key or move the mouse to start your computer again. Your computer returns to normal operation more quickly than it does from Suspend mode. Standby doesn't save as much power and is noisier because your computer's fans may continue to operate.

You can use this function on both laptop and desktop computers. No default GNOME icon or menu allows you to use the power-saving mode without being the root user. Therefore, use the GNOME Terminal to use APM:

1. **Click the GNOME menu and choose System Tools⇨Terminal.**

2. **If you're not already logged in as root, do so now:**
   ```
   su -
   ```

3. **Run this command to suspend your computer, saving the maximum amount of power:**
   ```
   apm -s
   ```
   Note that the case of the apm option is important: Using a lowercase *s* suspends the computer, and an uppercase *S* places it in Standby mode.

   Alternatively, you can use Standby mode:
   ```
   apm -S
   ```

When you want to return your computer to a working state, press the power button to return from Suspend or press any key or move the mouse to come back from Standby.

Chapter 10

Gnowing More Applications

In This Chapter

▶ Introducing Nautilus, the GNOME file and integration manager

▶ Introducing the Ximian Evolution e-mail and personal organizer

▶ Introducing more useful GNOME applications

Many applications help make your Red Hat Linux computer useful. In this chapter, you find out how to use several of the most useful applications that come packaged with Red Hat Linux. The first one is the Nautilus file manager, an integral part of the GNOME desktop system. The second application is the new e-mail and organizer application named Evolution. We also introduce several other useful applications.

Chapter 11 describes how to use the Mozilla Web browser. Chapter 13 introduces the OpenOffice desktop productivity suite, which gives you Microsoft Word-compatible word processing, a spreadsheet program, a Power Point-compatible presentation program, and other functions. These programs, combined with Evolution, give you all the functions you need to make your Red Hat Linux computer a fully functioning workstation.

Navigating with the Nautilus File/Internet Integration Manager

Being the boss doesn't make you a bad person. It's just a job. Right? Well, that little GNOME guy is a good worker and doesn't get paid much. Just press a key here, click a button there, and you can boss him around like any worthy pointy-headed Dilbert manager. GNOME even comes with its own file and integration manager that saves work and makes time for those long lunches.

Nautilus is the GNOME file and Internet navigator system. Nautilus follows in the tradition of all good file managers by graphically displaying the files and directories on your computer. You can copy, move, delete, and execute files by pointing and clicking; creating directories and viewing file details are a snap, too. Nautilus even goes a step further: You can use it to configure your GNOME desktop. And that's not all! Nautilus can also navigate the Internet, access multimedia, and slice and dice! Not a bad deal, considering that it works for free.

Waking up Nautilus

Red Hat Linux configures Nautilus to start automatically when you log in. Nautilus appears toward the end of the login process and works as a file manager (see Figure 10-1, showing the contents of your home directory). If you want to start it manually — after you have closed it, for example — right-click anywhere on the desktop background and choose New Window.

The main menu follows familiar menu formats (File, Edit, and so on) and does all the things you would expect those menus to do. The toolbar immediately below the main menu enables you to quickly move up one directory (Up) and skip back to previous moves (Back and Forward). It also lets you rescan a directory, go to your home directory, and change the way icons are displayed.

The Reload function is useful if you create a new file — for example, via a terminal emulator. The file doesn't show up in the File Manager until you move to another directory and return, or else reload.

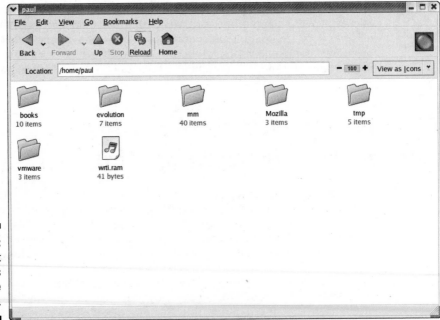

Figure 10-1:
Nautilus at
work as
a file
manager.

Moving files and directories

Moving a file or directory is as simple as clicking and dragging the item you want to move to the directory you want to move it to. Release the button, and you have moved your file or directory.

You can move multiple files by clicking and dragging the mouse cursor over the files you want. The mouse cursor creates a rectangular outline and highlights all the files within that box. Next, click anywhere within the highlighted box and drag the mouse cursor to the directory you want. Release the mouse button and the files move to the specified directory.

Copying files and directories

Copying a file or directory is a bit more complicated than moving one. Rather than simply click and drag an icon someplace, you need to right-click the file or directory icon and choose Copy from the menu that appears. Next, enter the directory you want to copy to by double-clicking its icon. When the directory opens, right-click anywhere on the background and choose the Paste option. The file or directory is copied to the new location.

You can copy multiple files and directories in the same manner that you copied individual ones. Trace a box around the files or directories you want to copy by clicking and dragging the mouse cursor. Next, right-click any of the blue highlighted icon names (but not the white space around the icon and names themselves) and choose the Copy option. Double-click the directory to copy to. Right-click the background and choose Paste. Release the mouse button and the files are copied to the specified directory.

Deleting files and directories

Deleting files and directories is much the same process as copying them. You right-click the file or directory icon you want and choose Move to Trash from the menu that appears. The file or directory is moved to the Trash directory.

"Trashed" files and directories are not immediately deleted. When you use the Move to Trash option to delete a file, for example, the file is moved to the Trash folder. Open the Trash directory by double-clicking its icon and then right-clicking the file or directory to delete. Choose the Delete from Trash option. The Delete From Trash? warning window opens and prompts you to confirm deletion. Click the Delete key and the file is erased.

You can delete multiple files and directories. Again, you trace a box by clicking and dragging the mouse cursor. Right-click the blue highlighted icons or icon names (but not the white space around the icon and name). The files or directories are moved to the trash directory.

Creating directories

Right-click anywhere in a Nautilus window and choose New Folder to create a new directory. A new folder appears with the name Untitled folder. Enter any name for the directory as you please.

Viewing files and directories

By default, files and directories are displayed onscreen as icons. The only information an icon shows is the name and whether an item is a file or directory (directory icons also show the number of files and directories they contain). You can display additional information by clicking the View as Icons, View as List, or View as buttons that appear when you click the View Menu button at the top of the screen.

This list describes the differences between views:

- **Icons view:** The default display option; shows the icon and indicates whether an item is a file or directory. Regular file icons take several forms, but text and configuration files look like pieces of paper with a corner folded. Files containing specific types of data have small subicons overlaid on the file icon. For example, PDF files have a PDF subicon. Links, devices, and so on take other forms. Directories take the form of a partially open manila folder. Icons are evenly placed across the entire File Manager screen. Icons tend to make distinguishing files and directories easier but take up more space onscreen.

- **List view:** Displays the size and time stamp of each file and directory in addition to their names.

- **View as:** Enables you to select icons or lists as your default folder view for all or specific directories. You can also associate MIME types with specific applications.

You can use Nautilus to create shortcut icons on your desktop that point to files or applications. In Nautilus, just click and drag any file or application to any blank part of the desktop and then release the mouse button. An icon is placed on the desktop. You can then start the application by double-clicking its icon. If the icon points to a data file (such as a text file, for example) and Nautilus knows how to handle its MIME type, Nautilus launches the appropriate application to open the file. Otherwise, Nautilus prompts you to tell it which application to use to open it.

Nautilus is programmed to recognize numerous Multipurpose Internet Mail Extensions (MIME) types, and they define what type of information a file stores — in other words, MIME keeps its own Rolodex of sorts. Each MIME type is associated with certain file extensions. For example, when you double-click a .doc file, Nautilus recognizes that the .doc file suffix corresponds to a Word document MIME type and starts up the OpenOffice word processor (described in Chapter 13), which loads the .doc file.

Nautilus provides the ability to bookmark your favorite locations. The Nautilus bookmark function works just like Mozilla's or any other Web browser. Go to any directory and click Bookmarks⇨Add Bookmark. You only have to click on Bookmarks and select the particular bookmark to go to that location. You can modify existing bookmarks by choosing Bookmarks⇨Edit Bookmarks.

Running programs

Nautilus is such a hard worker that it happily launches commands for you. Right-click the icon you want to run to open a submenu, and then choose Open. For example, if you click the xclock icon in the /usr/bin/X11 directory, the xclock appears on your desktop. (Double-clicking the icon also works.)

Managers are generally not very smart. But Nautilus is smarter than the average manager, and it knows what to do when it encounters various file types. If you open a nonexecutable file, such as a PDF file, the file manager knows which program to use in order to view it.

Come the Ximian Evolution Revolution

The Ximian Evolution system is the new workhorse of the GNOME and Linux world. Evolution provides the next significant step in the evolution of the Linux desktop by combining excellent e-mail and calendar clients with other functions to create a single, integrated package. Evolution provides these capabilities:

- Calendar
- Contact manager
- E-mail client
- Personal Digital Assistant (PDA) manager
- Task master (to-do list)

The following two sections describe how to configure the Evolution e-mail and PDA functions.

Using Evolution for your e-mail

Red Hat uses Evolution as its default e-mail client. Evolution makes it easy for you to configure one or more e-mail accounts. The following instructions describe how to configure Evolution to send messages to and receive messages from your ISP e-mail account:

1. **Log in to your Red Hat Linux computer.**

2. **Click the Evolution icon on the left side of the GNOME panel.**

   The first time you start Evolution, the Setup Assistant (wizard) starts, as shown in Figure 10-2.

3. **Click the Next button.**

4. **Enter your name and e-mail address in the appropriate text boxes in the Identity window and click Next.**

   You can optionally enter your organization and *signature file* (a file where you keep personal or business information to be appended to the end of every message you send).

   Figure 10-3 shows some sample entries in the Identity window.

   The Receiving Email window appears, as shown in Figure 10-4.

5. **Click the Server Type pull-down menu and choose the option that matches your ISP's e-mail system. Most ISPs use the Internet Message Access Protocol (IMAP) server type.**

   The Receiving Email window expands so that you can enter more information about your ISP email system.

Figure 10-2:
The Evolution Setup Assistant window.

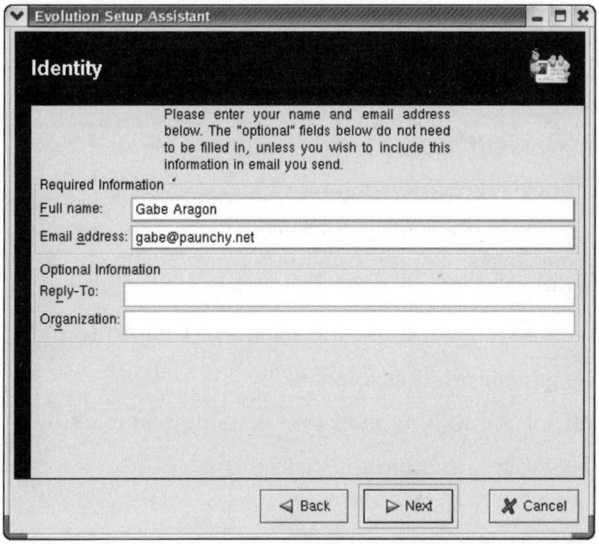

Figure 10-3:
The Identity
window.

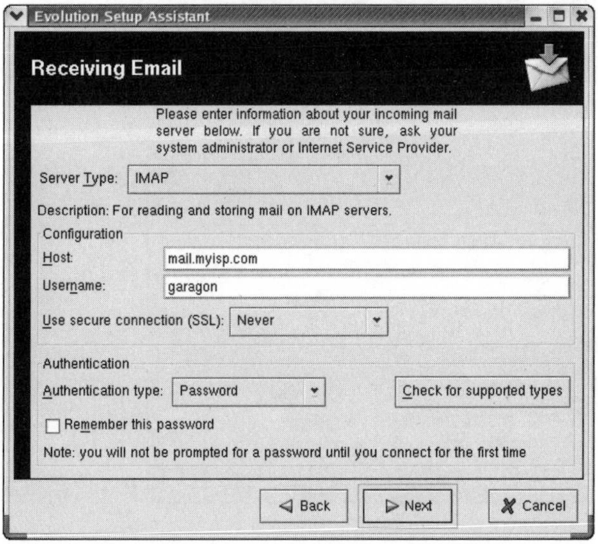

Figure 10-4:
The
Receiving
Email
window.

6. Enter the host name of your ISP e-mail server and your ISP user name.

Your ISP provides you with the name of its incoming and outgoing e-mail
servers when you first subscribe. You need to enter the incoming server
name in the Host text box. For example, your ISP incoming server may
be `mail.myisp.com` or `imap.myisp.com`.

Your ISP username may be different from your username on your Linux computer. For example, your ISP username may be based on your first initial and last name — *garagon* — but your home Linux computer user name may be just your first name — *gabe.*

7. **Click the Next button.**

   A second Receiving Email window appears.

   You can change options, such as having Evolution automatically look for incoming messages, by checking the Automatically check for new mail radio button.

8. **Make any changes you want and click the Next button.**

   The Sending Email window appears.

9. **Enter your ISP's outgoing mail server name and click the Next button.**

   Figure 10-5 shows a sample screen in this window.

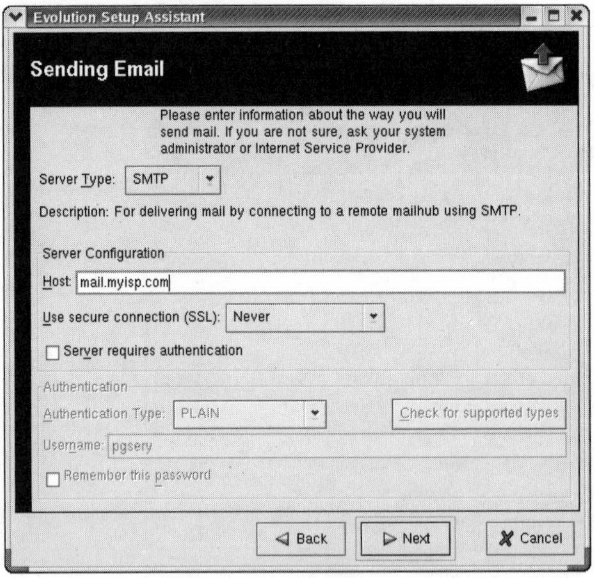

Figure 10-5:
The Sending
Email
window.

The default outgoing Evolution e-mail protocol is SMTP. SMTP is used frequently by ISPs, so you may not need to change it. Your ISP should supply you with the protocol it uses.

A few ISPs may use encrypted Secure Service Link (SSL) connections and require authentication. Again, you need to obtain this information from your ISP and use those options, if necessary.

The Account Management window opens. The account you're creating is called by this name. Evolution uses your e-mail address as the default name. You can change the name if you want, but it's not necessary.

Your new account is your default account if it's your only one. Otherwise, you can choose to make it your default by clicking the Make This My Default Account radio button.

10. **The final configuration step requires you to pick your time zone. Click the closest dot to your location.**

A bigger map appears, as shown in Figure 10-6, which enables you to fine-tune your location, if necessary. It's the same system you used in Chapter 3 to set your computer's time zone.

11. **Click the Next button.**

The Done window pops up.

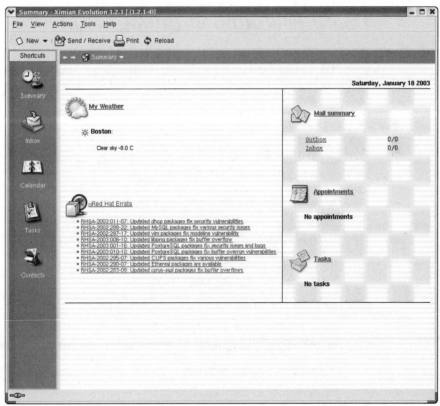

Figure 10-6:
The Evolution Summary window.

12. **Click the Finish button and you're finished.**

Evolution starts and displays a Summary window. Shortcuts to the Evolution function are on the left side of the window. Click your e-mail account shortcut to see your new e-mail account listed. (You can also access your account by clicking the Summary button, located toward the upper-left corner of the window.) Select your account to make it active. You can then send and receive messages. You can also perform any other typical actions on your account, such as sorting, moving, and deleting messages.

You can add new e-mail accounts as desired. You can also go back and modify or delete existing accounts. Click your e-mail account shortcut icon and then choose Tools⇨Settings. The Mail Settings window opens, and you can modify your account, add new ones, and delete old ones. Note that the Evolution Account Assistant starts when you click the Add button.

Using Evolution with your PDA

You can use the Evolution' calendar, to-do manager, and contact manager with your PDA. In this section, we concentrate on using Evolution to back up your PDA because that's one of more interesting and fun things you can do. You can find out more about using the calendar by reading the online Evolution documentation (click Help or visit `www.gnome.org/gnome-office/evolution.shmtl`) or simply by experimenting with it.

You can use the Evolution pilot-link utility to back up your PDA databases to your computer. To do so, follow these steps:

1. **Plug your Pilot cradle into your computer's serial port.**

The cable attached to your cradle has a female 9-pin (called a DB9) plug attached to it. Most, if not all, modern computers have a 9-pin male plug that connects to a serial port socket controlled by the `/dev/ttyS0` Linux device. (In the Windows world, `/dev/ttyS0` is equivalent to COM1, `/dev/ttyS1` is COM2, and so on.)

2. **Click the Evolution icon on the GNOME panel.**

The Ximian Evolution (revolution?) application starts up.

3. **Click the Contacts button.**

4. **Choose Tools⇨Pilot settings.**

The Welcome to GNOME Pilot Wizard window opens.

5. **Click Next and the Cradle Settings window, as shown in Figure 10-7, appears.**

You need to tell Evolution where to find your PDA. Click the Port menu and choose the serial device.

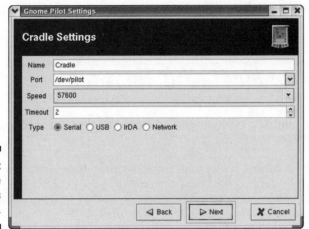

Figure 10-7:
The Cradle
Settings
window.

The device is probably /dev/ttyS0 or /dev/ttyS1. There's no shame in trial and error, so choose each port in order until you find the right one.

Don't worry about selecting the speed. The default value is adequate unless you have a very old computer.

6. **Click the Next button.**

   The Pilot Identification window opens.

7. **Click the No, I've Never Used Sync Software with This Pilot Before button.**

   Your user name is inserted into the User Name text box. (For example, if you're logged in as paul, paul is your default Pilot ID.)

8. **Click the Next button to accept the user name; otherwise, type the name you want to use for your Pilot ID.**

9. **Press the synchronize (for example, HotSync for a Palm Pilot) button on the PDA cradle.**

   The calendar database is copied to your Red Hat Linux computer.

Evolution can also synchronize your contact list and address book. Pretty cool, eh?

Checking Out Some Handy Linux Programs

GNOME not only does the work described in the previous sections of this chapter, but also works overtime. Many cool programs are bundled along with Red Hat Linux. A few of the particularly useful ones are described in this section.

Going graphical with The Gimp

The Gimp is more than just a graphics-viewing program — it's also a great graphical manipulator. Click the GNOME Menu button and choose Graphics⇨ The GIMP to start The Gimp.

The Gimp opens several screens, including a Tip window. If you choose File⇨Open, you can open, view, and even modify your graphics files. You can also copy any window or your entire screen by using The Gimp's Acquire function. Choose File⇨Acquire⇨Screen Shot. You can then save any images you want. (This method is how most of the figures in this book were obtained.)

Reading PDF files

You can view portable document format (PDF) files with xpdf. PDF files are used to provide lots of documentation on the Web because they aren't editable and look the same on every machine. PDF files are useful because they enable you to page forward and backward through a document rather than have to view the whole thing at once.

Here's what you need to do:

1. **Start xpdf by logging in as any user, clicking the GNOME Menu button, and then choosing Graphics⇨PDF Viewer.**

   What you see isn't very interesting — it's just a blank page with some buttons pushed off to the bottom of the window.

2. **To open a file, you need to right-click your mouse button anywhere on the blank page and choose Open.**

   The xpdf: Open window pops up.

3. **Download or copy a PDF file of your choice and open it.**

   You can press the forward and backward buttons to page through the document.

   You can also click the Print button to print all or parts of a document. The binocular button is used to search for text. Have fun!

You can see other applications by clicking the GNOME Menu button and choosing All Applications. You see the menu of applications waiting to be used. New applications are continually being added to the GNOME universe. Go to www.gnome.org/applist to see what's available.

Chapter 11

Surfin' the Net and Groovin' to Tunes

*I*n this chapter, we introduce the open source Mozilla Web browser. Mozilla provides all the capabilities of other popular browsers. We show you how to set up Mozilla for your Red Hat Linux computer so that you can surf the Net. You can use your computer as a multimedia device. After working with Mozilla, we describe how to configure your Linux box to listen to music and create CDs.

Our goal in this chapter is to describe how to use the basic Mozilla features. However, we want you to know that Mozilla can do far more than we describe here. For more information about Mozilla, check out the features available on the Help menu, such as the Reference Library or Help contents.

Making the World Wide Web Possible

Once upon a time, a company named Netscape created a browser to surf the Internet. The browser was originally named Navigator, and later, Communicator. Millions of people downloaded it from the Internet for free. Netscape put in the hands of millions of people (including us, your authors) the power to access the exploding number of Web servers. Netscape made history and changed the world because it changed the Internet from a medium that served scientists into a tool that anyone can use.

Even though Netscape Communicator is freely distributed to anyone who wants it, Netscape Communicator isn't Open Source software in the same way that Linux is. Quite simply, Netscape Communicator is a moneymaking venture, and Netscape considers the way the software works to be proprietary.

On the other hand, Netscape recognizes the importance of the Open Source dynamic, which is why it released an Open Source version of Netscape named Mozilla. Now, countless numbers of people are developing and enhancing Mozilla, the default browser for Red Hat Linux computers.

The CD-ROMs that come with this book include Mozilla, the Open Source brother to Netscape Communicator. Netscape and Mozilla are quite similar, although they have a slightly different look and feel.

Surfin' the Net with Mozilla

If you have ever browsed the Internet (and who hasn't, these days?), the first thing you want to do is to tailor Mozilla to your preferences. You can do this task without connecting to the Internet. Follow the steps in this section to customize Mozilla to your liking and set up Mozilla to be your e-mail client.

When you connect to the Internet, the first page you see is your home page. You have the option to set your home page to a Web page you want to see rather than look at a page that someone else wants you to see. And you may also want to tweak your history settings for whatever reason (but certainly not a paranoid one). These steps explain what you need to do:

1. **Start Mozilla by clicking the blue globe icon on the GNOME Panel.**

   The Welcome to Red Hat Linux screen appears in Mozilla, as shown in Figure 11-1. You can use this page to find out more information about Red Hat and its products.

   We want to concentrate on configuring Mozilla and skip over all the Red Hat information; there's lots of good information, however, so explore its world at your leisure.

2. **Choose Edit⇨Preferences.**

   On the left side of the Preferences window is a list of categories, which you can think of as a map of where you are in the Preferences window.

3. **Click the plus sign (+) next to the Appearance category to expand it.**

   Here, you determine which font sizes and other options to use. Next, examine the Navigator category, which is already expanded. This section determines which Web page appears when you start Mozilla and which Web page loads when you click the Home button on the Navigation toolbar.

Figure 11-1:
Mozilla
displays info
about Red
Hat Linux.

4. **In the Home Page area of the Preferences window, fill in the Location field with the URL of the Web page you want to be your home page.**

   You can also surf to the site of your choice, click Preferences, and then click the Use Current Page button.

   For example, type **www.linuxworld.com**, and you see interesting information about Linux whenever you start up your browser or click the Home button in the upper-left corner of the Mozilla window.

Mozilla remembers where you have been and lets you select (and go to) a previous location. How long Mozilla remembers (and then how big the list becomes) depends on how many days of history you choose. The History configuration option determines the length of time in days that the locations you visit are saved. If you're short on disk space, choose a lower History number, such as 1 or 2 days. Otherwise, leave the default setting alone.

If your Linux computer is connected to a network with a proxy firewall, you have to configure Mozilla to work with it. To do so, from the Preferences window choose Advanced⇨Proxies. Click the Manual Proxy configuration radio button and enter the name of your firewall. For example, enter **proxy.mynetwork.com** in the HTTP Proxy text box (if that is the name of your firewall) and enter **80** in the Port text box. You don't have to perform this configuration if you're using the Red Hat default firewall or the packet-filtering firewalls we describe in this book.

Plugging In Plug-Ins

Mozilla performs the tasks you expect from a browser, like displaying graphics along with text. Without help, Mozilla doesn't go the extra mile and display things like animation and JavaScript. When it comes to special functions, Mozilla is a blank slate.

However, with a little help from friends such as you, Mozilla can go that extra mile. That help comes in the form of plug-ins. A *plug-in* is software Mozilla uses when needed to perform extra functions. To make use of plug-ins, all you need to do is — sorry — plug it in.

The plug-in process is straightforward:

1. **Obtain the plug-in.**
2. **Place it in the Mozilla plug-in directory.**
3. **Optionally, configure the Mozilla preferences to use the plug-in.**

We describe how to download and install several popular — and in today's world, necessary — plug-ins. Let's start with the popular Macromedia Flash plug-in. Mozilla can show animation and other cool stuff. Here's what to do:

1. **Start up Mozilla and your Internet connection (if necessary).**
2. **Check to see what plug-ins Mozilla already has access to by clicking the Help⇨About Plug-ins menu.**

   The Mozilla window shows that only the default *libnullplugin.so* is installed. You can download and install some useful plug-ins.

   Clicking the Netscape.com link at the top of the page sends you to the Netscape plug-in Web page. That page describes what plug-ins do and what popular ones are available.

3. **Enter the** www.macromedia.com/go/getflash **address in the Location bar and press the Return key.**

   The Macromedia download page opens.

4. **Click Macromedia Flash Player in the Macromedia Web Players section (the upper third of the page).**

5. **Click the Download Now button, and the Downloading install_flash_player_6_linux.tar.gz window opens.**

   You need to save the file that contains the Flash software, so click OK.

6. **A second window, Enter name of file to save to, opens.**

   Mozilla saves to the directory you're working from by default, generally your home directory. Click the Save button and the software is saved to your computer. (The Download Manager window shows the progress of the download.)

7. **Now you need to unpack and install the Flash plug-in. Open a Gnome Terminal window.**

8. **You need to become root (the superuser), so enter this command in the terminal window:**

   ```
   su
   ```

   Enter the root password when prompted.

9. **Enter this command to unpack the Flash Media software:**

   ```
   tar xzf install_flash_player_6_linx.tar.gz
   ```

   The directory `install_flash_player_6_linux directory` is created, in which the Flash plug-in is placed.

10. **Copy the Flash plug-in to the Mozilla plug-in directory:**

    ```
    cp install_flash_player_6_linux/libflashplayer.so/usr/
           lib/mozilla*/plug-ins.
    ```

    We specify using the asterisk (*) in this command because you may be using a different version of Mozilla than we are. The asterisk substitutes for the Mozilla version number.

11. **Click the Help⇨About Plug-ins menu, and the window shown in Figure 11-2 opens.**

    The Mozilla window described in Step 2 opens and displays the new Flash Player plug-in you just installed.

Your Mozilla browser handles any Web page that uses Flash content.

Installing the Macromedia Flash Player plug-in helps you a great deal. The following list shows some more common plug-ins, available for Linux, that you should consider installing:

✔ **Adobe Acrobat:** Reads the Adobe Portable Document Format (PDF) files. Many Web sites provide information via PDF files rather than HTML or other formats. You can download the Adobe Acrobat plug-in from `ftp://ftp.adobe.com/pub/adobe/acrobatreader/unix/4.x`. (Note that you can use the Open Source xpdf program to view PDF files.)

✔ **Macromedia Shockwave:** Provides multimedia, graphics, and game-oriented support. You can download the Shockwave plug-in from `www.macromedia.com/software/shockwavelayer/`.

✔ **RealAudio RealPlayer:** The RealPlayer plug-in allows you to play the RealNetworks audio and video streams. Many Internet radio stations still use the RealNetworks protocols to stream their content. You can download the RealPlayer plug-in from

```
http://proforma.real.com/real/player/unix/unix.html?src=d
     ownloadr,000814rpchoice_c1.
```

✔ **Sun Microsystems' Java:** Java is a programming language that many Web sites use to provide dynamic content. Although dynamic content comes in many forms, it's basically anything that changes over time. Java is good at providing those interesting and often annoying Web thingies that spin around and such. Download the Java 2 Platform, Standard Edition (J2SE) RPM for Linux from `java.sun.com/j2se/ 1.4.1/download.html`.

Speaking of tunes, the next section shows how to play music from your CD-ROM.

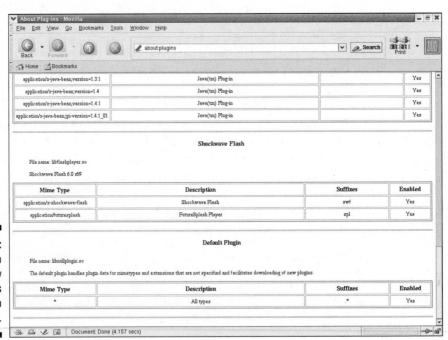

Figure 11-2: The Plug-in window shows the Flash plug-in.

Groovin' to Tunes with CD Player

Imagine that you're sitting alone, working at your computer. Or you could be reading a book that is really making you feel bored. It's Saturday night too, of course. What a drag. Want some diversion? Music helps, eh? We can't provide music, but we can show you how to use your computer to listen to some tunes.

In the following sections, we show you the tools Red Hat Linux provides to make your workstation into a sound system, including all the necessary applications to play CDs, and tools for connecting your PC to a sound card and speakers. Start by making sure that your computer can play music.

Setting Up Your Sound System

Red Hat Linux should have automatically configured your computer's sound system during the post installation described in Chapter 3. However, you may run into problems — especially on older computers — so Red Hat provides a sound card detection utility.

You can configure and test your sound card at the same time by following these steps:

1. **Log in to your Linux computer.**

2. **Click the GNOME Menu button and choose System Settings⇨ Soundcard Detection.**

   Enter the root password if prompted.

   The Audio Devices window opens, as shown in Figure 11-3.

3. **Click the Play test sound button.**

   If you hear some mellow music, your computer is ready to rock.

4. **Click OK and you're ready to go.**

Figure 11-3: A sample Audio Devices window.

If you're plugged in correctly and you repeated the steps, but you *still* didn't hear any sound, one of these reasons may explain why:

- ✔ Your computer has an old, unrecognizable sound card.
- ✔ You don't have a sound card.
- ✔ Someone else's stereo is way too loud.

You definitely have to purchase a sound card if you don't have one. Using old sound cards is generally difficult, so we also recommend purchasing a replacement. We can't help you much with the third possibility.

The Red Hat Esound daemon (referred to as *ESD*) is designed to allow multiple applications to use your computer's sound system at the same time. Sometimes, however, an application may not be able to take advantage of this elegant system. For example, when you start XMMS, you may have to turn off the ESD daemon. You can turn ESD off by starting a GNOME Terminal window and entering this command:

```
killall -1 esd
```

Playing CDs

Everyone wants a little music in her life. But you went ahead and bought a computer rather than a stereo system. D'oh! But it happens that you indeed spent your money wisely because your Red Hat Linux computer functions well as a stereo system. This section describes how to set up your computer to play music CDs.

Red Hat bundles two Open Source CD players for Linux users: CD Player and XMMS. We describe the CD Player in this chapter because it automatically starts when you insert a CD in your computer. (We don't ignore XMMS, however, because we use it in Chapter 12 to play Internet audio streams.)

Anyway, these instructions show how to start playing music:

1. **Log in as any user and pop a CD into the CD drive.**

   The Gnome CD Player application appears.

2. **Listen as your CD starts playing.**

Those are the easiest instructions in this book. However, if you exit from the CD Player, you have to restart it manually (unless you insert another CD, in which case CD Player starts automatically again.) You can start CD Player by clicking the GNOME Menu button and choosing Sound & Video➪CD Player. Nothing to it.

The CD Player controls should be familiar territory for anyone born in the 20th century. Here's a quick refresher for those cavepeople out there:

- ✔ To change the volume, click the vertical slide bar on the right side of the CD Player window. Hold the mouse button while you adjust the volume.

- ✔ Click the crossed tools (a screwdriver and wrench) button, toward the middle-left area of the window, to open the Preferences window. You can then select how the CD Player reacts when you start and stop it. You can also control the default CD device (the default is `/dev/cdrom`, but you many want to change it to `/dev/cdrom1`, or other devices, depending on your computer hardware). You can also select the theme of the CD Player skin. A simple help system is available too.

- ✔ The remaining controls are self explanatory: start, stop, forward, yada-yada.

As you can see, playing CDs is pretty simple. Note that in Chapter 12 we show how to use simple XMMS and the more general-purpose MPlayer players to play Internet music streams and files.

Ripping CDs

Are you paranoid? If not, do you want to be? Well, `cdparanoia` can help fulfill all your fears. Just kidding. Really, `cdparanoia` is used for ripping the audio information — music files — from CDs to your hard drive or to other CDs. *Ripping* refers to the process of copying audio from a CD to your computer.

The following steps show how to use the Gnome RIP (Grip) interface to simplify using `cdparanoia` to copy music from a CD to your hard drive:

1. **Insert your favorite CD in the drive.**

2. **Click the GNOME Menu button and choose Sound & Video⇨More Sound & Video Applications.**

3. **The Grip window, as shown in Figure 11-4, opens.**

4. **Click the Rip column (right side of screen) of each track you want to use.**

   A check mark appears next to each track you select.

5. **Click the Rip tab at the top of the window (next to the Tracks tab).**

6. **Click the Rip Only button.**

Figure 11-4:
The Grip
window
shows a
CD's tracks.

Grip starts the `cdparanoia` program and feeds it the options you just selected. The music is stored in the up-and-coming Open Source protocol, Ogg. By default, Grip creates the `ogg` directory in your home directory (assuming that you haven't changed the defaults). Grip creates a subdirectory (in `ogg`) named after each CD that you record. Individual tracks are stored in files named after each song; those files live in the directory named after the CD.

After you create the music file, you can listen to it with XMMS or GNOME-CD.

Entering the Ring of Fire: Burning CDs

Back in the 1980s, when vinyl melted away under the invasion of CDs, it cost megabucks to build the factories to create the CDs; back then, it took a huge effort to make a CD. Today, for roughly the $100 it costs to purchase a CD burner (to *burn* means to record to CD), you can build your own, personal factory. Amazing.

If you don't have a CD burner (or writer), this section doesn't do you a bit of good. Sorry.

A one-time recordable CD is referred to as a *CD-R;* a rewritable CD is a *CD-RW.* CD burners look like regular read-only drives and are connected with either an IDE or SCSI interface.

Burn, baby, burn: Burning CDs

These instructions describe how to create, or *burn,* a CD-ROM. You can copy any kind of file to your CD-R/RW:

1. **Log in as any user and insert a CD-R or CD-RW disc into your CD writer.**

   What can you burn? The world's your oyster, and you can make a CD of anything you want — data, software, or music. A good place to start is by backing up your /home directory on CD.

2. **Click the GNOME Menu button and choose System Tools⇨More System Tools⇨CD Writer.**

   The Information window opens. Click the OK button to continue.

   The GNOME Toaster window also opens, as shown in Figure 11-5.

3. **Click the Folder icon near the lower-left side of the window.**

   Gtoaster contains its own file manager.

4. **Find the file or directory you want to record by clicking the directory where it's stored.**

   For example, double-click /home and then the paul/ogg/Pat Metheny directory.

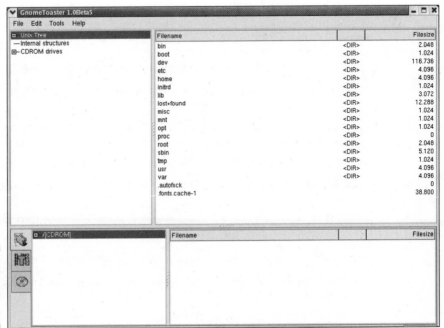

Figure 11-5:
The GNOME
Toaster
window.

5. **Click and drag the files or directory — the** `rh18fd` **directory, in this example — to the Folder subwindow you opened in Step 3.**

   You don't have to use GNOME Toaster's file manager to select the file or files to record. You can open a Nautilus window and drag the file over to the Track subwindow.

6. **Click the CD icon immediately below the Track button in the lower-left corner of the window.**

   The Record subwindow opens and replaces the Track subwindow. You're presented with several options that control the CD-R drive. The defaults should work for your ISO image.

7. **Click the Record button and the CD recording process counts down.**

   You have nine seconds to abort your mission.

8. **You can stop the process by pressing the Stop button.**

   Your home directory is burned to the CD, creating a simple, reliable, and effective backup system. It's easy to use.

Working with multiple CD-ROM drives

Many computers come packaged with two CD-ROM drives. This can cause problems because programs like Gtoaster may not recognize the correct drive — for example, the default CD-ROM may not have any recording capabilities. These instructions may help you if you have trouble getting the recording started:

1. **Click the Preferences button toward the top of the window.**

2. **When the GnomeToaster Preferences window opens, click the CD-ROM and Recorder Setup tab.**

3. **Click the ScanBus button at the bottom of the window and then click the appropriate drive.**

4. **Click the Edit button, and the Please enter drive data window opens.**

5. **Click the This Drive is a CD writer radio button and then the OK button.**

   In this case, we're using a writable DVD drive, which Gtoaster doesn't know can write CD-R and CD-RW.

6. **Control returns to the GnomeToaster Preferences window.**

7. **Click Apply and then the OK button, and you go back to the Gtoaster window.**

   Try writing your CD-R or CD-RW again.

Burning CDs the old-fashioned way

The cdrecord application is a command-line (nongraphical) system that writes CDs. Sometimes you may prefer to use this system for its simplicity and reliability. These instructions describe the process:

1. **Log in as root and insert a CD-R or CD-RW disc into your CD writer.**

2. **Start a GNOME Terminal window.**

3. **Determine the location of your CD-ROM drive by entering this command:**

```
cdrecord --scanbus
```

The output shows information similar to this code:

```
Cdrecord 1.10 (i686-pc-linux-gnu) Copyright (C) 1995-2001
        J!!rg Schilling
Using libscg version 'schily-0.1'
scsibus0:
    0,0,0    0) 'IDE-CD ' 'R/RW 4x4x24      ' '1.04'
             Removable CD-ROM
    0,1,0    1) *
    0,2,0    2) *
    0,3,0    3) *
```

You see this output if you have an IDE/ATAPI CD-ROM drive. SCSI-based systems, however, may show up with other values depending on their configuration. You recognize SCSI drives by their controller, target, and slice numbers. *Slice numbers* correspond to the three numbers in the preceding output. For example, if you have a SCSI-based CD-ROM drive that's connected as the third target on the first controller, it shows up as: 0,3,0 in the preceding code. (Slices are not used in this configuration and are always 0.) Whatever the numbers are, you simply need to use them in the dev= parameter described in the next step.

SCSI doesn't mean that it's a dirty (it's pronounced "scuzzy") interface: This acronym stands for *Small Computer System Interface*. Most inexpensive to moderately priced computers use an IDE interface to control both the CD-ROM drive and hard drive. SCSI interfaces also control hard drives and CD-ROM drives. You find SCSI interfaces on high-end computers because they provide higher performance and are more expensive.

The cdrecord utility is designed to interact with a SCSI-based CD-R drive. Red Hat Linux installs a kernel module named ide-scsi that allows cdrecord to interact with an IDE-based CD-R drive; most PCs use IDE devices. You may need to install the ide-scsi module if the cdrecord -scanbus command doesn't show a CD-R device. Run the command **modprobe ide-scsi** to insert the module.

4. **Use the** `scsibus` **values from Step 3 with the** `cdrecord` **command by entering this command:**

```
cdrecord -v speed=n dev=scsibus_values -isosize filename
```

where *n* is the speed of your CD-ROM drive and *scsibus_values* are the virtual SCSI values obtained from Step 3. *-isosize* specifies that you're recording raw data, and *filename* is the name of the file that is created.

For example, if you have a 24X speed ATAPI/IDE CD-ROM drive and want to create a CD from the `mydir/31jan03.raw` file, run this command:

```
cdrecord -v speed=24 dev=0,0,0 -isosize mydir/31jan03.raw
```

The scsibus values from Step 3 — for example `0,0,0` — are used with the `dev=` parameter. The `0,0,0` value is combined with `dev=` to create the `dev=0,0,0` parameter.

You need to set your speed according to what your CD-ROM drive can handle. You need to obtain the speed value from the documentation that came with your recordable CD-ROM drive in order to enter it as part of the `speed` parameter in the `cdrecord` command. Look for a value like *4X, 8X, 12X,* or *24X.* Don't worry if you can't find your documentation or don't know the values. If you set the speed too high, your CD is just recorded at the lower level.

That's it! Your computer writes the information to CD. Congratulations! You have created a new CD.

The process changes just a little bit if you want to burn music. You don't need to create an ISO image. The following example shows how to create an audio CD:

```
cdrecord -v speed=32 dev=0,0,0 -audio tom_waits.wav
```

Chapter 12

Live from the Net

In This Chapter

▶ Using XMMS to listen to Internet audio streams

▶ Using XMMS to work with MP3

▶ Listening to live radio and playing DVDs with MPlayer

The invention of audio and video streaming technology is one of the great Internet innovations. Streaming technology provides the ability for anyone to create a radio or TV station unlimited in terms of geography and governmental approval; it also can be done inexpensively. Using streaming technology, computer users can listen to or view those broadcasts from anywhere.

This chapter describes how to use your Red Hat Linux machine as both an audio radio receiver and a DVD video player. We use the Open Source XMMS and MPlayer applications to listen to the Net.

Using the XMMS Audio Player

The Open Source XMMS (X MultiMedia System) application is a great tool for listening to audio streams and files. XMMS plays WAV files produced by `grip/cdparanoia` by default. It can also play the up-and-coming Ogg/Vorbis format (codec).

The Ogg codec doesn't contain any proprietary or patented algorithms. Ogg is free for anyone to use, and people and organizations that don't want to depend on proprietary systems are discovering it; Ogg also produces higher-fidelity audio streams. Why depend on another corporation's whims when you don't have to?

You can use XMMS to listen to some of the music you may have saved in Chapter 11. If you used `grip` to save music to your home directory and you want to listen to it, start XMMS and right-click the window. Choose Open⇨File and select any of the WAV files you created.

Ogg is the system used to format audio streams, and *Vorbis* compresses the information. Unlike most other technological systems, Ogg/Vorbis isn't an acronym but rather is named after science fiction characters. For more information about Ogg/Vorbis and similar Open Source multimedia systems, go to www.vorbis.com.

Now that you have a bit of technological background, you can start using XMMS to listen to Ogg/Vorbis streams:

1. **Open Mozilla and go to** www.vorbis.com/music.psp.

2. **Click any of the Track links.**

3. **When the Downloading window opens, click the OK button.**

   For example, click the first one, Lepidoptera.

   The Enter the Name of File to Save To window appears.

4. **Click the Save button and Mozilla saves the music stream to disk.**

5. **Open a GNOME Terminal window and enter this command:**

   ```
   xmms
   ```

   An XMMS window opens. Figure 12-1 shows the player.

6. **Right-click the XMMS window and choose Open⇨File.**

7. **Enter the filename you just saved to disk.**

   XMMS starts playing the music.

Figure 12-1:
The XMMS
window.

The Vorbis Web page provides links to other Ogg-capable sources. For example, click the New Music Sites link, near the top of the www.vorbis.com/music.psp page. You see a page with links to other sources. For example, click the WCPE link to go to a Web page that streams classical music.

Now is a good time to describe how to configure Mozilla to automatically start XMMS whenever you click Ogg/Vorbis sources and streams:

1. **Open Mozilla.**

2. **Click the Edit⇨Preferences menu.**

   The Preferences window opens.

3. **Choose Navigator⇨Helper Applications.**

   The Helpers Applications subwindow opens in the Preferences window.

4. **Click the New Type button in the upper-right corner of the window.**

   The New Type window opens.

5. **Enter the following options. This information tells Mozilla to use XMMS whenever it encounters Ogg/Vorbis–formatted media:**

   - **Description of type:** Enter any information that helps you understand the MIME type.

   - **File Extension:** Enter the file type extension in this field. In this case, Ogg files use the ogg extension.

   - **MIME type:** This field describes the MIME type (Multipurpose Internet Mail Extensions) associated with the helper application. If you read Chapter 10, you know that MIME types help your computer decide how to handle different media formats and types. Enter **audio/x-ogg** in this field.

   - **Application to use:** Enter the program you want to handle this MIME type. In this case, enter **xmms**.

6. **Figure 12-2 shows the Ogg information entered in the New Type window.**

7. **Click the OK button to return to the Preferences window.**

8. **Click the OK button in Preferences to return to Mozilla.**

Mozilla now launches XMMS whenever you click a link to an Ogg/Vorbis source. XMMS starts and connects and then plays the stream.

XMMS uses the Enlightened Sound Daemon (esd) process by default to access your computer's speakers. Designed to allow multiple audio players to simultaneously use your computer's speakers, sometimes esd gets confused and you need to restart it. Log in as root, open a GNOME Terminal window, and run the command **killall -HUP esd**. If that doesn't work, you can configure XMMS to use another output system. Right-click the XMMS window and choose Options⇨Preferences. Click the Output Plugin subwindow and select the OSS Driver 1.2.7 plug-in. Click the Apply button and then the OK button.

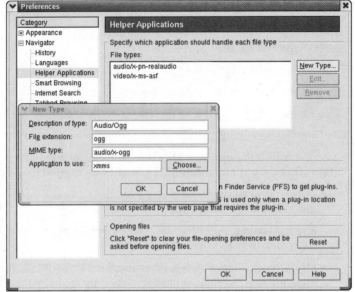

Figure 12-2:
Creating a
new helper
application
in the
New Type
window

Modifying XMMS to Work with MP3

MP3 (MPEG audio layer 3), a popular medium for storing music and other audio information, can also be used to stream multimedia across the Internet. The Open Source media player, XMMS is installed by Red Hat Linux by default. However, because of copyright and patent considerations, Red Hat doesn't include MP3 support in any of its software any more.

This section describes how to install MP3 support from the XMMS people themselves. We include these instructions because XMMS is easy to use and comes bundled with Red Hat Linux. The MPlayer program described in this chapter also supports MP3, but you may only need to use MP3 and prefer to use one system.

You can obtain an MP3 plug-in for XMMS from `www.xmms.org`. Follow these steps:

1. **Start Mozilla and go to** `http://staff.xmms.org/priv/redhat8/`.

2. **Click the** `xmms-mpg123-1.2.7-13.rpm` **link in the area dedicated to XMMS for Red Hat.**

   The Enter the name of the file to save window opens.

3. **Click the Save button.**

4. **Open a GNOME Terminal window by right-clicking a section of the desktop and selecting the New Terminal menu.**

5. **If you're not already logged in as root, enter this command in the Terminal window:**

```
su
```

6. **Enter the root password when prompted.**

7. **Install the MP3-enabled XMMS player by entering this command:**

```
rpm -ivh rpm-mpg123* (This should be rpm -ivh xmms-
        mpg123*)
```

8. **Start XMMS by entering this command at the prompt:**

```
xmms
```

9. **You can see that the MP3 plug-in was installed by clicking the XMMS window and choosing Options➪Preferences.**

The Preferences window opens and shows the new additions. Figure 12-3 shows the new plug-ins.

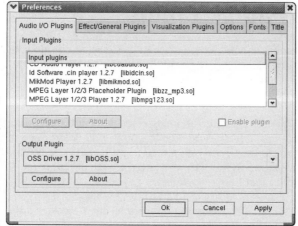

Figure 12-3:
The XMMS
Preferences
window
displays
the new
plug-ins.

Now, you only need to locate a streaming audio source over the Internet to use XMMS to listen to MP3s. A good place to find streaming MP3 locations is www.shoutcast.com. It provides links to numerous streams. To listen to some MP3s, follow these steps:

1. **Start Mozilla and go to www.shoutcast.com.**

2. **Click any one of the Tune-in links.**

For example, check out the Jazz stream.

3. **A window opens and you're prompted to either save the file to another location or specify an application to deal with the connection.**

4. **To have XMMS make the connection, click the Advanced button.**

   Another window opens.

5. **Click the Application field and enter** xmms.

6. **Click OK.**

7. **Click the Ask Me Before Opening Downloaded Files of This Type button.**

   This step is a quick alternative to defining a new Helper Application for the MP3 MIME type. (The preceding section "Using the XMMS Audio Player," describes how to create a new Helper Application.)

8. **Click OK and you return to the preceding window. Click OK again.**

Mozilla starts XMMS in order to process the MP3 streams. You can now use XMMS to listen to any type of music and any news you want.

Using the Fabulous Mplayer

Whenever a desperate need exists, the Open Source movement comes in to save the day. Until recently, you couldn't use any single Linux application to listen to and view most of the popular streaming formats. Now, MPlayer has burst on to the scene and fills that gap.

MPlayer can play most popular (and many obscure) audio and video streaming formats. Although it hasn't reached the point that it has been officially released, it's close to that point and already quite usable. At the time this edition of the book was written, the second release candidate (the final form of beta testing) had just become available. Expect Version 1.0 soon.

This list shows some of the streaming formats that MPlayer can play:

- **MPEG-1/Layer 3 (MP3):** MP3 is a popular but proprietary codec used for both storing and streaming audio.

- **Ogg/Vorbis:** This new and upcoming Open Source streaming format is unencumbered by any copyrights or patents, like other formats are.

- **Microsoft Media Server (MMS):** You can listen to radio broadcasts that use the popular MMS format with Mplayer. Previously, you needed to use the Microsoft client to listen to MMS streams.

- **Digital Versatile Disc (DVD):** You can play DVDs from your computer with Mplayer.

- **RealAudio:** You need to download, compile, and install the RTSP package to use RealAudio.

MPlayer is not now included in the Red Hat Linux distribution. We hope that it will be later, but for now you have to obtain it from its developers. These instructions describe how to download, install, and use Mplayer:

1. **Log in and open Mozilla.**

2. **Go to** `http://www.mplayerhq.hu/homepage/dload.html`.

3. **Click the latest Red Hat RPM version.**

   At the time this book was written, Red Hat 7.x is the latest version. The instructions work on Red Hat 9, however.

4. **Download these packages from either the i386 or i686 directories:**

   ```
   mplayer-0.90rc5-1
   mplayer-common-0.90rc5-1
   ```

5. **Download these packages from the noarch directory:**

   ```
   mplayer-gui-0.90rc5-1
   mplayer-skin-default-1.6-3
   ```

   and any one of these font packages:

   ```
   mplayer-font-iso1-1.0-3
   mplayer-font-iso2-1.0-3
   mplayer-font-iso9-1.0-3
   ```

   At the time this edition of the book was written, the most recent MPlayer version is `rc5` (Release Candidate 5). You may see — and should use — the most recent version available.

6. **Open a GNOME Terminal window and change to root:**

   ```
   su -
   ```

   Enter the root password when prompted.

7. **Install the packages in this order:**

   ```
   rpm -ivh --nodeps mplayer-common*
   rpm -ivh mplayer-0.9*

   rpm -ivh —nodeps mplayer-skins*
   rpm -ivh mplayer-gui*
   rpm -ivh mplayer-fonts*
   ```

8. **Run the MPlayer program. You need a source to listen to, so we have a suggestion:**

   ```
   mplayer http://64.236.34.141:80/stream/1005
   ```

   Unfortunately, we can't guarantee that this stream will work by the time you try it. We found this URL at `www.shoutcast.com`, and suggest that you use it to find additional streams.

9. **Mplayer also plays playlists and files.** *Playlists* **are files that store the locations of one or more audio and/or video streams. For example, if you click any of the Shoutcast streams, Mozilla asks you to save it. After saving the file, you can use Mplayer to play it:**

```
mplayer -playlist playlist.pls
```

Shoutcast uses the name `playlist.pls`, but a playlist is just a file and can have any name.

10. **You can use Mplayer to play music files too. Suppose that you used** `grip` **in Chapter 11 to save some music to a file named** `track1.wav`. **Use this command to play that file:**

```
mplayer track1.wav
```

11. **Press the Control and C (Ctrl-c) keys at the same time to end the session.**

That's it! You can use Mplayer to listen to all sorts of streams. The entire world of Internet radio and — hopefully, soon — video broadcasts is open to you. Mplayer will only become more versatile and useful with time.

The first Mplayer RealAudio (using the RTSP protocol) plug-in was just recently released from www.live.com/mplayer. The plug-in is still too young for easy use, but it soon will be. Keep an eye on this system.

Using gmplayer to play DVDs

MPlayer works well, but a graphical version is available too. We all expect graphical interfaces in today's world. However, MPlayer has a graphical front-end, and you may have installed it in the preceding section. We use gmplayer now to put on a friendly face to enhance your listening and viewing pleasure:

1. **Pop your favorite DVD into your DVD drive, crack open a soda, and make some popcorn.**

2. **Put your feet up.**

3. **Log in as root and open a GNOME Terminal.**

   You need to tell gmplayer where to find your DVD drive, so run this command:

```
dmesg | grep -i dvd
```

   This line should display the information, such as that shown below, about your DVD:

```
hdc: TOSHIBA DVD-ROM SD-C2402, ATAPI CD/DVD-ROM drive
hdc: ATAPI 24X DVD-ROM drive, 128kB Cache
   The failed "Send DVD Structure" packet command was:
```

   In this case, Red Hat recognizes the computer's DVD drive as the device `hdc`. That translates to the file `/dev/hdc`.

4. Create a link (technically called a *soft link* in Linuxspeak) to the DVD drive that gmplayer, or any Linux application, can understand:

```
ln -s /dev/hdc /dev/dvd
```

If, for example, the output of Step 3 shows the DVD as hdd, you would enter this command:

```
ln -s /dev/hdd /dev/dvd
```

5. Start gmplayer. Enter this command (you can exit from the root user login by pressing the Ctrl-D keys):

```
gmplayer
```

6. gmplayer opens two windows.

The first window, Display Window, is used to display graphics whenever they're available. The second window, as shown in Figure 12-4, is the control system — Control Window. You can right-click either window to open files, DVDs, VCDs (Video CDs), and URLs.

Figure 12-4:
The two
gmplayer
windows.

7. Right-click either of the gmplayer windows and choose DVD⇨ Open Disc.

The gmplayer Display Window plays the DVD. You can control the DVD action with the Control Window just like you can on a stand-alone DVD player.

That's it. You now have a video entertainment system. Just add a Surround Sound system plus an overstuffed couch, and you'll never need to leave home again!

The graphical MPlayer isn't limited to playing DVDs, of course. You can use it to play any audio or video source that MPlayer can — gmplayer is just a graphical front end to MPlayer actually. Right-click either of the gmplayer windows and select any media source you want.

When the Live.com RTSP plug-in for MPlayer becomes easily available, you can listen to an outstanding interview with The Man himself — Linus Torvalds — by opening this URL from gmplayer or MPlayer:

```
rtsp://audio.npr.org/fa/20010604.fa.rm
```

Audio by proxy: Getting XMMS to work through your firewall

Firewalls are necessary to fight the evil guys who lurk on the Internet, but they can really put a kink in your listening pleasure. A *firewall* is used to prevent unauthorized access from outside — in most cases, the Internet — from reaching your computer or network.

The firewall we build in Chapter 8 and the default Red Hat firewall don't affect either of the players described here. However, many LANs are connected through *proxy* firewalls, which intercept packets sent to the Internet and rewrite them according to certain rules; our firewalls are filter packets based on their source and destination addresses and ports.

If your Red Hat Linux workstation sits on a network with a packet-filtering firewall, such as the one installed in Chapter 8, you don't need to modify XMMS. The key is that the filtering firewall allows all outgoing TCP/UDP connections (or ports). However, if your network uses a proxy-based firewall, you may have to modify XMMS (gmplayer doesn't have any mechanism specifically designed to work with proxies).

To configure XMMS to work with proxy firewalls, follow these steps:

1. **Start XMMS.**

2. **Right-click the XMMS window and choose Options➪Preferences.**

3. **Click the Ogg Vorbis plug-in in the Input Plugins subwindow.**

4. **Click the Configure button and the Ogg Vorbis Configuration window opens.**

   You need to enter the address of your proxy server. You may need to contact your friendly neighborhood systems administrator to get that information.

5. **Click the Use Proxy button and enter the proxy server address in the Host subwindow.**

   The following figure shows the configuration window with the proxy server information added.

6. **Click the Use Authentication radio button and enter your username and password in their respective subwindows if your proxy server requires them.**

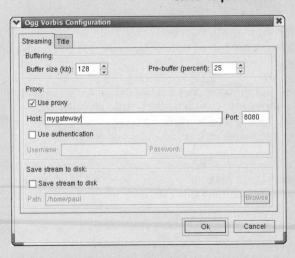

In this clip, Terri Gross conducts an interview during the summer of 2001 on her program, "Fresh Air." Linus discusses the development of Linux, his life in Silicon Valley, and other matters.

Launching gmplayer from the Panel

Until now, we have been manually launching mplayer and gmplayer . Now it's time to put gmplayer in its place on the GNOME Panel. You can create an applet launcher (an icon to click) for gmplayer on the GNOME Panel.

The *Panel* is the gray bar that rests along the bottom of your screen.

Follow these steps to create a launcher applet for gmplayer:

1. **Right-click any blank section of the GNOME Panel and choose Add to Panel⇨Launcher menus.**

2. **Type a name for the gmplayer launcher icon.**

3. **Press the Tab key to go to the Generic Name text box.**

   Enter any name you want. An entry such as *Radio Player* or *Streaming Audio/Video player* describes what the launcher is meant to do.

4. **Press the Tab key again and enter a descriptive comment in the Comment text box.**

   The comment is displayed whenever you place the cursor over the MPlayer icon.

5. **Press the Tab key one more time and type** /usr/bin/gmplayer **in the Command text box.**

6. **Click the Icon button at the bottom of the Launcher window to pick an icon for the launcher.**

   The Browse icons window appears and displays the generic GNOME icon images. You can select any image you want by clicking the image and then clicking the OK button. You return to the Create Launcher window.

   Selecting an icon image here means that you can skip steps 7 through 9, which helps you find custom icon images. Go to Step 10.

7. **Click the Browse button to select a custom image.**

   The Browse window opens.

8. **Select any generic icon you like and click the OK button.**

   The gmplayer icon is displayed in the Launcher window, ready and waiting to launch the program.

9. **Click the Close button and the gmplayer icon is placed on the GNOME Panel.**

10. **Click the OK button in the Launcher window.**

    The new icon is inserted into the GNOME Panel.

11. **Click the new gmplayer launcher you just created on the GNOME Panel.**

    The gmplayer window appears.

You can also reach gmplayer from the GNOME menu. Click the GNOME Menu button and choose Sound & Video⇨More Sound & Video Applications⇨ gmplayer.

You can easily copy the gmplayer icon (or any icon) from the GNOME Panel to your desktop. Click and hold the gmplayer icon in the GNOME Panel and drag it to your desktop. Release the mouse button, and the icon is copied to your desktop background. You can then right-click the desktop icon and choose Properties from the menu that pops up. The gmplayer Properties window opens and enables you to modify the icon's look and feel.

Finding radio stations

"What else can I play with this thing?" you may be asking, or more importantly, "How do I find stuff to play? Mom, I wanna play!" You can find streaming radio content in several ways and places, including

- ✔ Search with Mozilla Search (click the Mozilla Search button) to find individual stations and radio station databases and to find which ones provide streaming content.

- ✔ Stumble across Ogg/Vorbis, Windows Media, RealAudio, and MP3 files and streams all around the Internet (look for the blue Real logo — you see them everywhere when you start looking).

- ✔ Browse a radio locator service, such as the one at www.radio-locator. com/cgi-bin/home. This page, for example, allows you to search for a station based on its city, state, country, call letters, or frequency. The search results display lists of stations you can try connecting to.

Chapter 13

Going to the Office

*R*ed Hat Linux is a useful product that comes with a large base of services and applications. It has always been an outstanding platform for providing services and technical applications, but until recently has lacked a presence on the desktop. The problem was its lack of a full-blown office suite to work with word processing documents, spreadsheets, and similar documents. Fortunately, desktop suites — such as OpenOffice and its sister application, StarOffice — have taken Linux out of the back office and into the front.

Opening Your Office

The OpenOffice desktop productivity suite does nearly everything Microsoft Office does, but for less money. How much less? Well, 100 percent less because it's 100 percent free. Sun Microsystems, Inc., sells the version named StarOffice but provides an Open Source version named — you guessed it — OpenOffice. OpenOffice is licensed under the GPL/LGPL and SIISL licenses. What do all those letters mean? They mean f-r-e-e, and they also mean that Linux can integrate office productivity features from OpenOffice because Linux and OpenOffice share the GPL license. You can find more information about the licenses at this URL:

```
www.openoffice.org/project/www/license.html
```

OpenOffice is not only free (did we mention that it's free?), but it's also powerful, providing you with these functions:

- **Word processor:** A full-function what-you-see-is-what-you-get (WYSIWYG) word processor named *Writer*. OpenOffice Writer, as shown in Figure 13-1, comes with many functions you would expect — formatting, cutting and pasting, graphics, spell check, and more. It uses its own format but can also read from and write to Rich Text Format (RTF) plus it handles Microsoft Word 6.0, Word 95, and Word 97/2000/2002 files.

- **Spreadsheet:** A full-function spreadsheet program, named *Calc,* used by Wall Street brokers to calculate their option strike prices and such items. If you're familiar with spreadsheet software, Calc should be straightforward to use. Figure 13-2 shows the initial Calc window.

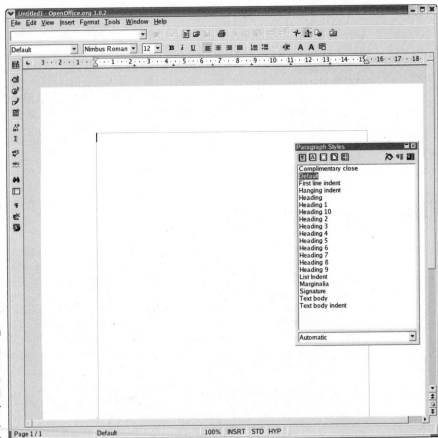

Figure 13-1:
The OpenOffice word processor window.

✔ **Presentation:** A graphics program named Impress with all the bells and whistles for creating presentations. You can also import and export PowerPoint documents with Impress. Figure 13-3 shows the Impress window.

✔ **Drawing:** The OpenOffice Draw program, as shown in Figure 13-4, gives you graphics tools for creating anything from a novice drawing to a masterpiece. Draw provides your creative side with a tool for creating graphics.

✔ **Miscellaneous:** OpenOffice provides other functions, such as an HTML editor, a Math editor for supernerds, and label and business card creation tools. You can also create word processing templates.

Figure 13-2:
The OpenOffice spreadsheet window.

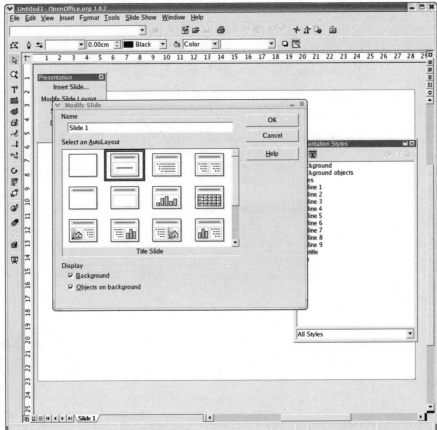

Figure 13-3:
The
OpenOffice
Impress
window.

Okay, so OpenOffice has lots of great features. How good are they? Can they get the job done? Well, we wrote this edition of the book using OpenOffice, and we wrote the preceding edition using StarOffice. That's not a bad testimonial to the capabilities of OpenOffice.

Figure 13-4:
The
OpenOffice
graphics
program,
Draw.

Getting to Know OpenOffice

If you're familiar with Microsoft Office, you should be able to find your way around OpenOffice. The look and feel are a little different, but the idea is the same. OpenOffice is also morally superior to Office because it's free *and* a part of Open Source. This section briefly describes some of the most common functions of OpenOffice.

The next few sections provide only a basic introduction to the things you can do with OpenOffice. No, we're not lazy; it's just that it would take too much space to describe it all in detail. Please experiment with your own test documents and consult the online help for more information.

Firing up and using OpenOffice

Red Hat includes OpenOffice and installs it by default. OpenOffice is easy to access. Click the GNOME Menu button and then choose Office⇨OpenOffice Writer. You can choose some, but not all, of the other OpenOffice functions from this menu too. After thinking about life for a while, the OpenOffice window appears.

The first time you start OpenOffice, it asks whether you want to use the workstation or personal model. The former installs the OpenOffice programs in a central location accessible to all users; the latter option installs a copy of OpenOffice in your home directory. We use the workstation configuration here, but you can select the personal model if you want.

When you use OpenOffice for the first time, you're also asked a few questions about importing an address book. We cancel the operation because we prefer to use the Ximian Evolution address book.

You can access all the OpenOffice functions by clicking the File button, in the upper-left corner of the window, and then the option you want.

The following list introduces the functions. You're probably familiar with the layout and operation of the menu if you have used Microsoft Office.

- ✔ **File:** As you may expect, you can open, close, save, and otherwise manipulate OpenOffice documents with the File menu. Writer files have the .sxw extension. Other file formats, such as Microsoft Word and HTML, must be imported and exported.

- ✔ **New:** You can create a new document for any OpenOffice function. When you choose File⇨New, you're given the option to create a new text document, spreadsheet, presentation, or other function.

- ✔ **Edit:** This menu provides all the functions you need to modify documents. Functions such as cut, copy, paste, and delete are all provided here. The functions that are active at any time depend on whether you're editing a document, spreadsheet, or presentation. For example, the cut, copy, and paste options aren't active if you're not editing a document (like just when you first start up OpenOffice and have not opened any files).

You can also track changes, just like with Microsoft Word. Choose Edit⇨Changes, and you can track changes on a character-by-character basis. You can display the changes or keep them hidden from view. When you're satisfied with your edits, you can make the changes permanent and save only the finished document to disk. Pretty cool.

OpenOffice also provides the Find and Replace function from the Edit menu. The Find and Replace feature enables you to find text strings and either replace them with another string or delete them. You can search forward or backward through a document. You can replace one instance or all instances.

✔ **Spell check:** OpenOffice provides a spell checker, of course. You can tell the spell checker to check an entire document by choosing Tools⇨Spell Check⇨Check. You're prompted to act on each possible spelling error the checker detects.

Alternatively, you can set the spell checker to operate continuously. Choose Tools⇨Spellcheck⇨AutoSpellCheck to toggle on the real-time spell checker; when activated, a check mark appears next to the menu option. The continuous option tells OpenOffice Writer to checks each word that you enter and underlines possible misspellings with a squiggly red line. The red line disappears when you successfully correct the mistake.

✔ **View:** This menu displays or hides the various menu bars. You can display a document's formatting characters and also increase or decrease the size — zoom in or out — of the text displayed on the screen. The zoom function enables you to make smaller fonts more readable without changing the document.

✔ **Insert:** This menu enables you to insert special characters, objects, files, and macros into your documents. Special characters include various symbols (accents and umlauts, for example) that aren't part of the everyday character set (unless you happen to use words like café frequently). Objects include graphics, symbols, and figures. (You can create your own figures with Draw.) You can also insert macros and hyperlinks into your documents.

You can insert tables into documents with any number of rows and columns. OpenOffice can automatically adjust the row height, or you can do it manually. Choose Insert⇨Table and play around with this feature.

✔ **Tools:** From this menu, you can access the spell checker, thesaurus, various OpenOffice configuration settings, and other functions. Tools such as the spell checker are self explanatory. We examine some of the configuration options in this list.

✔ **Window:** This menu enables you to control the look of your desktop. In addition to enabling you to modify and move windows, the menu provides other manipulation capabilities.

✔ **Help:** OpenOffice provides pretty good online help services. Many are context sensitive. If you're editing a text document, click the Help menu to get access to information related to the Writer module.

For example, choose Help➪Help Agent, and the Help Agent is enabled. The Help Agent provides assistance in several areas of interest to new users, including

- **Introduction to Writer:** Provides an introduction to the word processor

- **Basic tips text documents:** All you ever wanted to know (and then some) about reading, writing, and printing text documents

- **Advanced tips:** Extends the previous basic text document tip to more advanced subjects

- **Menus:** Describes how all the OpenOffice menus work together

- **Toolbars:** Describes the toolbars that provide information and shortcuts

- **Shortcuts:** Describes what key combinations can be used to perform various word processing functions

- **New stuff:** Describes what's new since the last OpenOffice version

- **Support:** Displays brief information about getting support from Sun Microsystems

Printing with OpenOffice

Printing from OpenOffice is a simple process after you have configured Red Hat Linux to use a printer. OpenOffice uses the default Linux printer, so all you have to do is configure it. This section first describes how to configure a Red Hat Linux printer and then shows you how to set up OpenOffice to use that printer.

Configuring a printer attached to your Red Hat Linux computer is a simple process. All you have to do is run the `printconf-gui` printer configuration utility and enter the information about your printer. These steps describe how to do it:

1. **Log in to your Red Hat Linux computer as root.**

2. **Attach a printer to your Linux computer's parallel (printer) port.**

The parallel port is a 25-pin female connector on the back of your computer case. New computers usually label the parallel port with some kind of printer icon (although sometimes it's hard to imagine how they came up with the symbol). If yours isn't marked, there's no harm in finding the appropriate port through trial and error.

3. **Start the printer configuration tool by clicking the GNOME Menu button and choosing System Settings⇨Printing.**

   Enter the root password if prompted. The printconf-gui window opens.

4. **To add a printer, click the New button.**

   When the introductory Add a new print queue window appears, click the Forward button.

5. **The new print queue window, as shown in Figure 13-5, appears.**

   Enter a descriptive queue name — for example, Epson777 — and optionally a description of the queue. (You can, of course, use the default name — `printer` — but we prefer to use descriptive names.)

6. **Click the Forward button and you go to the Queue type window.**

7. **Assuming that your printer is directly connected to your computer, you see the device name `/dev/lp0` in the Queue type window. Select the `/dev/lp0` device and click the Forward button.**

   The Printer model window opens. You can choose from various manufacturers or generic models.

8. **Click the Generic (click to select manufacturer) button.**

   Select your printer's manufacturer from the pull-down menu.

9. **Use the vertical slide bar to locate and select your particular model.**

   Click the Forward button.

10. **When you finish, the new print queue window opens.**

11. **Click the Apply button.**

    A Question window opens. You're asked whether you want to print a test page. Click the OK button and a test page is printed.

    An Information window opens and you're prompted to check whether the test page printed successfully.

12. **Click the OK button and you return to the Printer Configuration window. You can create an additional print queue or modify existing ones.**

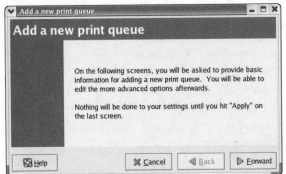

Figure 13-5:
The Add a
New Print
Queue
window.

The GNOME Print Manager window opens and shows an icon for the new print queue you just created. Double-click the new icon and a status window opens that shows current and past print jobs.

Now that you have a printer connected to your Red Hat Linux computer, you can print from OpenOffice without any further configuration. OpenOffice uses the Red Hat Linux printer configuration by default. Open a file you want to print. From the OpenOffice desktop, choose File⇨Print. You can choose to print the entire document, individual pages, or a range of pages.

Part IV
Revenge of the Nerds

The 5th Wave   By Rich Tennant

"Drive carefully, remember your lunch, and always make a backup of your directory tree before modifying your hard disk partition file."

In this part . . .

In the great tradition of slackers and procrastinators, we have put off the real work as long as possible. In this part, you find out about how to make a server out of your Red Hat Linux computer. These chapters don't turn you into a Linux guru capable of commanding six-figure consulting fees, but they do introduce you to the technical side of Linux.

We start by describing in Chapter 14 how to build a simple Local Area Network (LAN). Building a LAN isn't as difficult as it first sounds. You need to connect your computers by using cables or wireless technology and then configure the computers to recognize each other. Finally, you need to create an Internet gateway.

Chapter 15 shows how to use your Red Hat Linux computer as a network server on your newly created network; you can also provide the services to the Internet, if you want. You learn how to create a Web server, a Samba file server (so that both Linux and Windows computers can use a common file system), a network printer server, a DHCP server, and a domain name server.

Chapter 16 tells you how to make your network and your computers more secure by using specific methods and utilities.

And if (okay, when) you need to troubleshoot Red Hat Linux, check out Chapter 17. It provides some detailed help in fixing computer problems, with a special focus on networking. When you're done with this part, you'll be wearing pocket protectors with the best of us!

Chapter 14

Building Your Own, Private Network

A *private network* is a group of two or more computers linked so that they can communicate with each other; also referred to as a *Local Area Network* (LAN). The computers are generally located close together within a room or building. Unlike the Internet, which is designed to allow the world's computers to talk with each other, LANs are designed to keep the communication local and private. (Of course, you can always connect your LAN to the Internet, but we talk about that topic elsewhere.)

Building a private network isn't as difficult as it may sound. First, you need to decide on a general network layout. Second, you need to connect the computers with cables and/or wireless devices. Finally, you need to configure each computer's network settings. Design, connect, configure — one, two, three — it's as simple as that.

This chapter shows how to build a simple LAN. If you want to know how to add a Linux computer to an existing network, check out Chapter 7. To find out about adding a firewall to your LAN, check out Chapter 8.

In this chapter, we show you how to wire computers together; you should depend on the Linux networking instructions from Chapter 7 to get your computers connected on your network. The instructions in Chapter 7 are also designed to work with the new LAN you're building here.

In this chapter, we describe how to connect computers to form a LAN. However, you can connect many other devices to a network. Devices such as broadband Internet modems (cable and DSL), routers, switches/hubs, network-capable printers, and even some personal digital assistants (PDAs) can all be connected to a network. In the future, we fully expect that it will be possible to connect nearly every electronic device to a LAN. We talk about computers only in this book because our emphasis is on Red Hat Linux workstations. However, remember that you're not limited to just networking computers.

Designing and Building Your Private Network

Private networks take many shapes and sizes. As you may expect, the design of a LAN for a large- or medium-size organization is different than for a small office or home. Individuals and small organizations generally don't require complex systems unless they perform complex work. For the purposes of this book, we assume that you need and want a simple network. We describe how to design a basic LAN that is both powerful and reliable. This network can be used for many small- or medium-size businesses and most households.

This chapter shows you how to design a flat network. *Flat* refers to the fact that all the computers connected to the network communicate over a single subnetwork (subnet, for short). Subnets can be combined within a single LAN, but that makes the network more complex to design, build, and maintain. The network we describe here is also designed around a Red Hat Linux Internet gateway. The *Internet gateway* is a computer that acts as a portal, connecting the private network to the Internet. The networked computers in the private network — also referred to as *hosts* or *clients* — are connected through one of two methods:

- ✔ **Wired connections:** Hosts are connected to the LAN through a device called an *Ethernet hub* or *Ethernet switch* (hub or switch, for short). Switches are superior to hubs in performance and are becoming the standard. For your LAN, we suggest that you connect all computers (hosts), including the Internet gateway, by using a switch. Figure 14-1 shows an example of our private network where the interconnecting fabric is the Ethernet switch. (In the past two years, Ethernet switches have become inexpensive and common.)

- ✔ **Wireless connections:** Wireless devices make it possible to build a network without interconnecting cables. Wireless networks can take two forms:

- **Using an access point:** Using a device called an *access point,* you can connect wireless hosts to a LAN. This design has the hosts connect to the access point via radio frequency (RF) signals. The access point also connects to a wired network, and the wireless hosts communicate to the wired network through that connection.

  Access points have become the most popular system for creating wireless LANs. You can find access point devices in consumer electronics stores in the $100 range.

- **Using Ad-Hoc mode:** The alternative wireless-connection method, called *Ad-Hoc mode,* doesn't require a separate access point other than a wireless device for each host. Wireless hosts communicate directly to each other when using Ad-Hoc mode. (You can read more about Ad-Hoc mode in the section "Wiring your network with wires," later in this chapter.)

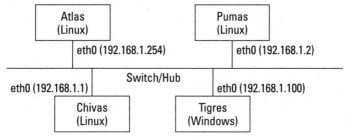

Figure 14-1:
The diagram of a private network.

The ABCs of switches and hubs

Switches are slightly more expensive than hubs because they do a little more work. Suppose that you have a network consisting of three machines — A, B, and C — that are all connected to a switch. When machine A wants to communicate with machine B, the switch transmits the network traffic from A directly to B. Machine C is totally out of the loop. By making sure that C doesn't know what A and B are saying, the switch keeps network communication private. Hubs, on the other hand, broadcast the network traffic from one machine to all the machines connected to the hub. When A sends information to B, the hub broadcasts that information to both B and C.

The next sections describe how to build a wired network; the following section shows a wireless one. You can mix wired and wireless networks, but, for simplicity, we describe how to build a pure wired or wireless network.

Wiring your network with, uh, wires

Way back in prehistoric times (circa 1996), you had to be technically savvy to wire your own network. Wiring consisted of coaxial cables like those used for cable TV connections. Coaxial cables are bulky and require you to use special tools to attach the connectors to the cable ends.

Life is easy now. Wiring your network requires that you obtain Cat 5 cables, which are similar in appearance to telephone cables. Cat 5 cables are manufactured with telephone-like connectors that are a snap (pardon the pun) to use. No muss, no fuss.

You can buy Cat 5 cables at any electronics store. They come in all colors and sizes. Cat 5 cables aren't cheap, but they aren't terribly expensive, either. They're reliable and much easier to work with than coaxial cables.

You need to use a network switch or hub in conjunction with Cat 5 cables. Switches and hubs are the glue that holds your network together. Both switches and hubs connect individual computers so that they can communicate with each other.

Most — if not all — of today's networking equipment is based on the Ethernet protocol. Ethernet is inexpensive and readily available. You can purchase it from any consumer electronics store, mail-order catalog, or online computer seller. You don't need to know any of the technical aspects of Ethernet because it requires no configuration. You need to know only that an Ethernet connector looks similar to a telephone jack. However, Ethernet and telephone jacks aren't compatible.

One byproduct of a switch's design is that it effectively makes your network faster. Network traffic flows only between the machines that are talking to each other. The computers that aren't talking to each other don't use the switch's bandwidth. For example, when machine A is sending information to B, machine C doesn't see any of the traffic.

For your network, start by connecting your machines to a central switch. (You can use a hub if you want.)

Although you can connect as many computers as your switch/hub can handle, to keep the job as simple as possible, the following steps wire two computers, Chivas and Atlas. The following instructions also assume that you have a switch or hub, plus at least two Cat 5 cables:

1. **On the first computer, plug one end of a Cat 5 cable into the Ethernet network interface connector (NIC) on the back of the machine.**

2. **Plug the other end of the cable into the switch.**

   A green light should appear near the connector you used on the switch. The green light indicates that you have link status. *Link status* means that an Ethernet connection has been established — you have an active connection between the computer and the switch.

   If you don't get a link status, make sure that both connectors on the cable have been properly inserted. Pull each connector out and firmly press it back in (called *reseating*).

   If this suggestion doesn't fix the problem, make sure that the cable is working correctly. Check the cable for breaks, cuts, and so forth. Check the cable's connectors for loose wires. Substitute another cable if possible; using a cable that you know works can help you determine whether the suspect cable is at fault.

   If neither of these options works, you may have either a broken switch or Ethernet NIC or both. You may have to replace either or both devices to determine the real problem.

3. **Repeat Steps 1 and 2 for each additional computer.**

After you have successfully connected all your computers to the switch, you can proceed to the "So You Want to Build a Gateway" section, later in this chapter. This section describes how to build an Internet gateway on a Linux computer. The Internet gateway connects your entire private network to the Internet.

Wiring without wires

Life has gotten easier in the past few years (circa 2000). Wireless networking is the best technological advance for home or small-business network users in the past five years, and it's now affordable for consumers.

Going wireless means

- ✔ **Not having to string cables around the house or office.** You don't have to spend money and/or time pulling wires through walls, ducts, cellars, and so forth. You also save the cost of the cables themselves.

- ✔ **Geographical freedom:** You have the freedom to use your computers anywhere, regardless of where your server or Internet gateway or printers are located.

- ✔ **Looking good:** You look high-tech even if you're not. You can impress your friends and family.

The process of constructing a wireless network is straightforward. You need to decide on how your wireless devices will connect into your private network. You can do this in two ways:

✔ **Use a wireless access point:** A *wireless access point* (WAP) is a device through which wireless devices communicate. An access point provides a single point of contact for all other devices to communicate through.

An access point uses two network connections. One is an Ethernet port that connects to your private LAN through a Cat 5 Ethernet cable, and the other point connects to your wireless devices. The access point serves as a common connection point to your LAN.

The other connection point is the access point's wireless receiver. The wireless "port" communicates with all the other wireless devices on your network.

To summarize, an access point acts like a traditional wired Ethernet hub or switch. The hub or switch is the network at an electronic — or physical — level. All the network communication for the subnet that the switch/hub controls goes through that hub or switch. The device provides the infrastructure for the subnet. Accordingly, using a WAP means going into *Infrastructure* mode. Also accordingly, you pay more for the more complicated network setup.

✔ **Use point-to-point (Ad-Hoc) communication:** Counter to popular opinion, you can create a wireless network without an access point. Wireless NICs are designed to communicate directly with each other as well as through an access point. You configure each NIC to know a common network name and a common encryption key, and the NICs form their own ad hoc network by communicating directly with each other. We show you how later in this section.

Point-to-point communication is referred to as *Ad-Hoc mode.* The term *ad hoc* means that you put something together with what you have in whatever way you can. Using wireless Ad-Hoc mode means that each wireless device can communicate with the other wireless devices. (Setting up a network with wireless NICs is less expensive than using WAPs.)

You can purchase an access point to construct your wireless LAN. That's simple and quick, if a little expensive. If you choose that route, we leave it up to you to follow the access point's instructions for connecting other computers to it. You can follow the instructions in Chapter 7 for configuring your Red Hat Linux wireless NIC to an access point.

We describe how to save a few bucks and use a Linux computer to build an ad hoc network. Building an ad hoc network requires you to put a Wi-Fi NIC on a Linux gateway. You then configure every computer, on your private network, to use the same network name and encryption key. The computers can then communicate directly with each other through the Linux gateway to the Internet. Figure 14-2 shows this simple, inexpensive, and elegant design.

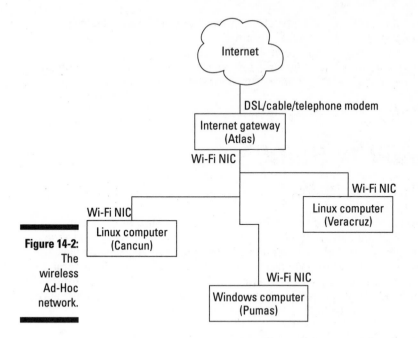

Figure 14-2:
The
wireless
Ad-Hoc
network.

Follow these steps to create a wireless LAN:

1. **Install both a Wi-Fi and Ethernet NIC on the Internet gateway computer.**

   Each of your private network's computers can talk to the Internet gateway through the wireless NIC. The Ethernet connects the gateway to the Internet through either a DSL or cable modem; you can substitute a telephone modem for the Ethernet NIC, if necessary.

   The next section in this chapter describes how to build an Internet gateway.

2. **Install a Wi-Fi NIC on each of your Linux and Windows computers.**

3. **Configure each Wi-Fi NIC to use the same network name and encryption key.**

   Refer to Chapter 7 to find out how to configure a Wi-Fi NIC; use the network IP addresses, netmasks, and so on that are described there.

4. **Configure your Internet gateway to forward your private network traffic to the Internet.**

5. **Configure a firewall on your Internet gateway.**

   Refer to the section "Protecting your LAN with a firewall," later in this chapter.

One advantage of using Infrastructure mode is that a wireless device can move from access point to access point without reconfiguration. Access points provide mobility and flexibility, which can be a good thing if you happen to work on a large, dispersed network. For example, if your company is spread across several locations, you want to be able to use your computer anywhere.

So You Want to Build an Internet Gateway

Okay, you have built your LAN. Woo-hoo! That wasn't too hard. The next question is "What can you do with it?" One answer is that every computer on your private network can communicate with all the others and share information and services. (We describe in Chapter 15 how to share some useful network-based services. You find out how to share files and printers, dole out IP addresses to your LAN devices, configure a Domain Name Server (DNS), and — ta-da! — build a Web server.)

One essential network function is to be connected to the Internet. Chapters 5 and 6 show you how to connect a single, stand-alone Linux computer to the Internet. Now we expand that process a step further and turn the Internet connection into one that can be used by the whole private network. Any computer connected to your LAN will subsequently have Internet access. Sharing is good, and your mom will be pleased.

The remainder of this chapter assumes that you have a working Internet connection, as described in Chapters 5 and 6. This connection is the conduit from your LAN to the Internet. You only have to configure a Linux computer to redirect Internet-bound traffic from your LAN to the Internet — a process called *routing*.

Understanding IP forwarding and network address translation

An Internet gateway requires a Linux computer that has two network connections. You need one Ethernet or wireless NIC to connect to your LAN. The other network connection is used for the Internet connection; this connection may be a traditional telephone-based modem or a DSL or cable modem. You need an Ethernet NIC for this second connection type.

Suppose that you open Mozilla on Chivas (with an IP address of 192.168.1.1), which is a Linux workstation on your LAN, and enter the URL www.redhat.com. NAT on the Internet gateway works like this:

1. Mozilla works with Linux to look up the address — via the Domain Name Service (DNS) — which translates to 216.148.218.195 or 216.148.218.197.

2. Chivas compares the address to its internal routing table. The operating system directs network traffic to the default route if the address doesn't match its local networks.

   In this case, neither 216.148.218.195 nor 216.148.218.197 matches any internal route, so all traffic for the browsing session is directed to the default route.

3. On your private network, the default route of each host is directed toward the Internet gateway, Atlas. All the network packets that Chivas produces that are destined for the Internet, for example, are sent to Atlas.

4. The Internet gateway Atlas receives the outbound packets from Chivas on its internal connection and forwards them to its external connection. Packets going through its external connection are directed to the Internet.

5. Atlas (192.168.1.254) also converts the source address of packets from Chivas (192.168.1.1) to the source address of its external connection. For example, if Atlas has a DSL Internet connection with an address of 10.0.0.213, the source address of Chivas packets is changed to 10.0.0.213. (This supposedly external Internet address has been changed to protect the innocent.)

6. The packets go to their intended destination. The www.redhat.com server responds to the query and sends back the requested information.

7. Atlas receives the return packets, converts their destination address back to that of Chivas, and forwards them to the private network.

8. Chivas receives the packets, and the browser displays the information.

When Atlas is wearing its gateway hat, it performs two primary functions: It routes network traffic between its internal and external network connections, and it converts internal LAN addresses to external Internet ones. The following section describes how to configure your gateway to perform these functions.

Forwarding network traffic through your gateway

This section describes how to configure a Linux computer to work as an Internet gateway. The process requires you to configure the Linux kernel to forward packets from one network interface to another — between the LAN port and the Internet port. Because Red Hat Linux turns off forwarding by default, the following instructions describe how to turn on forwarding (you also need a Linux computer with two network connections in order to construct a gateway):

✔ One network connection should be either an Ethernet or wireless NIC that connects the gateway to the LAN. We refer to it as the *internal network connection.*

✔ The other connection is either the telephone-based modem or an Ethernet NIC connected to a DSL or cable modem. We refer to it as the *external network connection.*

Turn off your external network connection for now. You will turn on IP forwarding to enable the transmitting of network traffic between the Internet and your private network, which can be a security hazard. Disconnecting your Internet connection removes the insecurity: Unplug your modem's (DSL, cable, or telephone) external (Internet) cable.

These instructions describe how to configure a Linux computer as the Internet gateway for a LAN:

1. **Add the appropriate internal and external network connections to your intended Internet gateway.**

   For example, the internal network connection is eth0, and the external network connection is eth1.

2. **Log in to your Internet gateway as root.**

3. **Click the GNOME Menu button and then choose Run Program.**

4. **Edit the** sysctl.conf **file by entering** gedit /etc/sysctl.conf **in the Run Program window.**

   The gedit program displays the contents of sysctl.conf, as shown in Figure 14-3.

5. **Locate the following line (which should be close to the top of the file):**
   ```
   net.ipv4.ip_forward = 0
   ```

6. **Change the zero to a one:**
   ```
   net.ipv4.ip_forward = 1
   ```

7. **Click the Save button.**

8. **Choose File➪Quit to exit gedit.**

   You can view the change by clicking the Nautilus Refresh button. You have to restart Linux networking in order for the change to take effect.

9. **Open the Service Configuration Druid by clicking the GNOME Menu button and choosing Server Settings➪Services. Locate the Network service, as shown in Figure 14-4.**

10. **Click the Restart button to turn on IP forwarding.**

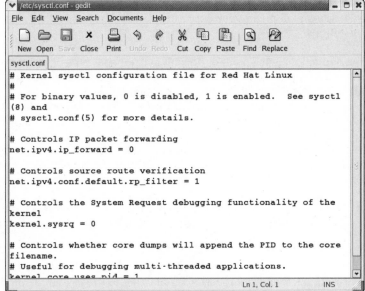

Figure 14-3:
The gedit editor opens the `sysctl.conf` file.

Figure 14-4:
The Service Configuration utility.

Connecting your Internet gateway

After you configure your Internet gateway to forward network traffic from your private network to your Internet connection (see the preceding section), you need to make that connection. In this section, we describe how to use the Internet connections introduced in Chapters 5 and 6. We build on those instructions to connect your entire network to the Internet through these connections.

From a functional viewpoint, it doesn't matter what type of Internet connection you use because all Internet connections send and receive the same network traffic. (Practically speaking, however, speed and latency are two different things.) For this reason, we can treat the Internet connections from Chapters 5 and 6 as interchangeable.

The forwarding described in the preceding section takes care of routing the packets to and from the Internet via your Internet gateway. Follow these steps to configure the Internet gateway:

1. **Install the first NIC (Ethernet or Wi-Fi) on your Red Hat Linux Internet gateway; the second NIC connects your private network to the gateway.**

2. **Connect the gateway to its Internet connection.**

   You either connect the second Ethernet NIC to the DSL or cable modem or connect your computer's serial cable to the telephone modem (or simply the internal telephone modem).

3. **Configure your Internet gateway to allow packet forwarding.**

   (Refer to the section "Forwarding network traffic through your gateway," earlier in this chapter.)

4. **Assign an IP address to each NIC.**

   When you're using a telephone or cable modem, this action is done automatically for you; some DSL modems also perform this action for you. Telephone modems use the Point-to-Point Protocol (PPP), whereas cable and some DSL modems use DHCP, which assigns an IP address to their respective interfaces.

5. **Assign a default route that points to the Internet connection device.**

   Again, the PPP and DHCP protocols do this automatically.

Follow these steps to configure computers or network devices on your private network to connect to the Internet through the gateway:

1. **Configure your computer with its network parameters.**

   In other words, assign an IP address and netmask (and optionally, but highly recommended, a host and network name) to each computer when using an Ethernet-based LAN. On a wireless network, you need to assign the IP address, netmask, common network name, and encryption key.

   For example, Chapter 7 describes how to set up the sample computer Cancun. We assign it the host name `cancun`, the network name `paunchy.net`, the IP address `192.168.1.1`, and a netmask of `255.255.255.0`.

If we use a Wi-Fi NIC on Cancun, we can assign the network name (ESSID) *wifi* and the encryption key *iamnotanumber*.

2. **Configure the default route on each device to point to the Internet gateway.**

3. **Rinse and repeat these steps for each computer on your private network.**

After you have configured your Internet gateway and each additional computer on your private network, you should test whether they can communicate with the Internet. Consult Chapter 18 for pointers on troubleshooting network problems if you encounter difficulties. After you're satisfied that you have your LAN happily connected to the Internet, turn that puppy off. You still need to set up your firewall (described in the next section) because you don't want to stay connected without one.

Protecting your LAN with a firewall

After you have configured your gateway for IP forwarding, you need to protect yourself from the Internet. This section describes how to turn your gateway into a firewall. We use the same process and many of the same rules we describe in Chapter 8; however, this firewall is designed to protect your entire network, whereas the one in Chapter 8 is oriented toward protecting a single machine.

The firewall script contains both of the filtering rules that help to prevent hackers from invading your computer and network. The firewall also provides the network address translation (NAT) function, which allows the computers on your private network to access the Internet. NAT, if you recall, converts the nonroutable source IP addresses (192.168.1.1, for example) into the routable source IP address of your Internet connection.

Network address translation is also referred to as IP masquerading, or simply masquerading.

The basic configuration of the firewall we describe in Chapter 8 works in the new configuration. The firewall performs these functions:

✔ **Block all incoming, outgoing, and forwarded packets:** Start by blocking all network traffic by default. This firewall completely protects your private network but also makes it completely useless! Start with this policy to ensure that the firewall blocks all except the connections you explicitly allow.

✔ **Allow all loopback traffic:** You must allow all network traffic on the Internet gateway's loopback interface. The loopback interface is used by the Linux operating system for its own, internal communication.

✔ **Allow all internal NIC traffic:** Machines on the private network use the internal NIC to communicate with the gateway. You don't want to restrict traffic on the private network, although you may decide to do so if your security policies demand it.

✔ **Allow all outgoing traffic through the firewall:** Allow all machines on the private network to connect to the Internet through the gateway's external NIC. The firewall allows all outgoing connections. Because the firewall is *stateful* (it keeps track of which connection each packet belongs to), it allows the return packets back into the private network. You can add extra rules to restrict outgoing traffic if your security policies require it.

✔ **Use NAT for outgoing connections:** Create a NAT rule to make all connections originating on the private network appear to be coming from the Internet gateway. All private network machines will have their source address and port numbers changed to that of the gateway.

The network address translation isn't necessary if your Internet connection device (telephone, DSL, or cable modem) performs NAT. However, by providing a NAT filtering rule, you ensure that your Internet gateway will work with any connection device — whether or not it performs NAT.

✔ **Allow incoming SSH connections:** Secure Shell (SSH) is a protocol for encrypting network connections.

The firewall on the Internet gateway is identical to the firewall we describe in Chapter 8, except that you must create an extra set of rules for the second NIC.

Enter each filtering rule on your Internet gateway. Be sure that you enter the rules from the Linux computer's console because if you use a network connection, you may accidentally block your connection while modifying the firewall.

After you complete the process, save the rules so that they're started automatically every time you boot the computer. This command saves the rules to the `/etc/sysconfig/iptables` file:

```
iptables-save > /etc/sysconfig/iptables
```

You can now restart your Internet connection. Your private network can now access the Internet and be reasonably — but not completely — protected from the bad guys.

Chapter 15

Creating Basic Linux Network Services

*L*inux was built from scratch with networking in mind and, therefore, its networking is both integrated and sophisticated. Linux also comes bundled with software that provides file sharing, printer sharing, and other functions. Thus, Linux gained initial popularity by inexpensively and reliably providing network services. (Linux moved to the desktop only when applications such as word processing were written for it.)

In earlier chapters, we show how to use a Red Hat Linux computer with an existing network. We also show how to build a private network by using a Linux computer as the Internet gateway and firewall. In this chapter, we describe how to configure a Linux box to provide some popular services to the private network.

Preparing a Network Server

All the examples shown in this chapter can be run from any Red Hat Linux computer, such as the one we describe in Chapter 3. (The Red Hat Linux computer we describe there was configured as a personal workstation — we recommend using either the Workstation or, optionally, the Personal Desktop installation type. You can also use the Server type if you want to build a computer that provides Linux services.) However, Linux doesn't really care what your intentions are when you build your computer. Linux calmly does what it is told and even works as a server if you want.

Linux works equally well whether it's running a word processor or a Web server; the difference between them is just the software that's used and how it's configured. For example, you start the OpenOffice program when using your computer as a word processor, or you use the Apache program for Web services. In fact, you can run both programs at one time and do word processing while running a Web server.

Regarding performance, maintenance, and security: Workstations and servers should be run on dedicated machines, if possible. Workstations require a wider range of software than do servers. Your workstation is a jack-of-all-trades by nature. Servers work better when they're configured to do just a small — preferably one or two — jobs.

When you get to the point where your business and livelihood depend on providing network services, you want to build and dedicate machines for this purpose. However, until that time comes, you can use the simple workstation we describe in Chapter 3, which is what we assume you're doing for this book.

You can configure the Red Hat Linux computer from Chapter 3 to provide services to a private network like the one we describe in Chapters 7 and 14. This chapter provides instructions on how to make the Apache Web server visible to the Internet. Services such as Samba, printers, and DHCP, however, should definitely be kept private and not be shown to the Internet.

We also assume in this chapter that you're connecting to the Internet through a private network as described in Chapters 7 and 14. (Chapter 14 provides instructions for using a Red Hat Linux computer as an Internet gateway and firewall.) This chapter assumes that you'll be using this same computer to provide services to your private network. This assumption is a reasonable one for small-office and home-office (SOHO) networks because the demands put on a modern PC by a small network aren't excessive. Using a single computer for multiple purposes greatly simplifies the work you must do and is the most efficient way to use your resources. (Otherwise, you have to start adding routing rules to the gateway.)

Using a single Linux computer to act as an Internet gateway and provide network services is a cost-effective way of using your limited resources. However, this type of configuration is more difficult to secure. Each function you place on a single machine increases the potential number of vulnerabilities. Think of adding functions like adding doors and windows to a house: Building a house with a single door and no windows is more secure than a house with 5 doors and 15 windows. However, who wants to live in a dark house? Security, like everything else in life, is a matter of compromise. Please consult Chapters 5 through 8, 16, and 19 for discussions on how you can increase security.

Building an Apache Web Server

The Web is the Internet, and the Internet is the Web. Well, that's not completely true because the Internet provides the foundation for widely used functions, such as e-mail. However, the Internet became immensely popular because of the World Wide Web (WWW).

The Web isn't as mysterious as it may seem at first. It's essentially all the world's Web servers that are connected to the Internet. The Internet serves the same function as the world's telephone system: It interconnects everyone. You can think of Web servers as the telephones that allow people to contact each other, businesses, and other organizations. Just as you can start a business or organization and let people contact you via your phone, you can also allow people to contact you via your Web server. This section describes how to construct a simple Web server.

Describing how to set up anything more than a simple Web server is beyond the scope of this book. Needless to say, you can configure Apache to provide a whole world of Web services. If you want to utilize the powers of Apache, consult such books as the excellent *Apache Server 2 Bible,* by Mohammed J. Kabir, published by Wiley Publishing, Inc.

Installing and starting the Web server

Linux provides the ideal platform for providing Web services. The Apache Web server system is bundled with Red Hat Linux. Apache is easy to set up and use. These instructions show you how to install and configure a basic Web server:

1. **Log in as root and mount the appropriate CD that accompanies this book.**

2. **Install the Apache RPM packages. Consult Appendix D for instructions on installing RPM packages.**

   You can manually install the Apache packages by starting a GNOME Terminal emulation window and running this command:

   ```
   rpm -ivh /mnt/cdrom/RedHat/RPMS/httpd*
   ```

3. **The Apache RPM package puts all the configuration files in place, so all you have to do is start the appropriate daemon. Enter this command from the GNOME Terminal window:**

   ```
   /etc/init.d/httpd start
   ```

Linux uses the term *daemon* when referring to a process that runs continually in order to provide a service. The Apache daemon is named `httpd`, which is short for HyperText Transport Protocol Daemon. The HyperText Transport Protocol (HTTP) is the system used to coordinate the transfer of Web pages between the server and client (for example, the Mozilla browser). HTTP is the common language that both sides speak.

4. **Start your Mozilla Web browser and enter** localhost **in the URL window. Your new Web server is displayed, as shown in Figure 15-1.**

5. **If you want your Web server to start automatically every time you boot your computer, enter this command in the terminal emulator window:**

```
chkconfig --level 35 httpd on
```

The *level 35* option configures the Web server to start in either non-graphics mode (system level 3) or graphical (system level 5) modes.

This command creates *soft links,* which are roughly analogous to a pointer. In this case, the soft link `S99httpd` is run automatically whenever you boot your computer.

Your Web server should now be visible on your private network. (If your computer isn't connected to a LAN — for example, if it's a stand-alone machine with a telephone, cable, or DSL Internet connection — you can still use your Web server from the machine itself.) However, keeping your Web server all to yourself isn't much fun. The following section describes how to allow access to your Web server from the Internet.

The OpenOffice suite includes an HTML editor you can use to create Web pages. It's simple to use and can produce great documents. Open any OpenOffice programs — Writer or Spreadsheet, for example — and choose File⇨New⇨HTML Document. The HTML editor window opens, and you can create Web pages.

Accessing your Web server through your firewall

This section describes how to open your firewall to allow access to your Web server. Exactly how you allow access depends on whether you're connecting to the Internet directly from your Linux computer or through a LAN. The instructions describe how to modify your firewall and a DSL Internet connection to allow the Internet to view your Web page.

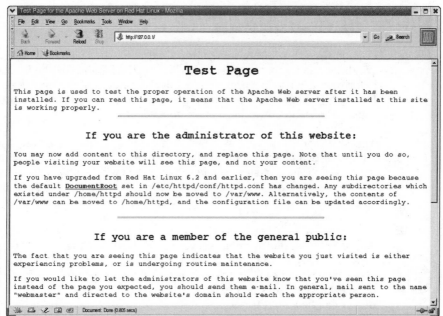

Figure 15-1:
Your first
Web server!

You must modify the network address translation (NAT) configuration if you're using a DSL modem like the one we describe in Chapter 6. Connect to the DSL modem as described in Chapter 6 and run these commands:

1. **If your Web server is directly connected to the Internet via a telephone, cable, or DSL modem, add this rule to the firewall (as described in Chapter 8):**

   ```
   iptables -A INPUT -p tcp -m state --state NEW,ESTABLISHED
           -j accept -dport 80
   ```

2. **If your Web server is indirectly connected to the Internet via a private network, add the following rule to the firewall we describe in Chapter 16. The firewall may or may not be the same machine as your Web server.**

   ```
   iptables -A INPUT -p tcp -m state --state NEW,ESTABLISHED
           -j accept -dport 80
   ```

Amazons of the world, watch out! Okay, it takes just a bit more than the default Apache Web page to upset the big boys, but you have the basics in place. All you need to do is figure out what to sell. How about a great Linux book?

Building a Samba File Server

Early in the game, Linux gained popularity by acting as a file server for both Windows and Linux computers by dancing the Samba. Samba is more than just a dance: It's also a program (a suite of programs) that speaks the same file-sharing language — or *protocol* — as Windows. Using Samba produces a way to share the Linux file system on a network.

This section describes how to install and configure Samba on any Linux computer. Samba comes bundled with Red Hat Linux, of course, so installation is a breeze. Samba is also configured to automatically share the ubiquitous /home directory on a Red Hat Linux computer, so configuration is also easy. The instructions in the following section describe how to get Samba running on a private network.

Samba is based on the client-server model in which a computer (server) provides services to one or more computers (clients). Samba uses the term *share* (which comes from the Microsoft Windows world) to refer to any object that, as a server, it exports to a network or, as a client, mounts. An object can be a directory or printer.

Installing and starting Samba

Samba consists of several programs, configuration files, and documentation files. Samba is packaged in four RPM files on the CDs that accompany this book. This list describes the purpose of each RPM file:

- ✔ **samba-client:** This package contains the utility and other supporting software to connect a Linux computer to a Samba server. You can use an interactive utility, smbclient, to connect to a Samba share. The default Red Hat Linux installation installs this package by default.

- ✔ **samba:** The Samba server software is included in this package. All the programs for sharing files, directories, and printers are included here; the two essential daemons are smbd and nmbd; the essential configuration file is smb.conf. The utilities for controlling the daemons are also included.

- ✔ **samba-swat:** You can manually configure the Samba configuration file, smb.conf, if you're an expert. However, Samba provides a Web-based system that is much easier to use and produces clean and readable configuration files.

- ✔ **samba-common:** All the software required by the other three packages is included in this file. This package is also installed by default.

Samba was originally designed and coded by Andrew Tridgell, in Australia. Samba almost instantly became popular worldwide and became too much for a few people to handle. Thus, the Samba project was started in order to take care of the phenomenon. You can find more information about Samba at www.samba.org.

These instructions describe how to dance the — er, install, configure, and use — Samba:

1. **Log in as root and insert CD1.**

2. **Open a terminal emulator window and enter these commands:**

```
rpm -ivh /mnt/cdrom/RedHat/RPMS/perl-CGI*
rpm -ivh /mnt/cdrom/RedHat/RPMS/samba-2*
rpm -ivh /mnt/cdrom/RedHat/RPMS/samba*
```

3. **Eject CD1.**

4. **Insert CD2 and install the Samba SWAT package:**

```
rpm -ivh /mnt/cdrom/samba-swat*
```

You can use the Red Hat Package Manager, described further in Appendix D, to install these packages. However, it's almost as easy, and less confusing to describe, to use the manual method.

The Samba server consists of two daemons: smbd and nmbd. You must start both daemons before anyone can access your Samba server.

5. **Enter this command to start the daemons:**

```
/etc/init.d/smb start
```

You can stop the daemons by substituting the *stop* option for the *start* option. You can restart the Samba server by using the *restart* option:

```
/etc/init.d/smb restart
```

6. **Automate the startup of the Samba daemons by creating these soft links with the** chkconfig **utility:**

The following command tells Linux to automatically start Samba for level 3 (nongraphical) and level 5 (running the graphical X server); Samba is started whether your Linux computer starts in graphical or nongraphical mode:

```
chkconfig --level 35 smb on
```

Samba is configured by default to use its own password file. You must create the password file using the mksmbpasswd.sh script.

7. **Use the** mksmbpasswd.sh **script to create the Samba user account and password.**

The -a **option tells the script to add the user account to the smbpasswd file:**

```
smbpasswd -a paul
```

You're prompted to enter a password twice.

8. **The acid test: Run this command to look at user Paul's file system.**

```
smbclient //cancun/paul -U paul
```

9. **Enter the password you entered in Step 6, and you gain access to Paul's home directory, which should look similar to this:**

```
added interface ip=192.168.1.1 bcast=192.168.1.255
        nmask=255.255.255.0
Password:
Domain=[MYGROUP] OS=[Unix] Server=[Samba 2.2.7]
smb: \>
```

10. **Enter** help **at the** smb:\> **prompt and you see all the commands at your disposal.**

    For example, enter **dir** and you see all the files in your home directory.

11. **You can mount Samba file systems from a Linux computer. Enter this command from either the Samba server or another computer (client) on your LAN:**

```
mount -t smbfs -o username=paul //cancun/paul /mnt
```

12. **You can unmount the share by entering the command** unmount/mnt.

Your home directory is now mounted on the /mnt directory. This is great! Now you can use your Linux computer to provide files and directories to the rest of your network!

Configuring Samba with SWAT

Call in the SWAT team! (Sorry, that couldn't be helped.) No, not the guys who say "huh" in Chicago, but rather the guy who configures Samba for you. (Sorry again.) SWAT, which stands for Samba Web Administration Tool, is used to graphically configure Samba. SWAT helps you to configure all aspects of a Samba server and also to start, stop, and look at Samba's status.

You must configure the inetd.d daemon to start up SWAT. These instructions show you how to get xinetd.d to run SWAT:

1. **Log in to your Samba server as root and open a Terminal emulator window (refer to Chapter 4 for instructions).**

2. **Edit the** /etc/xinetd.d/swat **file.**

3. **Change the last line from** disable=yes **to** disable=no.

4. **Restart** `xinetd.d`.

```
/etc/init.d/xinetd restart
```

5. **Start Mozilla on your Samba server and enter this address in the URL window:**

```
localhost:901
```

SWAT starts and prompts you for a user name and password. SWAT is configured — via the `/etc/xinetd.d/swat` file — to use the root user and password.

6. **Enter** root **at the User Name prompt and the root user's password at the Password prompt.**

Mozilla shows the SWAT configuration system, as shown in Figure 15-2.

You can now use SWAT to configure any aspect of Samba. These steps describe how to use Samba to export your CD-ROM drive:

TIP

Samba comes configured to export users' home directories and printers on the server where it resides, so the basics are already covered. One good share to provide users on your LAN is your CD-ROM drive.

7. **Click the Shares button.**

The Shares window opens.

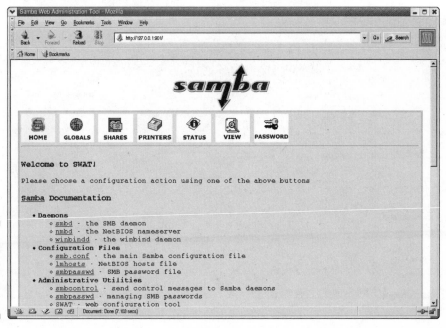

Figure 15-2:
The SWAT configuration system.

8. **Enter the word** cdrom **next to the Create Share button and then click the Create Share button; the word** cdrom **is arbitrary but descriptive.**

   The configuration window for the new cdrom share opens.

9. **Enter** /mnt/cdrom **in the path window, as shown in Figure 15-3.**

   Optionally, you can enter a comment to describe what you're exporting.

10. **Click the Commit Changes button, and the new share is saved to the** /etc/samba/smb.conf **file.**

    The changes also take immediate effect because a new smbd daemon is spawned every time a share request is made to the Samba server. You can now mount the new Samba share from any machine on the LAN, including the server.

11. **Try mounting the share by entering this command from the server:**

    ```
    mount -t smbfs -o username=paul //cancun/cdrom /mnt
    ```

    Note that when you mount a file system over an existing file system, only the newly mounted file system is visible. In this case, we mounted the CD-ROM on /mnt. This covers over the initial CD-ROM mount.

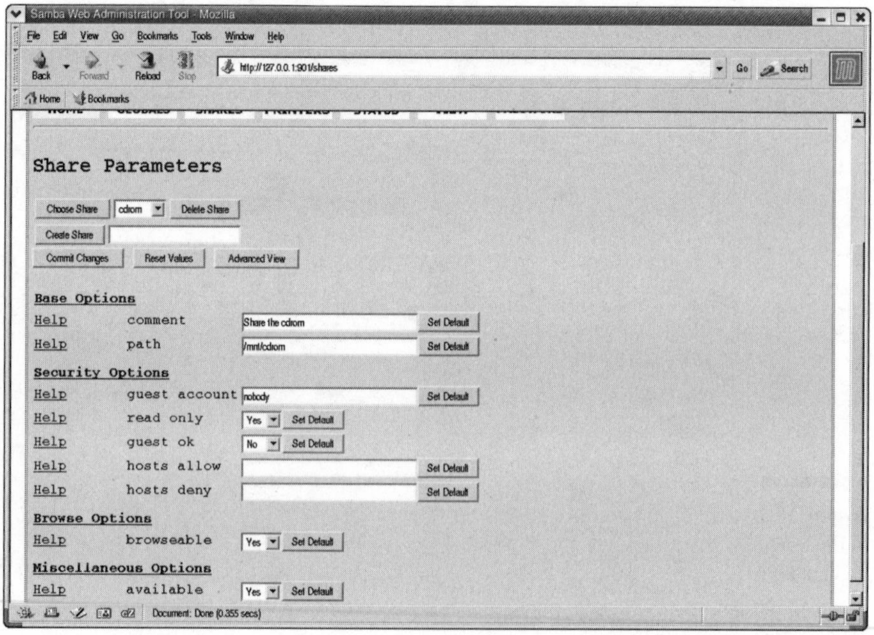

Figure 15-3:
Configuring
a new
share.

Building a Print Server

Linux can share printers to other Linux (and Unix) computers without using Samba; you can select the Unix Style print queue to create a Linux print server. However, Windows doesn't speak Unix, and using Samba enables Linux, Unix, and Windows computers to all use the Linux print server.

You must complete these steps before your Linux computer acts as a print server to your entire network:

1. **Connect a printer to the Linux computer.**

2. **Configure the Linux print server to use the printer.**

3. **Configure a Linux client to print through the server.**

The following sections describe how to complete each of these steps so that every computer on your private network can print through your Linux print server.

Connecting a printer to your Linux computer

Choose from two types of printers when you're creating a print server:

- ✔ **Networked printers:** Printers that can be connected directly to a LAN are networked printers. They have their own Ethernet (and, in the future, wireless) NIC. Networked printers are divided between those that can act as their own print server (also called a *print spooler*) and the ones that need to be connected to a print server.

- ✔ **Nonnetworked printers:** Traditional printers need to be connected to a computer through a printer (parallel) or Universal Serial Bus (USB) port.

Nonnetworked printers outnumber networked printers because they cost less. Traditional printers are less flexible than networked printers because they must be connected to a computer; networked printers can be located anywhere that a network connection exists.

This section describes how to use non-networked computers because they're so common. The process is simple: You connect your printer to the Linux print server via the USB or parallel port. After you're connected, the Linux computer can be configured to send print jobs to the printer.

Using a parallel port requires no configuration of the Linux operating system. The USB connection, however, requires that Linux load a USB kernel module (essentially a driver, in Windows terminology). Loading the kernel module should be automatic. However, if you encounter problems, you can load the module manually:

1. **Log in as root.**

2. **Open a terminal emulator window (refer to Chapter 4 for instructions).**

3. **Enter this command:**

```
modprobe printer
```

Linux loads the printer kernel module.

Configuring the Linux print server

After you connect a printer, you need to configure Linux to act as a print server. Red Hat provides an excellent print configuration utility. (Red Hat refers to its configuration systems as *utilities*.) Building a Linux print server requires you to configure the printer as a local device. However, every print server client — the computers on the LAN that send their print jobs to the print server — configure their print queues to use the Windows Printer type. The print server sees the printer directly through its USB or parallel port, but the print clients see the printer as a Samba (Windows) share on the server.

Red Hat Linux can handle five printer types. The printer configuration druid allows you to configure each type. The following list describes the printer types:

- **Local Printer:** Use this type if your printer is connected directly to your computer. The print server is configured using this type because the printer is connected directly to it.

- **Unix Printer:** Use this type if you're creating a print server that only other Linux and Unix computers will use. Windows computers can't use Unix printers. Unix printer queues don't require Samba to work.

- **Windows Printer:** Use this type if you're printing to a Windows print server. Samba makes the print server look like a Windows print server, and the clients on the private network use this setting.

- **Novell Printer:** Use this type if you're printing to a Novell print server.

- **JetDirect Printer:** Use this type if you're printing to a Hewlett-Packard (HP) JetDirect printer. The HP JetDirect interface is built into many HP and other printers. You can also purchase JetDirect print server devices that connect to non-networked, traditional printers. JetDirect print servers convert traditional printers into networked printers.

The following instructions describe how to configure an Epson Stylist printer because it's a good, inexpensive inkjet printer. The configuration utility can configure many different types of printers, so select the model that's appropriate for you.

1. **Log in to your Red Hat Linux print server.**

2. **Click the GNOME Menu button and then choose System Settings⬦ Printers.**

3. **Enter the root password if you're prompted to do so.**

4. **Click the New button and the Add a new printer queue wizard starts.**

5. **Click the button and you're prompted to enter a queue name.**

   Figure 15-4 shows the Set the Print Queue Name Forward description window.

   The queue name is the name clients use to access the print server's printer. You can enter any name you want for the queue name. For example, Epson777 clearly indicates that you're accessing an Epson Stylist 777 printer.

6. **Enter the printer name in the Name text box and, optionally, a description.**

7. **Click the Forward button and the Queue type window opens.**

   Linux should detect the printer attached to either the USB or parallel port.

   Linux parallel (printer) ports correspond to Windows printer ports. Linux lp0 is equivalent to LPT1: and /dev/lp1 is equivalent to LPT2:.

8. **Click Next and the Select a Print Driver window pops up.**

   You can select a network-based printer connection, if that's what you have, by clicking the Locally connected pull-down menu in the upper-middle area of the window. Select the type of network printer you have.

9. **Click Forward and the Printer model window pops up.**

   Click the Select the printer manufacturer and model pull-down menu. Scroll down the list and click your printer's manufacturer.

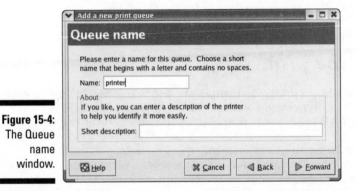

Figure 15-4:
The Queue name window.

10. **The manufacturer's model list appears in the Printer model window.**

    Scroll down the manufacturer's model list and select your printer model.

    Figure 15-5 shows the print driver selected for the Stylus Color 777 printer.

11. **Click the Forward button and you see the Finish, and create the new print queue window.**

12. **Click the Apply button and a Question window opens.**

    You can click the Yes button to test your new print queue. Click No to skip the test.

13. **Control returns to the Printer configuration window.**

14. **Click the Apply button and the Linux print daemon, lpd, restarts and makes the new configuration active.**

15. **Close the configuration utility by choosing Action⇨Quit.**

The printer configuration druid allows you to go back and edit or delete a printer configuration.

You can configure your print server to control more than one printer. Revisit Steps 4 through 12 to configure each new printer. Click the Default button to make one of the printers the default printer.

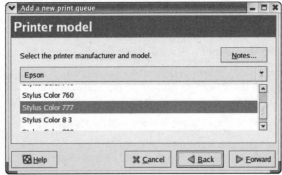

Figure 15-5:
Selecting
your printer
driver.

Configuring a Linux client to print through the print server

Samba makes sharing a printer to Linux, Unix, and Windows computers easy because all of those types can speak the Server Message Block (SMB) protocol; SMB is a Windows way of spreading the wealth (yeah, right).

Samba comes configured to automatically export the default Linux printer. Half the battle is won! You don't have to configure the server; you only have to configure each client.

Configure a Linux client to print through the Linux print server by repeating the instructions given in the preceding section, "Configuring the Linux print server." The instructions are the same except that you select the Windows queue type rather than Local. You select the Windows type because the client is sending its jobs to the server via Samba; Samba makes the server act like it's a Windows queue type.

You can print a test PostScript page to test your printer configuration by choosing Test⇨US Letter Postscript Test Page in the Printer Configuration utility.

Building a DHCP Server

The Dynamic Host Configuration Protocol (DHCP) is a system that provides configuration parameters such as IP addresses a nd DNS addresses to computers. DHCP is used to simplify the process of connecting computers, printers, and other devices to networks. Rather than find and attach an IP address to each device on a network, you can use DHCP to automatically do the job for you.

Chapter 3 discusses the steps in configuring the Red Hat Linux computer's network configuration. In that process, you have to decide on an IP address (for example, 192.168.1.1), the netmask, default gateway, DNS servers, and so on. That process isn't terribly difficult when you have a network of two or three machines. But when you start working with larger networks, you start duplicating a great deal of work.

Using DHCP simplifies your job as a part-time network administrator. DHCP not only reduces the configuration work for every network device you configure, it also makes moving between networks easier. For example, if you switch your laptop between work and home, you need to switch network configurations, unless you use DHCP. If you use DHCP, your computer automatically picks up work or home network parameters.

The following sections describe how to set up a Linux DHCP server and client. We use the default DHCP server configuration. DHCP can be programmed to provide more information than just an IP address. However, the basic DHCP server works well "out of the box" at providing basic network parameters.

Installing and configuring the DHCP server

This section describes how to get your Linux DHCP server up and running. The basic DHCP system uses a dhcpd daemon to respond to client requests. The dhcpd daemon gets its configuration from the /etc/dhcpd.conf file.

These instructions describe how to install and configure the dhcpd daemon:

1. **Log in to the Linux server as root and insert CD1 that accompanies this book.**

2. **Open a terminal emulator window (refer to Chapter 4) and enter this command:**

   ```
   rpm -ivh /mnt/cdrom/RedHat/RPMS/dhcp*
   ```

   Alternatively, you can use the Red Hat Package Manager to install the dhcp package. See Appendix D for instructions about using the Package Manager.

3. **Create the /etc/dhcpd.conf file, as shown in the following example (you can use the sample configuration file /usr/share/doc/dhcp*/ dhcp.conf.sample as a template, if you want):**

   ```
   ignore client-updates;

   subnet 192.168.1.0 netmask 255.255.255.0 {
       option time-offset -18000; # EST
       option domain-name-servers      192.168.1.254;
       option routers                  192.168.1.254;
       option domain-name              "paunchy.net";
       range 192.168.1.140 192.168.1.180;
       host ns {

           fixed-address 192.168.1.254;
       }
   }
   ```

   This configuration sets up the Linux DHCP server to dole out IP addresses 192.168.1.140 through 192.168.1.180 to DHCP clients. The server also configures the client to use the Internet gateway address of 192.168.1.254 and the name server configuration pointing to 192.168.1.254. These arbitrary addresses should be configured to your gateway and, optionally, your name server (as described in the next section). For example, if you use your ISP's name server for your network, use its address in place of 192.168.1.254. (The DHCP server modifies the client's /etc/resolv.conf file with the name server addresses.)

4. **Automate the startup of the dhcpd daemon by creating these soft links with the chkconfig utility:**

   This command turns on the dhcpd for level 3 (nongraphical) and level 5 (running the graphical X server):

   ```
   chkconfig --level 35 dhcpd on
   ```

5. **Start the dhcpd daemon by running the DHCP daemon startup script:**

   ```
   /etc/init.d/dhcpd start
   ```

Your DHCP Linux server now provides any device (Linux, Unix, Windows, printers, and so on) with an IP address, netmask, and DNS addresses.

Installing and configuring the DHCP client

The Linux DHCP client looks to the DHCP server to get its network configuration parameters. The client runs the `dhcpcd` daemon, which communicates with the server `dhcpd` daemon. These steps describe how to set up and configure the DHCP client on a Linux computer:

1. **Log in to the Linux DHCP client as root and insert the appropriate CD that accompanies this book.**

2. **Open a terminal emulator window (refer to Chapter 4) and enter this command:**

```
rpm -ivh /mnt/cdrom/RedHat/RPMS/dhcpcd*
```

   Note that the `dhcpd` server RPM package includes a client daemon. However, the client packaged with the `dhcpcd` client RPM package works better and should be the one you use.

3. **Modify the client's network configuration. Click the GNOME Menu button and then choose System Tools⇨Network.**

   The Red Hat Network Configuration utility starts.

4. **Click the Edit button and the Ethernet or Wireless Device Configuration window appears.**

5. **Click the Automatically Obtain IP Address Settings with DHCP button. Enter the host name you want to assign to your client computer.**

6. **Click the Automatically Obtain DNS Information from Provider button, which forces your client computer to use the DNS information provided by the DHCP server. Click OK.**

7. **Back in the original Network Configuration window, click the Apply button and then click Close.**

8. **Restart the network configuration by running this command:**

```
/etc/init.d/network restart
```

Your client computer now gets its network configuration from the DHCP server. Life is made easy again.

Building a DNS Server

Every device connected to the Internet, including your Red Hat Linux computer, requires an Internet Protocol (IP) address in order to communicate properly. IP addresses are unique numbers and, therefore, difficult for us carbon-based humans to remember and use. The domain name system (DNS) solves that problem by converting numbers to names, making it possible to use names like `www.redhat.com` rather than `66.187.232.56`. In many ways, DNS makes the Internet usable and therefore popular.

DNS is an interdependent information sharing system — a distributed database. No centralized servers contain actual addresses, such as `www.redhat.com`. Instead, DNS is structured so that local servers store local addresses, and a few centralized servers store information about where to go to find local addresses.

Introducing DNS components

The overall DNS system is a complex system that contains many components. But because we show you how to build a DNS server for your private network, you can use a more simple system. Building your DNS server requires understanding only a relative handful of DNS components.

This list outlines the basic DNS components:

- ✔ **Domains:** You're probably familiar with the domains whether you realize it or not. *Domains* are the networks you access all the time on the Internet. For example, `redhat.com` is a domain (and `www.redhat.com` is the name of a server within the `redhat.com` domain.)

    Domains can optionally be divided into subdomains. For example, Red Hat has a subdomain, `beta.redhat.com`, used for its beta software development.

    Domains themselves are divided into domains. The ubiquitous `.com`, `.edu`, and `.org` are all top-level domains. They organize the Internet into business, educational, and not-for-profit arenas.

- ✔ **Zones:** Domains are divided into zones. DNS servers service zones. A zone can map directly to a domain; multizones can service a domain as well. The DNS server you're building in this section consists of a single domain that services the fictitious `paunchy.net` domain.

- ✔ **Authoritative name servers:** Every zone must have an authoritative name server. An authoritative name server holds the information for every host within the zone. You can create primary and secondary authoritative name servers. The secondaries back up the primaries.

- ✔ **Non-authoritative name servers:** You can create name servers that don't necessarily provide the most up-to-date information.

- ✔ **Caching name server:** Name servers can be configured to look up addresses from other name servers and temporarily save — or *cache* — the information. Caching name servers help spread out the load of servicing large domains.

✔ **Root name servers:** The authorities that control domain name registrations provide root name servers that hold the addresses of name servers for each domain. DNS queries go to root name servers to find out where to find authoritative name servers.

The following list describes the parameters found in DNS configuration and zone files. The parameters are called Resource Records (RR):

✔ **A Records:** Address (A) records map IP names to numeric addresses.

✔ **C Records:** Canonical (C) records define aliases for A records.

✔ **MX Records:** Mail exchange (MX) records specify the mail servers that service a domain.

✔ **NS Records:** Name server (NS) records specify the name server for a zone.

✔ **SOA:** Start of authority (SOA) creates a section that describes the generic properties of a zone file. The SOA configures parameters that set the serial number and various timeouts, plus the domain name of a zone.

Following a DNS address request

Look at how your browser finds the Red Hat Linux Web page:

1. You open your browser and enter the URL `www.redhat.com`.

2. The browser asks Linux for the Web page's numeric address.

3. Linux looks in its `/etc/resolv.conf` configuration file and finds the address of a name server.

   You can use any available DNS server on the Internet. For example, you can use the DNS servers of Albuquerque's fine ISP Southwest Cyberport, `198.59.115.2`, from anywhere on the Internet. You should use your own ISP's servers because it has fewer routers, or hops, to go through, which results in better reliability and speed.

4. Linux requests the IP address for `www.redhat.com` from the name server.

5. If the name server doesn't know the IP address of `www.redhat.com`, it asks a root server for the address of an authoritative name server for the `redhat.com` domain.

6. The root server returns the address of the Red Hat authoritative name server, the first of which is `ns1.redhat.com` (`66.187.233.210`).

7. The name server asks `ns1.redhat.com` for the address of `www.redhat.com`.

8. `ns1.redhat.com` returns the `www.redhat.com` address.

9. Using the numeric `www.redhat.com` IP address, your browser starts communicating with the Web server.

Building a DNS server

Enough theory. It's time to build a server. The following instructions describe how to build an authoritative name server for your private network. The server provides the addresses for the private, non-routable private network described in Chapter 14. Therefore, you don't have to register the addresses with any authority. The DNS server is authoritative for your private domain, but that information isn't available outside your network.

The following instructions show you how to install the DNS server software. You'll create the `/etc/named.conf`, `/var/named/local.zone`, `/var/named/paunchy.zone`, and `/var/named/1.168.192.zone` files.

Start by installing the bind RPM that contains the named server software:

1. **Log in to your computer as root.**

   Insert the CD1.

2. **Start the Red Hat Package Manager by clicking the GNOME Menu and choosing System Settings⇨Add/Remove Applications.**

   Enter the root password if prompted.

3. **Click the DNS Name Server radio button.**

4. **Click the Update button and the bind (DNS server) package is installed.**

Now you need to create the DNS configuration file, `/etc/named.conf`:

1. **Start the text editor by clicking the GNOME Menu button and choosing Accessories⇨Text Editor.**

2. **Enter this configuration in the gedit window (see Figure 15-6):**

```
options { directory "/var/named"; };

zone  "localhost" {
      type master;
      file  "localhost.zone";
};
zone  "paunchy.net" {
      type master;
      file  "paunchy.zone";
};
zone  "1.168.192.in-addr.arpa" {
```

```
        type master;
        file  "1.168.192.zone";
};
```

3. **This list describes the various parts of the /var/named file:**

   - The `options` section defines the `/var/named` directory as the location of the database files.

   - The first zone section sets the master server for the `paunchy.net` domain or zone to be found in the file `/var/named/paunchy.zone`.

   - The second zone section defines the reverse lookup master server to be found in the `/var/named/1.168.192.in-addr.arpa` file.

4. **Save the configuration to `/etc/named.conf` by choosing File⇨Save As.**

5. **Enter /etc/named.conf in the Selection box and click OK.**

   Gedit saves your DNS configuration file.

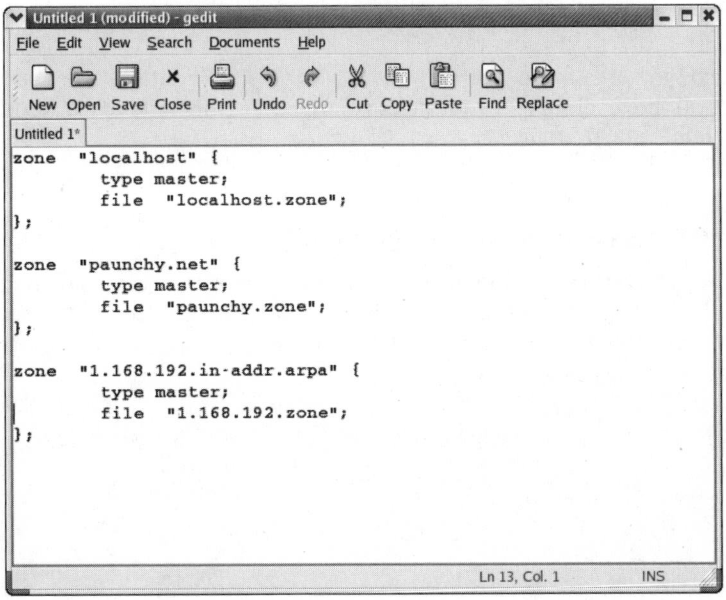

Figure 15-6:
Creating
/etc/
named.
conf with
gedit.

To create the local.zone file, follow these steps:

1. **From the gedit text editor, choose File⇨New from the menu.**

2. **Enter the following configuration.**

   (Of course, you can select the machine names you want. The names are arbitrary. In fact, the IP addresses are arbitrary too. You can select any nonroutable address space you want.)

```
$TTL 86400
@       IN      SOA     @ root.localhost (
                        1 ; serial
                        28800 ; refresh
                        7200 ; retry
                        604800 ; expire
                        86400 ; ttl
                        )


@       IN      NS      localhost.


@       IN      A       127.0.0.1
```

Semicolons (;) indicate comments. All characters following a semicolon are treated as a comment and don't affect the operation of the DNS configuration files.

3. **Save the configuration by choosing File⇨Save As.**

4. **Enter** /var/named/local.zone **in the Selection box and click OK.**

Next, you create the paunchy.zone file. This file contains the A and C records for all the machines in your zone (in this case, the zone maps directly to the paunchy.net domain.)

1. **From the gedit text editor, choose File⇨New from the menu.**

2. **Enter the following configuration:**

   (Of course, you can select your own machine names. The names are arbitrary. In fact, the IP addresses are arbitrary too. You can select any nonroutable address space you want.)

```
$TTL 86400
@               IN      SOA     paunchy.net.
        root.paunchy.net. (
                                200112211
                                10800
                                3600
                                3600000
                                86400 )
                IN      NS      ns.paunchy.net.
                IN      A       192.168.1.254

; servers
atlas           IN      A       192.168.1.254
www             CNAME           atlas
ns              CNAME           atlas
; workstations
chivas          IN      A       192.168.1.1    ; Linux
pumas           IN      A       192.168.1.2    ; Linux
tigres          IN      A       192.168.1.100  ; Windows
```

3. **Save the configuration by choosing File⇨Save As.**

4. **Enter** /var/named/paunchy.zone **in the Selection box and click OK.**

Figure 15-7 shows the new `paunchy.zone` file in the gedit window.

The final step is to create a reverse DNS lookup file for your zone. This file is optional but quite useful. Providing reverse lookup capability to your network means that you can specify a numeric IP address and get a name back:

1. **Back in the gedit text editor, choose File⇨New from the menu.**

2. **Create the reverse DNS configuration file parameters:**

```
$TTL 86400
@          IN      SOA     paunchy.net       root.paunchy.net
           (
                           2002030801
                           28800
                           7200
                           604800
                           86400
                           )
@          IN      NS      paunchy.net.

;          servers
254        IN      PTR     atlas

;          Windows workstations
1          IN      PTR     cancun
2          IN      PTR     pumas
3          IN      PTR     tigres
```

3. **Choose File⇨Save As.**

4. **Enter** /var/named/1.168.192.zone **in the Selection box and click OK.**

Again, the filename `1.168.192.zone` is arbitrary. You can call it `reverse.zone` or anything else you want as long as you match the name in the `/etc/named.conf` file — that is, `named.conf` would need to call the reverse IP address database `reverse.zone` rather than `1.168.192.zone`.

Starting your DNS server

After you have created the DNS configuration and zone files, you can start your server:

1. **Click the GNOME Menu and choose Server Settings⇨Services.**

2. **Locate the named service and click its radio button.**

   This step selects the server to be started at boot time.

3. **Click the Restart button.**

4. **Click the OK button in the Information window that pops up.**

   You now have a DNS server.

Configuring your DNS clients

To use your new DNS server, you need to configure the hosts on your LAN and modify the `/etc/resolv.conf` file on your Linux computers. Modify the network settings on your Windows machines.

Modify the `resolv.conf` file on Linux computers to look like this:

```
search paunchy.net
nameserver 192.168.1.254
```

You can specify as many as three name servers, so you may add your ISP's name server as an alternative:

```
search paunchy.net
nameserver 192.168.1.254
nameserver 198.59.115.2
```

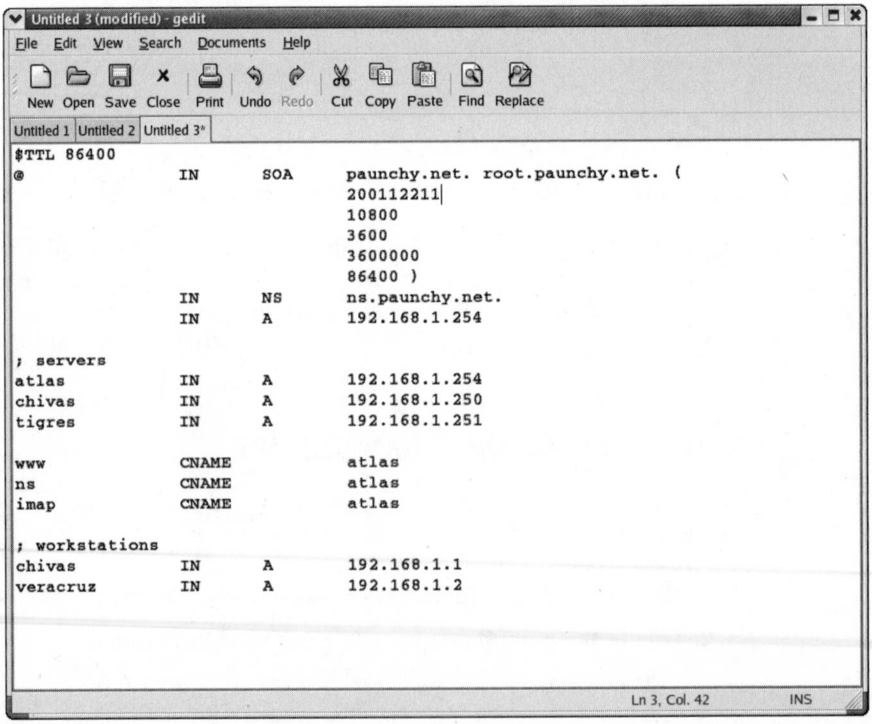

```
$TTL 86400
@               IN      SOA     paunchy.net. root.paunchy.net. (
                                200112211
                                10800
                                3600
                                3600000
                                86400 )
                IN      NS      ns.paunchy.net.
                IN      A       192.168.1.254

; servers
atlas           IN      A       192.168.1.254
chivas          IN      A       192.168.1.250
tigres          IN      A       192.168.1.251

www             CNAME           atlas
ns              CNAME           atlas
imap            CNAME           atlas

; workstations
chivas          IN      A       192.168.1.1
veracruz        IN      A       192.168.1.2
```

Figure 15-7:
Creating
paunchy.
zone with
gedit.

Open a GNOME Terminal and run this command.

```
host cancun
```

You see this result:

```
cancun.paunchy.net has address 192.168.1.121
```

The host command provides numerous options that provide more information about your query. For example, you can see information about where the host command gets its information. Add the verbose (-v) option to the preceding example and you see this information.

```
Trying "cancun.paunchy.net"
;; ->>HEADER<<- opcode: QUERY, status: NOERROR, id: 18016
;; flags: qr aa rd ra; QUERY: 1, ANSWER: 1, AUTHORITY: 1,
         ADDITIONAL: 0

;; QUESTION SECTION:
;cancun.paunchy.net.              IN      A

;; ANSWER SECTION:
cancun.paunchy.net. 86400   IN   A    192.168.1.1

;; AUTHORITY SECTION:
paunchy.net.          86400   IN   NS   ns.paunchy.net.1
Received 69 bytes from 192.168.1.120#53 in 263 ms
```

This list describes what the various sections in the preceding output mean.

- ✔ **QUESTION SECTION:** You see in the Question section that the query is cancun.paunchy.net. Note that we asked only for the address of cancun but that the search parameter in the resolv.conf file specifies that the paunchy.net domain be appended to cancun. You also see that an A record is part of the query — we're asking for an IP address.

- ✔ **ANSWER SECTION:** This is the answer to your query. The answer includes the host name and domain — cancun.sandia.gov — and its numeric IP address. The answer section also includes the time-to-live (TTL) value.

- ✔ **AUTHORITY SECTION:** This data shows where the information was found in the preceding ANSWER section. You got the answer from the name server — 192.168.1.254 — that you just built.

All the computers on your network can use your DNS server. Your DNS supplies addresses for all internal machines. The server forwards requests for external addresses as necessary.

Chapter 16

Securing Your Future

· ·

· ·

*P*rotecting your individual computers and collective network is an essential task in today's insecure world. Unfortunately, computer and network security is a big, complex job. This chapter provides several straightforward methods and utilities that will bring your security job down to size. We help you make both your computers and network safer.

This chapter describes security methods and systems. We have chosen several security tools and systems that give you the most bang for your buck. This chapter provides a starting point for making your computers and network safer. We encourage you to continue learning and evolving your security system.

Thinking Security

Computer security is best thought of as an ongoing process. No single method, tool, or system — a silver bullet — magically protects you from the wild Internet. Security, like exercise and diet, is just plain hard work.

Because no silver bullet exists, you need to layer your security measures — using "defense in depth." Each layer protects the other layers and vice versa. If and when one layer is breached, you fall back on the other. You can also add and remove layers as necessary.

Your layered security systems and measures fall under three categories:

- **Prevention:** Tools, utilities, and methods prevent any attacks from succeeding. Tools like passwords and the firewalls described in Chapter 8 are under this heading.

- **Detection:** Because not all attacks can be prevented, it's essential to detect them if possible. Intrusion detection is still more of an art than a science.

- **Process:** Most computer users would prefer to construct a security system and then sit back and forget about it. However, the hacker world changes as fast as the rest of the world, and the systems that work today won't necessarily work tomorrow. Therefore, you must keep learning and improving both your computer network and your own capabilities.

Preventing Intruders

We start by describing how to minimize your chances of being hacked. The following sections describe systems that increase your security:

- **Updating software:** The Red Hat up2date utility helps keep your computer's software up to date, which eliminates vulnerabilities as they are discovered.

- **Removing services:** Hackers can't take advantage of vulnerable software if you don't use it. Turning off services reduces your exposure.

- **OpenSSH:** Except for viewing average Web pages, you should never communicate over the Internet (or wireless LANs) without using encryption. The Open Source SecureShell (SSH) provides a simple and effective encryption system.

We describe each system in the following sections.

Reducing vulnerabilities by updating Red Hat Linux packages

Standard hacker operating procedure is to find and then exploit vulnerabilities. The method is simple but effective. That translates in real-life this way: Joe hacker goes around rattling doorknobs and occasionally finds one that's open. When no door is unlocked, the hacker looks to pick the easier locks. Your job is to make sure that your doors and windows are locked and not easily picked. The former option is taken care of by running firewalls and using passwords. The latter requires constant supervision. Today's software is powerful and, thus, necessarily complex. Complexity breeds errors, and with errors come vulnerabilities. Because the only certainties in life are death, taxes, and buggy software, the bugs need to be fixed whenever possible. We all need to constantly update our software when errors are found and corrected.

Red Hat provides an excellent method for updating its software. It created the Up-to-Date (up2date) system, which automatically detects new software and installs it for you. Next to passwords and firewalls, it's probably the most effective security system you can run.

If you read about the Firstboot post-configuration process in Chapter 3, you know that one of the Firstboot steps was registering with the Red Hat Network (RHN). You can register one computer with RHN at no cost. With RHN, you gain the ability to use up2date on one computer (you need to subscribe additional machines for a fee). Red Hat configures up2date to install new RPM packages on a daily basis.

You can register now if you haven't already done so. These instructions describe the process:

1. **Click the GNOME menu and choose Run Program.**

2. **Enter** up2date **in the subwindow and click the Run button. Enter your root password if prompted.**

   The Welcome to Red Hat Update Agent window, as shown in Figure 16-1, opens.

3. **Click the Forward button.**

4. **Read the privacy statement (yeah, right), as shown in Figure 16-2, and click the Forward button.**

5. **Enter the user name and password you want to use — plus your e-mail address — in the Step 2: Register or Update a User Account window (see Figure 16-3). Click the Forward button.**

6. **When registering for the first time, you need to create an account. In that case, the Step 2: Create a User Account window, as shown in Figure 16-4, opens.**

   Enter your personal information in the window.

   You have the option of creating a personal, corporate, or educational account. We use the personal option, so click the Create a personal account link.

Figure 16-1:
The Red Hat
Update
Agent
window.

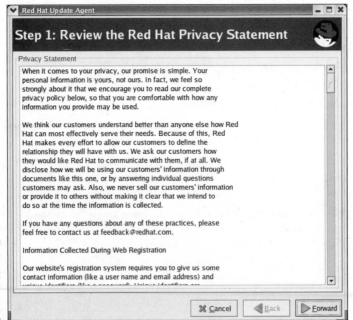

Figure 16-2:
The Red Hat
privacy
statement.

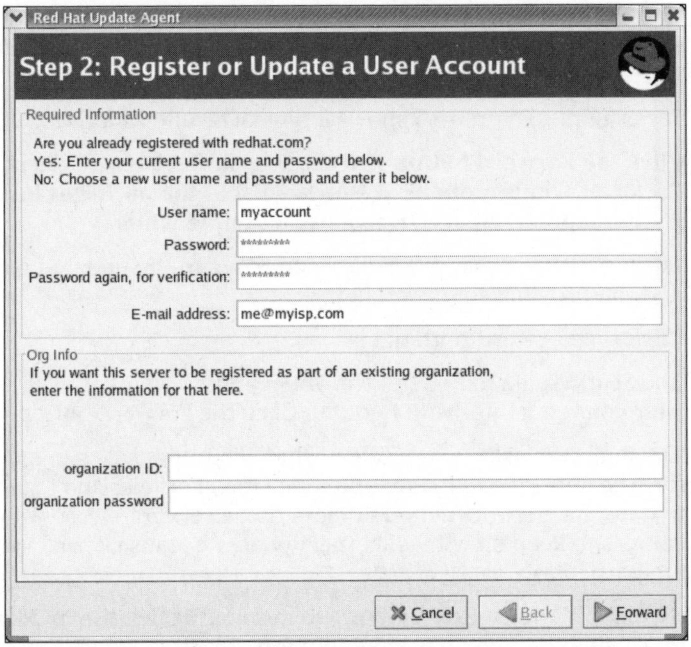

Figure 16-3:
The Register
or Update
a User
Account
window.

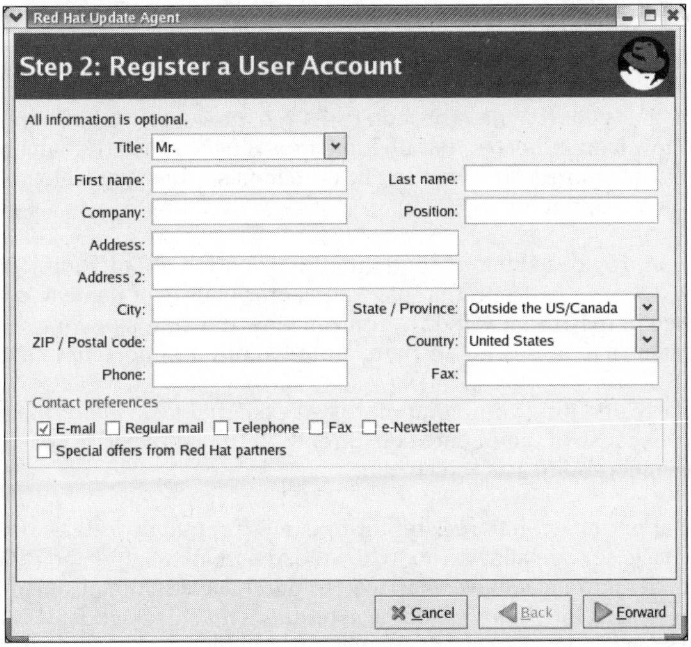

Figure 16-4:
Providing
your
personal
information
to get
the user
account.

7. **Red Hat reads the configuration machine off your computer and shows it in the next screen — Step 3: Register a System Profile – Hardware.**

   For example, Figure 16-5 shows a typical profile window.

8. **Click the Forward button and the Step 3: Register a System Profile – Packages window opens. It shows a list of the packages installed on your computer. Figure 16-6 shows a sample window.**

   These are the packages up2date compares to the updated packages that Red Hat provides for download.

9. **Click the Forward button.**

   The Send Profile to Red Hat Network window opens. You're ready to register your computer with Red Hat. Click the Forward button.

   The final step asks you to select what, if any, packages to ignore updates for. The default is to ignore updating Linux kernels. Don't ignore kernel updates for network servers unless those servers — you want all your servers to keep up with all kernel updates because kernel vulnerabilities are particularly nasty beasties.

10. **(Optional) You can skip having to manually click the up2date icon every time an update is available (oh, life is so hard). You can configure up2date to automatically update your system when it detects a new package.**

You now can regularly update your Red Hat Linux computer. The up2date icon is displayed on the right side of the GNOME Panel. When the icon is green, life is good. When the icon turns red, however, updates are available. (A yellow icon indicates that up2date doesn't know whether an update exists for your machine.) You want to click the icon so that it downloads and installs the updates.

Red Hat provides summary and other information about your account at rhn.redhat.com. Go to that page and enter your user name and password in the Sign in to RHN subwindow. You can view the status of your registered machine(s), modify your account, and read other important information.

Regularly updating your computer is an essential task. Many, many break-ins occur because of out-of-date software. With the help of RHN, you eliminate most vulnerabilities as they occur.

Red Hat permits you to register for free one computer for Basic update service. Basic service allows you to download and install updated RPM packages. To update more machines, you need to purchase additional subscriptions at $60 per year. Note that you can register more machines under the Red Hat None service, but they aren't eligible for updates.

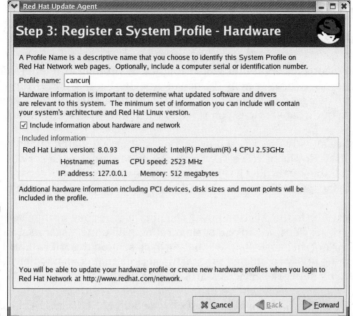

Figure 16-5:
The Register
a System
Profile –
Hardware
window.

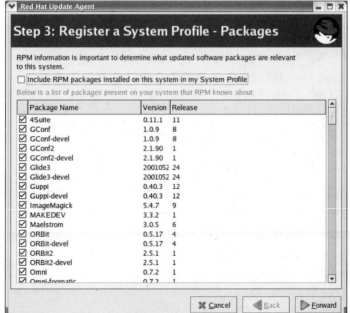

Figure 16-6:
The Register
a System
Profile –
Packages
window.

Reducing your exposure: Removing and reducing services

Hackers look for computer vulnerabilities by probing for vulnerable network services. Network services — such as Apache, Samba, and DHCP — are, of course, designed to respond to network queries. Therefore, hackers can readily find out what services you run and then find what, if any, attacks to use.

We have already described how keeping software updated minimizes their vulnerability. However, you can go one step better and make a service completely invulnerable by turning it off. One simple security rule is "Keep it simple." The simple fact is that if you don't need to run a service, you shouldn't.

We describe in this section how to eliminate or reduce both network and non-network services; we advise against running all unnecessary services, network or not, because simple is better. This section describes how to use the chkconfig utility to change the startup scripts that control when, how, and whether a network services starts at boot time:

1. **Click the GNOME Menu and choose Server Settings⇨Services.**

   Enter the root password if prompted.

2. **The Service Configuration window opens.**

3. **Select each unnecessary service and shut it off by clicking the Stop button.**

4. **Click the OK button when the confirmation window appears.**

5. **Next, click the check mark to the left of the service to toggle it off. The service doesn't start automatically at boot time when there's no checkmark.**

What services you turn off depends on your needs, of course. For example, if you're unintentionally running a Web server, turn off the httpd service. In general, you should be able to turn off these services.

- **The Advanced Power Management Daemon (APMD):** APMD is useful if you — like most people — regularly power off your personal workstation or laptop. However, APMD is generally unnecessary on servers that run continuously. You want to keep APMD in the former case (workstation or laptop) and remove it in the latter (server).

- **The job queue daemon:** The atd daemon is used to schedule one-time cron-like jobs. If you need atd, you know it. Otherwise, turn it off.

- **Network File Sharing (NFS) :** You only need services such as nfs, nfs-lock, portmap, and autofs when running an NFS server or client. The last thing you want to do is share files to the Internet, for example.

✔ **Print services:** Many people don't run the printer daemon on servers. Turn off cups or lpd when you don't need to print.

✔ **Samba:** Just like with NFS, you should turn off Samba if you don't need it.

The rest is up to you. Terminate services with a vengeance.

You can't modify a service when it isn't running. You can toggle off the check-mark on a non-running service, but it doesn't have any affect if it's not running.

You can use the CLI-based chkconfig utility. Open a GNOME Terminal and login as root (**su -**). List the services by running the chkconfig —list; list an individual service by specifying the service after the -list option **chkconfig - - list apmd**; stop a service with the - - add option: **chkconfig - - add apmd**; delete a service with the - - del option: **chkconfig - - del apmd**.

Using a secure shell client

You may be most familiar with graphical network communication applications like the Mozilla Web browser and Evolution e-mail clients. However, a world of text-based tools is available, such as Secure Shell, Telnet, and FTP. Those applications provide an interactive method for connecting to other computers across networks and the Internet using a command-line interface (CLI); refer to Chapter 4 for more information.

Interactive communications is effective for performing tasks on remote machines. For example, the primary way to work on Linux machines originally was via the CLI. The CLI is often the best way to perform remote tasks.

CLI-based communication used to be primarily carried out over the insecure Telnet, FTP, and rsh connections. All services used unencrypted connections, and passwords were readily detected. The rsh service also used a system of intermachine trust. That trust allowed hackers, like the infamous Kevin Mitnik, to break into one machine and then log in to additional ones without authentication.

Open Secure Shell (OpenSSH) provides an encrypted channel to perform all those tasks. Red Hat Linux bundles OpenSSH by default. We describe how to first use the OpenSSH client to communicate with other machines and, second, create an OpenSSH server.

You should (dare we say must?) use encrypted channels when communicating over the Internet and wireless networks. Both the Internet and Wi-Fi connections are inherently insecure, and you need to protect your communications.

Let's start with using OpenSSH as a client. Suppose that you want to log in to your ISP server — ssh.myisp.com — with OpenSSH:

1. **Open a GNOME Terminal.**

2. **Enter this command:**

```
ssh ssh.myisp.com
```

Your mileage may vary, of course. You may have to use the `-l` option if, for example, your ISP user account name is different from your local computer. If your user name on your local machine is `lidia`, but `lmaura` at your ISP, enter this line:

```
ssh -l lmaura ssh.myisp.com
```

3. **Enter your password and you're logged in.**

For example, you can now use a text-based e-mail client like pine to read your messages. This is useful if you want to read your e-mail securely but can't connect to your ISP with an SSL-enabled Mozilla or Evolution email client.

That's simple and useful, but you can do more. The OpenSSH client is automatically enabled to tunnel X across its connection. While logged on to your ISP, you can run X Window client software and view it on your local machine:

1. **Log in to your ISP (or any machine running an SSH server) as just described.**

2. **Run an X Window application, such as** `xclock`**.**

The simple xclock window is displayed on your desktop.

OpenSSH also bundles the file transfer applications scp and sftp. SCP is non-interactive and copies files to and from a remote machine. SFTP is a secure version of FTP and is also interactive. This list describes how to copy files between two machines:

- **Copy from a local to remote machine:** To transfer files from your local computer to a remote one, use Secure Copy (scp) as follows: **scp abc myacct@remote**. This command copies the filename `abc` from the directory you're working in to the `myacct` home directory on the remote machine. You can specify the local and remote directories on each machine. For example, this command copies the file `abc` from the `/tmp` directory to the `/var/tmp` directory on the remote machine and renames it to `xyz`:

```
scp /tmp/abcmyacct@remote:/var/tmp/xyz
```

The scp syntax is important. If you leave out the colon (:), your file isn't copied to the remote machine but rather simply renamed to `myacct@remote`.

- **Copy from a remote to local machine:** Reverse the order of the parameters to copy from a remote machine. The following example copies the file abc from the remote machine to the local one: **scp myacct@remote:abcd**.

The sftp program works like the old standby FTP but, of course, uses encryption. These instructions describe how to perform simple file transfers with sftp:

1. **Open a GNOME Terminal.**

2. **Enter this command:**

   ```
   sftp ssh.myisp.com
   ```

3. **Enter your user name and password.**

4. **Enter the help command at the** sftp **prompt.**

   You see a list of sftp commands. The ones you use most are cd, lcd, dir, ls, get, and put. These commands work in similar fashion to their Linux equivalents.

5. **Using** sftp **is self explanatory. Use** get **to transfer a file, files, or directory from the remote to local machine; put transfers from local to remote.**

 Another cool feature of OpenSSH is its ability to tunnel any protocol. You can potentially display an entire X window from a remote machine via X, for example. Consult the OpenSSH documentation for more information.

Configuring a secure shell server

Configuring an OpenSSH server is straightforward. You only need to modify the /etc/ssh/sshd_config file and run the /etc/init.d/sshd script. Look at the configuration file, the important parts of which are listed in these bullets:

- **Remove the older and faulty protocol version 1:** Version 1 has been broken and should not be used:

  ```
  Port 22
  Protocol 2
  # HostKeys for protocol version 2
  HostKey /etc/ssh/ssh_host_rsa_key
  HostKey /etc/ssh/ssh_host_dsa_key
  ```

- **Remove the comment from in front of the login grace time parameter:** This sets a limit on the time between when you start a login and complete it:

  ```
  LoginGraceTime 600
  ```

- **Disallow root logins:** You should prevent users, including yourself, from logging directly in as root. Forcing users to first log in as a regular user and then "su-ing" to root provides an audit trail that can be used to see who did what as the root user; it also forces everyone to jump through two hoops before becoming the all-powerful root user:

```
PermitRootLogin yes
StrictModes yes
```

✔ **Uncomment these parameters to allow the various authentication modes:**

```
# rhosts authentication should not be used
RhostsAuthentication no
# Don't read the user's ~/.rhosts and ~/.shosts files
IgnoreRhosts yes
# For this to work you will also need host keys in
          /etc/ssh/ssh_known_hosts
RhostsRSAAuthentication no
# similar for protocol version 2
HostbasedAuthentication no
# Change to yes if you don't trust ~/.ssh/known_hosts for
  RhostsRSAAuthentication and HostbasedAuthentication
IgnoreUserKnownHosts no
```

✔ **Finally, allow people to use password authentication, but don't allow unauthenticated access:**

```
# To disable tunneled clear text passwords, change to no
        here!
PasswordAuthentication yes
PermitEmptyPasswords no
```

To start the OpenSSH daemon, follow these steps:

1. **Make the changes and restart the sshd daemon:**

   ```
   /etc/init.d/sshd restart
   ```

2. **If you're running a firewall, add these rule to your iptables-based firewall:**

   ```
   iptables -A INPUT  -p tcp --dport 22 -m state --state
           NEW,ESTABLISHED -j ACCEPT
   ```

3. **Save your new firewall:**

   ```
   iptables-save > /etc/sysconfig/iptables
   ```

4. **Restart the firewall:**

   ```
   /etc/init.d/iptables restart
   ```

Now you can use OpenSSH to communicate to and from your Linux computer. Using OpenSSH, you can interactively log in to other computers, copy data between computers, and piggyback arbitrary communication stream — such as X Window — with this puppy. OpenSSH encrypts all your communication and prevents THE exposing of your passwords and data to prying eyes.

Exchanging keys makes your life easier

You can log in to remote Secure Shell user account by using the traditional passwords. This is the OpenSSH default authentication method. However, OpenSSH provides a second authentication method that takes a little bit of work to get started but saves work in the long run.

OpenSSH provides an authentication method called public-key cryptography. This system uses one public and one private key. You install the public key on the remote system and keep the private key on your computer. The public key can be shared with anyone — hey, it's public. The private key must be kept secret at all costs. In fact, OpenSSH encrypts the private key by default. You must use a pass phrase — essentially a password with spaces — to decrypt the private key before using it (more on decryption later).

When you want to log in or communicate with the remote computer, the keys are used to negotiate the process. The public/private key system guarantees that your user account is authenticated but also the initiating host; passwords authenticate only your login account, not the computer you're connecting from.

Setting up for a public-key cryptographic key exchange

To set up the key exchange, follow these steps:

1. **Log in to your user account on the local computer.**

   For example, log in as the user rod on cancun.

2. **Open a GNOME Terminal.**

3. **Run this command:**

   ```
   ssh-keygen -t dsa
   ```

   This step starts the program that generates your public and private keys. Several encryption methods exist: DSA (Digital Signature Standard) and RSA (named after Ron Rivest, Adi Shamir, and Len Adleman) are the most popular. DSA is a nonproprietary algorithm, whereas RSA was until recently patented. Even though RSA is available for public use, we use DSA.

4. **The program thinks for a moment and returns these output:**

   ```
   Enter file in which to save the key (/rod/.ssh/id_dsa):
   ```

   The keys are saved to the .ssh directory in your home directory. The default should be okay, so press the Return key.

5. **The ssh-keygen program asks you to enter a pass phrase that it will use to encrypt your private key:**

   ```
   Enter passphrase (empty for no passphrase):
   ```

6. **Enter your pass phrase and ssh-keygen generates the keys.**

   Use a phrase peppered with numbers and other characters. For example, you might try a pass phrase like this:

   ```
   Giv3 m3 @ bre@k!
   ```

7. **Verify the phrase by entering it a second time.**

The ssh-keygen generates your public and private keys. Those keys are stored by default in the .ssh directory. The .ssh directory is stored by default in your home directory; ssh-keygen creates the .ssh directory, if necessary.

Copying your public key to the remote computer

Now you need to copy the public key to the computer you securely communicate with. This steps describe how to copy and configure them:

1. **Log in to your user account on the local computer.**

   For example, log in as the user rod on cancun.

2. **Open a GNOME Terminal.**

3. **Copy your public key to your account on the remote computer. For example, if your account on the remote computer Chivas is rod, you can use the Open Secure Copy (scp):**

   ```
   scp .ssh/id_dsa.pub rod@chivas:
   ```

4. **Enter your account password when prompted, and the DSA public key is copied to your home directory on Chivas.**

5. **Log in to the remote machine. For example, use ssh:**

   ```
   ssh chivas
   ```

6. **Enter your password when prompted.**

   By default, OpenSSH looks for public keys in the authorized_keys file in the .ssh directory (in your home directory).

7. **Use these commands to copy the public key into the authorized_keys file (remember that you should still be in your home directory):**

   ```
   cat id_dsa.pub >> .ssh/authorized_keys
   ```

The cat command concatenates the contents of the id_dsa.pub to the Linux standard output (that's generally your console, which is the GNOME Terminal, in this case). The double "greater than" symbols (>>) append the standard output to the authorized_keys file in the .ssh directory. No preexisting keys are disturbed.

8. The `authorized_keys` file must have the right permissions. (See Appendix B for more information about file permissions.) In this case, loose permissions sink ships, and OpenSSH doesn't work with, for example, read/write/execute group permissions. Ensure the correct permissions as follows:

```
chmod 644 .ssh/authorized_keys
```

9. Make sure that the OpenSSH server configuration allows key exchange. These options should be set in the `/etc/ssh/sshd_config` file:

```
RSAAuthentication yes
PubkeyAuthentication yes
AuthorizedKeysFile        .ssh/authorized_keys
```

10. Restart the sshd daemon if you make any changes to the sshd_config file:

```
/etc/init.d/sshd restart
```

Connecting to the remote computer using key exchange

Ready to use the key exchange authentication system? From the host (local) computer, try these steps:

1. **Log in to your user account on the local computer.**

   For example, log in as the user `rod` on `cancun`.

2. **Open a GNOME Terminal.**

3. **Log in to the remote machine:**

```
ssh chivas
```

4. **Enter the pass phrase you used to encrypt your private key.**

The remote computer authenticates you and your host computer. Voilà! You're in.

Making life even easier with ssh-agent

That's not all! Red Hat automatically starts a system named `ssh-agent`. With `ssh-agent`, you enter your pass phrase and `ssh-agent` remembers it. You need to enter the pass phrase only once while logged in to your account. From then on, `ssh-agent` provides `ssh`, `scp`, `sftp`, or `ssh-agent` with the pass phrase and you no longer have to enter a password or pass phrase. Life is easy.

Setting up `ssh-agent` is simple. Follow these steps:

1. **Log in to your user account on the local computer.**

   For example, log in as the user `rod` on `cancun`.

2. **Open a GNOME Terminal.**

3. **Enter this command:**

   ```
   ssh-add
   ```

4. **You're prompted to enter your pass phrase:**

   ```
   Enter passphrase for /home/vm/.ssh/id_dsa:
   ```

5. **Connect to the remote machine — for example, Chivas.**

   ```
   ssh chivas
   ```

You get logged into your account on the remote machine without having to enter a password or pass phrase. This system is way cool.

Danger, Will Robinson! Detecting Intruders

Intrusion detection is the flip side of intrusion prevention. You can't depend on never getting hacked unless you turn off your computer and lock it in a safe. Remember, there's no silver bullet in the world of computer security. You have take measures to detect whether and when you do get compromised.

Many, many intrusion-detection systems (IDS) can help with your needs — far too many to review here. We concentrate on using three systems that are mature and relatively easy to use: Tripwire, Snort, and the Red Hat log reading utility. Both Tripwire and the Red Hat log reading utility are bundled with Red Hat Linux; You can easily download Snort from the Internet.

Setting up Tripwire

Tripwire is an IDS that creates a checksum for files and directories and stores them in a database. Tripwire periodically — daily, by default — re-creates checksums for the same files. Tripwire compares the new checksums to the originals, and any differences indicate that the file has been changed. The changed file list is e-mailed to you, and you then determine whether the changes are authorized.

Running a mathematical algorithm on a file creates a checksum. The algorithm creates a number — a very long number — that is unique to the file on which it is run. Thus, every checksum is unique, like a fingerprint. Checksums can be used to authenticate files and also to detect errors in the same files.

Tripwire is a simple, but effective intrusion-detection system (IDS). It calculates MD5 check sums of specified files and directories. The checksums are used to detect changes made to your file system. Unauthorized changes can mean that an intrusion has occurred. Follow these steps to set up a Tripwire:

1. **Log in as root and change to the /usr/local/src directory:**

```
cd /usr/local/src
```

2. **Start Mozilla by clicking the icon that looks like the Earth circled by a mouse.**

3. **Go to www.tripwire.org/downloads.**

4. **Click the rpm4 - tripwire-2.3-47.i386.tar.gz link.**

5. **When the Downloading tripwire-2.3-47.i386.tar.gz window opens, click the OK button.**

6. **The Enter name of file to save to window opens.**

   Click the Save button and the file containing Tripwire is saved to the /root directory.

7. **Extract the Tripwire RPM by entering this command:**

```
tar xzf tripwire*
```

   The tar command extracts the Tripwire RPM package from the file you downloaded.

8. **Install the Tripwire package:**

```
rpm -ivh tripwire*
```

Now you must configure Tripwire. Tripwire revolves around a policy file. The policy file tells Tripwire which files and directories to check and what to check for.

1. **Click the GNOME Menu button and choose Accessories➪Text Editor.**

   Open the /etc/tripwire/twpol.txt file.

2. **Leave the first 166 lines in the file unchanged. Delete everything after this line:**

```
# Commonly accessed directories that should remain static
        with regards to owner and group
```

3. **Add this Tripwire policy:**

```
(
rule name = "system files"
severity = $(SIG_HI)
)
{
/etc   -> $(SEC_CRIT) ;
/sbin  -> $(SEC_CRIT) ;
/bin   -> $(SEC_CRIT) ;
/usr   -> $(SEC_BIN) ;
/usr/lib                          -> $(SEC_BIN) ;
/lib                              -> $(SEC_BIN) ;
}


(
  rulename = "optional and extra files, libraries, etc.",
  severity = $(SIG_MED)
)
{
 /usr/local                       -> $(SEC_BIN) ;
 /opt                             -> $(SEC_BIN) ;
}


(
  rulename = "boot files",
  severity = $(SIG_HI)
)
{
    /boot                         -> $(SEC_CRIT) ;
    !/boot/System.map ;
    !/boot/module-info ;
}
```

This minimal configuration should be considered as a starting point. You should modify the files as you gain more experience with your Red Hat Linux computer.

4. **Configure Tripwire itself. Open a GNOME Terminal window and run the installation script:**

```
/etc/tripwire/twinstall.sh
```

5. **Enter the site keyfile pass phrase when prompted. The pass phrase is essentially a password and is used to encrypt the** `/etc/tripwire/` `site.key` **file, which is itself used to encrypt the checksum database.**

6. **Next, enter the local keyfile pass phrase. The script generates a file whose name is your fully qualified domain name with the string** `-local.key` **appended to it. For example, if your computer is cancun, the file is named** `cancun-local.key`.

You're prompted to enter the site key pass phrase you created in Step 5. Tripwire uses the site pass phrase to encrypt the *twpol.txt* file and saves it as *tw.pol*.

7. **Enter your site pass phrase.**

8. **Enter the local pass phrase when prompted.**

   The policy data file is signed after you enter the pass phrase.

9. **Initialize the Tripwire checksum database when the** `twinstall.sh` **script finishes. Enter this command:**

   ```
   tripwire -init
   ```

10. **Enter your site pass phrase when prompted.**

Tripwire does its work. It creates a database of checksums for all the files in the directories listed in the `twpol.txt` file. Tripwire is configured to check its checksum database on a daily basis. It e-mails a summary of its findings to the root user by default. You should log in as root and check the summary regularly.

Tripwire used to create unencrypted checksum databases. You had to save the database on some read-only media so that a successful hacker could cover his tracks. Tripwire now makes life much easier for you by encrypting the database. Unless you give up your pass phrases, a hacker can't modify your database without your knowing about it. Maintaining the Tripwire database on local media saves time and money.

Test Tripwire. These instructions describe how to change a file and run Tripwire. Tripwire detects the change and leaves it up to you to decide whether the change is legitimate:

1. **Change the time stamp on an important system file:**

   ```
   touch /etc/hosts
   ```

2. **Run Tripwire in check mode:**

   ```
   tripwire --check
   ```

3. **Tripwire computes the** `/etc/hosts` **checksum and compares it to the one found in the database. Tripwire takes minutes or longer to do its job. After Tripwire is finished, it shows that the** `/etc/hosts` **file was changed.**

After you're notified that a file is changed, you determine whether the change was valid or possibly caused by a hack. In this case, we changed the `/etc/host` file. You need to regularly check the Tripwire results and make sure that no unauthorized changes were made.

Traditionally, it was necessary to protect the Tripwire checksum database by storing it on read-only media. If the database is ever compromised, Tripwire can be made to give erroneous results, allowing a break-in to go undetected. However, the correct Tripwire version protects the database by encrypting it. Thus, the information stored in the database cannot be altered unless the encryption is broken — an unlikely occurrence. If the database file itself is modified, the signature doesn't match and the compromise is detected.

You can find more information about configuring Tripwire at www. tripwire.com.

Using that squealing pig: Intrusion detection with Snort

Snort is a network-based intrusion detection system. Snort complements the file-system-based Tripwire IDS. Using the two together provides fairly comprehensive IDS for your Red Hat Linux computer.

Snort monitors your network interface, looking for signatures of various hacks and probes. Snort uses a database of signatures that's updated on a daily at www.snort.org.

Downloading Snort

These instructions describe how to download Snort:

1. **Log in as root and change to the /usr/local/src directory.**

   ```
   cd /usr/local/src
   ```

   It's generally good practice to select a common location, such as the /usr/local/src directory, to place optional packages. Using this type of convention ensures that you can find software as time erodes your memory.

2. **Start Mozilla by clicking the GNOME Panel icon that looks like the Earth circled by a mouse.**

3. **Go to** www.snort.org **and click the Downloads link under the Resources heading.**

4. **Click the Binaries link near the top of the page.**

5. **Click the Linux link.**

6. **Click the most recent Snort package.**

7. **Numerous Snort versions are available. You should select the basic Linux version of Snort. For example,** snort-1.9.0-1snort.i386.rpm **is the current version.**

8. **The Downloading** snort-1.9.0-1snort.i386.rpm **window opens. Click the OK button.**

9. **Click the Save button when the Enter name of the file to save to window opens.**

Installing and using Snort

After you have captured the li'l squealer on your computer, you need to install and start it. These instructions describe how.

Because Snort relies on software — libpcap — that is not installed by default during the Red Hat installation process, you have to do so now.

1. **The software is included with the companion CD-ROMS, so insert CD2.**

2. **Install libpcap:**

```
rpm -ivh /mnt/cdrom/RedHat/RPMS/libpcap*
```

3. **Now you can install Snort (recall that the Snort package was stored in /usr/local/src):**

```
rpm -ivh /usr/local/src/snort*
```

Include the full path, just to ensure that Snort is installed.

4. **The default Snort configuration works quite well for basic intrusion detection.**

Eventually, you may need to modify the default configuration to use some of the sophisticated Snort features. For now, accept Snort as it is.

5. **Configure Snort to start automatically:**

```
chkconfig -level 345 snortd on
```

6. **Start Snort:**

```
/etc/init.d/snortd start
```

The pig squeals!

7. **Snort runs as a daemon and detects probes and other nasties directed against your computer.**

Snort saves its findings in the `/var/log/snort` directory. You should pay close attention to the `/var/log/snort/alert` log file. The alert file contains in its signature database every match that Snort makes. You may want to block offending IP addresses depending on their severity.

For example, getting probed by NMAP is a common occurrence. The NMAP tool sends TCP/IP packets in various tortured states at computers or networks to gain information about them. It's similar in concept to the linear particle accelerators that particle physicists use to probe subatomic particles with. Anyway, this excerpt from the alert log shows just such a probe:

```
01/25-20:10:00.642123  [**] [1:469:1] ICMP PING NMAP [**]
         [Classification: Attempted Information Leak]
         [Priority: 2] {ICMP} 192.168.128.253 ->
         192.168.1.1
```

For example, you could block the source IP address — 192.168.128.1 — if this alert were to appear dangerous (this address is fictitious, of course). Enter this command to add a blocking rule to your iptables based firewall:

```
iptables -A INPUT -s 192.168.128.1 -j DROP
```

Blocking offensive source IP addresses should protect you from danger. However, you should be aware that you may be blocking a friendly computer. Once again, no silver bullet exists, so you need to monitor your Snort logs and be ready to modify your firewall as necessary.

A nice script named Guardian — `www.chaotic.org/guardian` — dynamically blocks IP addresses based on information in the Snort alert log. The danger of using a system like Guardian is that a hacker can use it against you as part of a denial-of-service (DOS) attack. A hacker can systematically force you to block forged IP addresses after she realizes what you're doing. You computer's network connection grinds to a halt after it blocks too many IP addresses. It's a sort of ju-jitsu attack.

Reading your logs

You are your best IDS. Log files store information about nearly every one of your Red Hat Linux systems. Reading your logs lets you discover what has been happening on your computer and is one way to detect intrusions.

Unfortunately, exploring log files is somewhat akin to reading tea leaves. There's no mechanical method for sifting through log file tea leaves. You have to look for unusual and suspicious occurrences. As you read more, you learn about what is usual and, of course, unusual. Experience counts for everything.

Red Hat provides two reasonable systems for viewing log files:

- ✔ **Logwatch:** Logwatch is an e-mail-based log alert system. It sifts through the log files in `/var/log` and e-mails the root user any alerts or errors. You can configure the Logwatch operational parameters to better fit your operation. However, the default works well at alerting you to the happenings on your computer.
- ✔ **Red Hat Logviewer:** The Logviewer graphical utility provides one-stop shopping for all the standard log files. Logwatch is a manual tool that helps you to remember which log files to look at.

Using Logwatch

Logwatch is installed during the Red Hat installation process by default. Logwatch is a Perl script that's run nightly by `cron`. It reads through every log file in the `/var/log` directory and picks out items that it thinks are interesting.

The Logwatch Perl script is in `/etc/log.d/scripts/logwatch.pl`. The soft link — `00-logwatch` — in the `/etc/cron.daily` directory directs the `cron` system to run the script nightly.

Logwatch is controlled by the `/etc/log.d/conf/logwatch.conf` file. This file controls options like who is e-mailed the results. The logwatch configuration file is self documented and simple to configure.

Using Logviewer

Logviewer is a simple utility designed to display any of the standard Red Hat Linux log files in the `/var/log` directory. By default, it displays the raw log information and leaves sifting out suspicious entries to your eyes. Logviewer can also perform simple filtering based on simple text strings. Sart Logviewer by choosing GNOME Menu⇨System Tools⇨System Logs.

Nothing is special about Logviewer other than that is helps you to access the common log files and look at their data. Don't underestimate the value of that simple help. Our busy lives makes reading log files a difficult task. Like the mail in the U.S. postal system, they never stop coming and it's infinitely easier to blow them off than to read them every single, stupid day. Boring!

But if you're going to increase your changes of detecting an intrusion, you going to have to do it. Otherwise, the signs of intrusion that Tripwire and Snort may not detect will slip by.

The Internet provides an ideal medium for finding and taking advantage of vulnerable computers. A hacker doesn't have to leave the comfort of home to attack your machine. However, you shouldn't consider the Internet as the only danger. You should also consider the physical vulnerability of your computer. If you work with other people, someone can potentially try to break in.

Understanding the Security Process

The best way to look at security is as a process. The more you think about it and the more you study it, the safer you are. You should use the security systems described in this chapter as the foundation for your security process. However, you should continue to build your security process to meet your own computer system and network's need.

This section outlines some additional building blocks you might consider adding to your process:

- ✔ **Making backups:** Backups are part of the security process? Yes! Backups are essential security tool in the sense that you can never eliminate the possibility of getting hacked. If and when your security is breached, you may lose all sorts of information and configurations. For example, your computer may be completely erased or, worse, you may not know what files are good and bad. You must ensure your ability to recover from such catastrophes.

One good backup method is to use the GNOME Toaster application, described in Chapter 11. You can store your user account and configuration files to a CD-R/RW. It's reliable and should last forever. The only limitation is its ability to store only 700MB to 800MB; you can store more data with compression, however.

✔ **Security education:** Keeping up with security trends and topics helps you avoid getting bitten by new hacks. Knowing your adversaries and their techniques is essential.

✔ These URLs provide good security-based information; see Chapter 19 for some current top security holes:

- www.red.com/docs/manuals/linux/RHL-8.1-Manual/
  security-guide/

- www.linuxsecurity.com

- www.sans.org

- www.nmap.org

- www.securitytracker.com

- www.infosyssec.com

- www.cert.org

✔ **Physical security:** We focus on network-based security in this book. Our assumption is that your Red Hat Linux computer is running on your home network, in which case you need to worry most about Internet bad guys. However, in an office environment, you need to worry about physical security.

Physical security involves preventing people from walking up and gaining unauthorized access to your computer. You should set a BIOS password to prevent anyone from booting your computer into single-user mode, totally avoiding your Linux passwords. You should lock your computer in your office, if possible, to prevent anyone from stealing your hard drive. Don't, under any circumstances, write your passwords in any accessible place (like your desk or computer.)

You should also set the GNOME (or KDE) screen lock unless you want to log out every time you leave your desk. Choose GNOME Menu➪Preferences➪Screensaver and then click the Lock Screen After radio button. Select the amount time to wait before locking your screen and, finally, click the Close button.

✔ **Boring consistency:** Good long-term security depends on consistency. Making your backups, reading security logs and other such tasks all depend on your maintaining interest. It's just like staying in shape: You can't be good for a while but then forget about your exercise routine.

Chapter 17

Bringing In the Red Hat Linux Repair Person

. . . .

In This Chapter

▶ Understanding the philosophy of troubleshooting

▶ Gardening with the fault tree

▶ Diagnosing network problems

. . . .

*T*his book is perfect, and there's no way that anything described in it can ever go wrong. You'll be as lonely as the Maytag repairman if you expect trouble. (The trouble is, trouble never happens.) Errata (corrections) are as outdated as a bricks-and-mortar bookstore. This book makes setting up computers and networks so easy that you'll wonder why other people have so many problems! Blah, blah, blah, yadda, yadda, yadda.

Maybe not. For example, this guy named Murphy hangs out in both virtual and real bookstores. He's always jumping in just when things are starting to go well. The guy just can't keep his nose out of other people's business. This chapter is meant to smooth things out between you and Murphy in case he catches up with you.

One common problem involves getting your Red Hat Linux computer to work on a network. Not that you're having such problems after working through Chapter 7, but if the impossible happens and Murphy comes to visit, this chapter should help out.

The Fix Is In: Troubleshooting Your Network

Your Red Hat Linux machine is the foundation of your network and must be set up correctly for anything to run. If it isn't working, or if you have an unusual setup (or if Murphy is in a bad mood), you can check for several different causes.

We use the Red Hat Linux network as the troubleshooting example in this chapter. The Red Hat Linux network is one of the more difficult things to set up correctly because it depends on not only your Linux computer but also other computers. Suppose that your Red Hat Linux network isn't working. Use the following sections of this chapter as a simple fault tree that you can follow to troubleshoot your network.

Please see Part V for insights into other problems. Chapter 18 describes how to find information about your Red Hat Linux computer. Chapter 18 also points out where you can get help and solve some simple, frequently encountered problems. Chapter 19 describes ten security fixes.

Introducing Fault Trees

Troubleshooting is, as many people say, more of an art than a science. Sometimes it's easy to see what the problem is and how to fix it. At other times, it's not so easy. The degree of difficulty you have in fixing a problem depends on how complex the problem is and how well you know your stuff. Obviously, the better acquainted you are with computers and Linux, the better you are at troubleshooting.

Every problem has a solution. Computers are cause-and-effect-based machines. When something breaks or doesn't work, there's always a reason. The reason may not be easy to find, but it exists.

How do you find the cause? That's a million-dollar question. Getting a million bucks isn't easy unless you're willing to grind your teeth, plot against your fellow contestants for weeks on a remote island, purchase 10 million PowerBall tickets, or — believe it or not — work hard and work smart. Some people are willing to eat rats for the chance or are lucky enough to win the lottery, but most just have to work hard. Oh, well.

Working hard is conceptually easy, but how do you work smart? This is where the idea of the fault tree comes into play. The *fault tree* looks like an upside-down tree. The trunk of the tree represents the fault, or problem. The ends, or leaves, of the branches represent all the possible causes. The fault tree is a conceptual aid that helps you to eliminate all but the real cause of your problem. After that's done, solving the problem is virtually guaranteed.

For example, Figure 17-1 shows part of a fault tree that points out what major subsystems you should examine. To find the solution to a problem, you need to systematically identify what's working. You work your way to what's not working and then when you find it, you usually solve your problem. The fault tree simply helps to formalize the process of problem-solving.

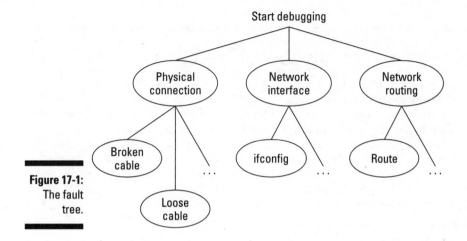

Figure 17-1:
The fault
tree.

Here are some possible faults:

✔ **The first branch on the left involves problems with the physical connection.** Do you have a network adapter? Is the cable connected properly to the adapter? Do you have a break in the cable? If so, you have to fix or replace the cable.

✔ **The second branch deals with the network interface configuration.** Have you configured the IP address for your Ethernet adapter correctly? If so, is the netmask correct?

✔ **The third branch helps you to decide whether the problem exists with the network routing.** Can your network packets be directed toward the correct network?

The fault tree helps you to break down any big problem into several simpler ones. By eliminating each simple problem one by one, you should eventually locate the root cause.

Ticking through Your Linux Networking Checklist

We describe the most common symptoms in order, from the most simple to the most complex. After cataloging the problems, we look at one of the branches of the fault tree to solve a problem.

The blind leading the blind

Paul's colleague Ken Hatfield once said, "One of the side benefits from lots of troubleshooting comes from what I call 'the value of blind alleys.' Most often in troubleshooting, you go down blind alleys or, in your tree example, the wrong branches of the solution tree. But in doing so, you learn something. In the future, when you encounter a different problem, that previous blind alley may be the road to the solution." Well said.

Here's an example: Paul recently had a server that was having lots of problems. The /var file

system had filled up, which caused some programs to fail. When space on /var was freed up, most of the programs started to do their jobs again. But one program didn't work. Paul spent a long time trying to figure out why it didn't work even after the problem was fixed. As it turned out, this particular program's real problem was that its license had expired. He had not only walked down a blind alley but also bumped into a wall and kept trying to go forward. D'oh!

Is the power turned on?

First, verify that you turned on the power. It sounds simple, but, hey, sometimes the simplest things go wrong.

Is your network cable broken?

Make sure that your network cables are not broken or cut. Check the connectors to make sure that they're okay. You should also make sure that you are using the correct network cable, which should be category 5 (8-wire) straight-through cable.

Is your Ethernet hub or switch working?

Your Ethernet hub or switch should also be turned on. Ensure that the network cables are also connected securely.

If you're stuck in the Middle Ages (with us!) and are using that coaxial network cable called Thinnet — or 10Base-2 for geeks — you don't have to check an Ethernet hub/switch because you don't have one. Thinnet connects each NIC (computer and printer, for example) to every other NIC on the subnet. In other words, each computer that is on a Thinnet cable is connected electrically to all other computers in the network. Each computer sees all the network traffic on that cable. If any part of that bus is compromised, all traffic ceases. For example, if you disconnect the terminator at either end of the cable, all communication ends. The best way to troubleshoot that type of problem is to start at one end and work your way down the line. Try to get just two computers working together, and then three, and so on. Eventually, you find the problem.

Determining whether your network cable has been compromised requires you to address these issues:

- ✔ If you're using Thinnet, make sure that the BNCs (Bayonet Nut Connectors) are securely attached.

- ✔ Look at the interface between the cable and Ethernet switch/hub — or the BNC connector, if you're using Thinnet — to make sure that they're in good physical contact. Sometimes the cable can pull out a little bit and break the connection.

- ✔ Look at the cable itself and make sure that it hasn't been cut or crushed.

- ✔ If you're using Thinnet, make sure that each end of the cable has a 50 ohm terminator attached to it. Thinnet must be terminated; otherwise, it doesn't work right, just as it doesn't work right if the cable is broken. The reason is that the radio frequency (RF) signal reflects from the unterminated end and interferes with the incoming signals. If you have a spare cable that you know is good, try substituting it. The idea is to eliminate as many segments that you are unsure about as possible. If you have just two computers in close proximity and you suspect a problem with the cable you're using, all you can do is try another cable. If the computers are far apart and rely on several segments or a long cable, try moving them closer together and using one short segment. If you have three or more computers, try getting just two of them working together. Then try adding another one. Proceed until you find the faulty segment.

"I is an enganeer"

An experienced electrical engineer and Linux author once got really angry with a cable TV company. His cable service went dead in the middle of a Philadelphia Eagles game. It didn't matter that the Eagles were losing — he wanted to see the game because the Eagles don't appear on TV often in Albuquerque. The engineer called the cable company immediately. Blah! Blah! Blah! My connection — Blah!

Blah! The nice support person guided the poor engineer step-by-step through his own fault tree. Step 1: Is your VCR or TV turned on? "Yes, of course." Step 2: Is the VCR button on your VCR toggled on? "Of course — ah, whoops, no, it isn't. Ah, yes, it works now, thank you very much. Goodbye." D'oh! What was five years of electrical engineering school good for?

Is your Ethernet adapter inserted correctly?

You have to have an Ethernet adapter to be connected to an Ethernet network. Make sure that your Ethernet adapter is plugged into your computer's motherboard — snugly. Sometimes it's necessary to pull out the adapter and then reinsert it. The process of pulling out an adapter and then plugging it back in is called *re-seating*.

Is your network adapter configured correctly?

Sometimes a startup script is misconfigured, which causes the startup screen to go by without your seeing an error message. If that happens, log in as root and from the shell prompt type this command:

```
ifconfig
```

You see a listing of two different interfaces, as shown in the following code, or three interfaces if you have PPP configured. The ifconfig command tells the Linux kernel that you have a network adapter and gives it an IP address and network mask. This is the first step in connecting your Linux computer to your network:

```
eth0      Link encap:10Mbps Ethernet  HWaddr 00:A0:24:2F:30:69
          inet addr:192.168.1.1 Bcast:192.168.1.255
                    Mask:255.255.255.0
          UP BROADCAST RUNNING MULTICAST  MTU:1500  Metric:1
          RX packets:16010 errors:18 dropped:18 overruns:23
          TX packets:7075 errors:0 dropped:0 overruns:0
          Interrupt:10 Base address:0x300

lo        Link encap:Local Loopback
          inet addr:127.0.0.1 Bcast:127.255.255.255
                    Mask:255.0.0.0
          UP BROADCAST LOOPBACK RUNNING  MTU:3584  Metric:1
          RX packets:115 errors:0 dropped:0 overruns:0
          TX packets:115 errors:0 dropped:0 overruns:0
```

Checking your wireless NIC

Linux provides several tools to work with Wi-Fi network interfaces. Red Hat installs the wireless-tools RPM package by default. The tools include iwconfig, iwspy, and other utilities. We describe how to use iwconfig to examine your Wi-Fi interface configuration.

Log in as root, open a GNOME Terminal shell (refer to Chapter 4 for more information), and run the `iwconfig` command. If your NIC is configured correctly, you see output similar to this example:

```
lo          no wireless extensions.

eth0        IEEE 802.11-DS  ESSID:"linky" Nickname:"..."
            Mode:Ad-Hoc  Frequency:2.437GHz  Cell: "..."
            Bit Rate:11Mb/s   Tx-Power=15 dBm   Sensitivity:1/3
            Retry limit:4   RTS thr:off   Fragment thr:off
            Encryption key:A654-6277-43D6-ACC3-E6ED-1C12-98
            Power Management:off
            Link Quality:0  Signal level:0  Noise level:0
            Rx invalid nwid:0  Rx invalid crypt:0  Rx invalid ...
            Tx excessive retries:0  Invalid misc:0   Missed ...
```

These are the important options to examine:

- ✔ **Mode:** You need to set this value to Ad-Hoc when connecting to an ad hoc network. (Refer to Chapter 7 for more information about this method.) You can use the value Any when connecting to an infrastructure network. The Any value can work for an ad hoc network in some cases; however, describe those cases is beyond the scope of this book, so use Ad-Hoc mode whenever necessary.

- ✔ **ESSID:** You need to use the same value on every machine connected to an ad hoc LAN. For example, every machine on our network is given the ESSID `linky`.

- ✔ **Encryption key:** You need to use the same encryption key on every machine connected to your wireless network. The key comes in two flavors: 40 bit and 128 bit. The 40-bit key is nearly useless because it can be readily cracked by hackers using widely available software.

Your wireless network should work as long as you set these parameters correctly and your computer is within range of the other devices on your LAN. The other parameters are either self-generating or unimportant in getting the card to work.

Maybe the physical connections aren't set up right

If you don't see the line containing `lo`, which is the loopback interface, or `eth0`, which is your network adapter, your physical network connections aren't set up right. The loopback interface isn't a physical device; it's used for the network software's internal workings. The loopback interface must be present for the network adapter to be configured.

If the loopback interface isn't present, type this command:

```
ifconfig lo 127.0.0.1
```

If the network adapter — generally an Ethernet card — isn't present, type this command:

```
ifconfig eth0 192.168.1.1
```

Because this is a class C network address, `ifconfig` automatically defaults to the `255.255.255.0` netmask. If you have an unusual netmask, which you shouldn't, type this command:

```
ifconfig eth0 192.168.1.1 netmask 255.255.255.0
```

Type **ifconfig**, and you should see your network adapter displayed correctly. If it's not, examine the manual page on `ifconfig`. You display this manual page by typing this command and then pressing Enter:

```
man ifconfig
```

You can page through the document in several ways: Press Enter to go line by line, press the Spacebar to go forward one page at a time, press Ctrl+B to page backward, or press **Q** to quit. The `ifconfig` man page shows a great deal of information about what `ifconfig` is and how it works. If you're still having problems, look at the Linux startup information by running this command:

```
dmesg | more
```

Note that we pipe (use the | symbol) the output from `dmesg` to the `more` command. Linux pipes are used to transmit the output command to the input of another. After you run the preceding command, you see the information that was displayed during the boot process. The `more` command shows one page of information at a time; press the Spacebar to display each subsequent page. Look for your Ethernet NIC, which should appear after the `Adding Swap` line in this code:

```
Freeing unused kernel memory: 60k freed
Adding Swap: 13651k swap-space (priority ?1)
Eth0:   3c509 at 0x310 tag1, BNC port, address ... aa,IRQ 11.
3c509.c:1.16 (2.2) 2/3/98
becker@cesdis.gsfc.nasa.govbecker@cesdis.gsfc.nasa.gov.
```

Or maybe you have a hardware problem

If you don't see your Ethernet adapter, you may have a hardware problem. Check your adapter. *Reseat* it (take it out and put it back in) and see whether it works. If not, you probably need a new NIC. If you do see the NIC, look inside the Linux kernel and see which devices it has. Type this command to change to a special directory named /proc where process information is located:

```
cat /proc/devices
```

You should see a line with your network adapter listed. If you don't, Linux doesn't know that it exists.

Try to run your Ethernet NIC again. If it still doesn't run, you need to find out more information.

Maybe you have an interrupt or address conflict

You may have an interrupt or address conflict. Look at the list of interrupts and then the IO addresses of all the devices that the kernel knows about by typing these commands:

```
cat /proc/interrupts
cat /proc/ioports
```

The IO address is the location in memory where the device, such as the network adapter, is accessed by the microprocessor (for example, your Pentium chip). The interrupt communicates to the microprocessor that it should stop whatever it's doing in order to process information that has arrived at the device sending the interrupt.

When your Ethernet adapter receives a packet, it sends an interrupt to the microprocessor to signal that an event has occurred. Your Pentium stops what it's doing and processes the new information. Actually, the microprocessor interacts with Linux to do the processing.

Type **cat /proc/interrupts** to show both the interrupts and the IO addresses with which Red Hat Linux is familiar. The output should look like this example:

```
 0:    378425    timer
 1:      1120    keyboard
 2:         0    cascade
10:     16077    3c509
13:         1    math error
14:     63652 +  ide0
```

This listing shows that Linux knows that the Ethernet NIC (3c509) exists. That is a good sign.

Typing `cat /proc/ioports` shows the input/output ports used by Red Hat Linux to interact with the computer's devices. This output shows the I/O ports used on this computer:

```
0000-001f : dma1
0020-003f : pic1
0040-005f : timer
0060-006f : keyboard
0080-009f : dma page reg
00a0-00bf : pic2
```

```
00c0-00df : dma2
00f0-00ff : npu
01f0-01f7 : ide0
0300-030f : 3c509
03c0-03df : vga+
03f0-03f5 : floppy
03f6-03f6 : ide0
03f7-03f7 : floppy DIR
```

Look for your network adapter. In this case, it's the 3c509. If the adapter is working, you shouldn't have any conflicts. If the IO ports of two devices overlap, a conflict exists and you have to reconfigure the adapter. Run your Ethernet NIC configuration program and set the adapter's parameters in its EEPROM. Older adapters may have jumpers or little switches called *DIP switches* to set. If you think you have to do this, remember to write down all the other devices' interrupts and IO addresses so that you don't end up conflicting with something else.

Or perhaps you have a funky kernel

You also may be using a kernel that doesn't have networking installed. This is virtually impossible with Red Hat Linux 9 because the Linux kernel automatically loads networking — and other modules — on demand (it's mature technology). But it's still informative to go ahead and look at these files to gain an understanding of how Linux works.

Display the networking devices by typing this command:

```
cat /proc/net/dev
```

The following output shows that the kernel is configured for loopback (lo) and Ethernet interfaces (eth0). The loopback interface is used only for internal networking.

If you don't see the Ethernet interface, you may have an unsupported network adapter or a defective or misconfigured one. The Red Hat Linux kernel, by default, automatically loads modules as they're needed. You can look back at the results of your boot process by using the dmesg command. Look for a message that says delaying eth0 configuration. This message most likely means that Linux wasn't able to load the network adapter module or that the adapter isn't working.

Display the information about your devices by using the cat /proc/net/dev command:

Inter-	Receive					Transmit			
face	packets	errs	drop	fifo	frame	packets	errs	drop	fifo
	colls	carrier							
lo:	116	0	0	0	116	0	0	0	0 0
eth0:	16292	19	19	23	19	7245	0	0	0	54 0

The next step is to make sure that your network routing is configured correctly. This is also a very easy thing to get confused. You don't need to set up routing outside your LAN yet, but Linux needs to know where to send packets on its own network. Look at your routing table by typing this command:

```
netstat -nr
```

You see a listing of your routing table, similar to this code:

```
Kernel IP routing table
Destination     Gateway         Genmask        Flags  MSS Window  irtt Iface
192.168.1.0     0.0.0.0         255.255.255.0  U       0 0          0 eth0
127.0.0.0       0.0.0.0         255.0.0.0      U       0 0          0 lo
0.0.0.0         192.168.1.254   0.0.0.0        UG      0 0          0 eth0
```

Here is a brief description of elements in the routing table:

- ✔ The destination is the location — IP address — to where you want to send packets. For example, the address 192.168.1.0 refers to my local network.

- ✔ The gateway is the address (computer or router) where the packets need to be sent so that they can find their way to their destination. In the case where the destination is the local network, the address 0.0.0.0 means no gateway.

- ✔ The genmask is used to separate from the host number the parts of the IP address used for the network address.

- ✔ The flags are used to indicate things like *U* for *up* and *G* for *gateway*. The metric is used as a measure of how far a packet has to travel to its destination (a number greater than 32 is considered to be infinite). The next two flags — Ref and Use — aren't important for this discussion.

- ✔ The Iface field shows which network interface is being used. (eth0 refers to an Internet adapter, and lo refers to the loopback interface. The loopback interface is used internally by the Linux kernel, and you shouldn't have any need to use it directly.)

The information about each interface — the routing table — is displayed below the headings. For example, the first line tells Linux to send packets destined for addresses of 192.168.1.0 through 192.168.1.255 to the Ethernet adapter (eth0). The second line deals with the kernel's internal loopback interface. The third and last line, with the address 0.0.0.0, is known as the default route. It defines where to send all packets not covered by a specific route.

If your table deviates from the example, you may have a routing problem. For example, if you don't have the default route — 0.0.0.0 — you can't communicate with any machines on your LAN or the Internet. If you lack a loopback — 127.0.0.1 — route, many internal processes will fail.

Defining a route to the loopback interface

You must have a route to the loopback interface (also referred to as lo), which is the 127.0.0.0 address. If you're missing either or both parameters, you must set them. To set the loopback device — which must be set for the network adapter to work — type this command:

```
route add -net 127.0.0.0
```

To set the route for the network adapter and your local network, type this command:

```
route add 192.168.1.0 dev eth0
```

This route is assigned automatically to your network adapter. You can assign the route to another NIC if necessary. For example

```
route add 192.168.1.0 dev eth1
```

Type **netstat -rn** to see your routing table. You should see entries for the loopback and the Ethernet. If you don't see a route to your network interface, try repeating the preceding steps. You may have to delete a route. To delete a route, type this command:

```
route del 192.168.1.0 dev eth0
```

Note that we use the network address instead of a host address here. The zero (0) designates the class C network address of 192.168.1.

Doing the ping thing

If the network adapter is configured correctly and the routing is correct, check the network. The best way to do it is to ping the loopback interface first and then the other computer. Type this command, let it run for a few seconds (one ping occurs per second), and stop it by pressing Ctrl+C:

```
ping 127.0.0.1
```

You should see a response like the one shown in this code:

```
PING 127.0.0.1 (127.0.0.1): 56 data bytes
64 bytes from 127.0.0.1: icmp_seq=0 ttl=64 time=2.0 ms
64 bytes from 127.0.0.1: icmp_seq=1 ttl=64 time=1.2 ms
64 bytes from 127.0.0.1: icmp_seq=2 ttl=64 time=1.1 ms
```

```
64 bytes from 127.0.0.1: icmp_seq=3 ttl=64 time=1.1 ms
?
--- 127.0.0.1 ping statistics ---
4 packets transmitted, 4 packets received, 0% packet loss
          round-trip min/avg/max = 1.1/1.8/4.6 ms
```

Each line shows the number of bytes returned from the loopback interface, the sequence, and the round-trip time. The last lines comprise the summary, which shows whether any packets didn't make the trip. This is a working system, but if you don't see any returned packet, something is wrong with your setup, and you should review the steps outlined in the preceding paragraphs.

Next, try pinging your Ethernet interface by typing this command:

```
ping 192.168.1.1
```

You should see a response like this code:

```
PING 192.168.1.1 (198.168.1.1): 56 data bytes
64 bytes from 198.168.1.1: icmp_seq=0 ttl=64 time=2.0 ms
64 bytes from 198.168.1.1: icmp_seq=1 ttl=64 time=1.2 ms
64 bytes from 198.168.1.1: icmp_seq=2 ttl=64 time=1.1 ms
64 bytes from 198.168.1.1: icmp_seq=3 ttl=64 time=1.1 ms
?
--- 198.168.1.1 ping statistics ---
4 packets transmitted, 4 packets received, 0% packet loss
          round-trip min/avg/max = 1.1/1.8/4.6 ms
```

Is there another computer or device to talk to?

Try to ping another computer — if one exists — on your network. Type the following command, let it run for 10 to 15 seconds, and stop it by pressing Ctrl+C. (This example assumes that another computer has an IP address of 192.168.1.2. Adjust the address you use to work with your network.)

```
ping 192.168.1.2
```

You should see a response like this code:

```
PING 192.168.1.2 (192.168.1.2): 56 data bytes
64 bytes from 192.168.1.2: icmp_seq=0 ttl=32 time=3.1 ms
64 bytes from 192.168.1.2: icmp_seq=1 ttl=32 time=2.3 ms
64 bytes from 192.168.1.2: icmp_seq=2 ttl=32 time=2.5 ms
64 bytes from 192.168.1.2: icmp_seq=3 ttl=32 time=2.4 ms
```

```
--- 192.168.1.2 ping statistics ---
4 packets transmitted, 4 packets received, 0% packet loss
round-trip min/avg/max = 2.3/2.5/3.1 ms
```

If you get a continuous stream of returned packets and the packet loss is zero or very near zero, your network is working. If not, the problem may be in the other machine. Review the troubleshooting steps again in this chapter. Note that the ICMP is taking about 1 full millisecond (ms) longer to travel to the external computer than to the loopback device. The reason is that the loopback is completely internal to the Linux computer.

If you can't locate the problem and you're using a PPP connection to an Internet Service Provider (ISP), establish a PPP connection and try to ping the computer where you have your account. It's considered a security breach — not to mention bad manners — to continuously ping someone else's computer, so don't leave this command running. Also, the ISP's firewall may not allow the Internet Control Message Protocol (ICMP) packets that ping uses. Even so, it's worth a try, and you have nothing to lose. ICMP packets are the simplest type of packet defined in the Internet Protocol. They're used for doing simple tasks, such as pinging.

Part V
The Part of Tens

The 5th Wave   By Rich Tennant

"We're here to clean the code."

In this part . . .

Ah, here's the part you find in every *For Dummies* book: The Part of Tens. Here's where we get to rummage around and come up with ten of this and ten of that.

In Chapter 18, we list some frequently encountered problems (and their solutions).

Unfortunately, the world is still a dangerous place. Chapter 19 outlines ten computer security threats. We describe how to be a little safer in the wild west otherwise known as the Internet.

Chapter 18

Ten Problem Areas and Solutions

*I*n any technical situation, people end up having problems and issues they need help with. The problems in this chapter are taken from a database of questions and answers created after hundreds of people installed the CD-ROMs. We answer some of these questions in the rest of this book, but because they still generate "What happened?" questions, we repeat the information here.

"Help! I Need Some Help!"

Before this chapter gets into solving specific problems, it first describes several sources of information. Because we cannot cover more than a few of the most common problems, we first point you in the direction where you can find more information and help.

Books and more books

When we were working with computers many years ago, the number of books about computers could fill little more than one bookshelf, and they were mostly about the electronics of the hardware itself. Networking texts concentrated on subjects such as the probability of two Ethernet packets colliding and not on how to build simple networks. Hardly any books about computers were ever in the popular bookstores. Thousands of books on computers are available now; most describe the software and its interactions, with the hardware taking a back seat. Books like the *Dummies* series aren't just for bookstores any more. You can also find them in mass-market venues, such as Wal-Mart.

One great source for information about *Dummies* books is the television series *The Simpsons*. That show loves *Dummies* authors in particular and provides an amazingly accurate portrait of us. D'oh!

Perhaps you looked at other books before you bought this one and were intimidated by their use of technical terms. Or you thought that the other books were too general for what you want to do and you want something more task oriented. You may want to look over those books again because your knowledge level will be higher after reading this book. TCP/IP networking, compiler design, operating system theory, formal language theory, computer graphics, and systems administration training are all topics you can study in greater depth when you have a Linux computer at your disposal.

Many books specifically about the Unix operating system are partially or completely applicable to Linux, such as books on Perl, a comprehensive interpreter. By getting one (or more) books on Perl and sitting down with your Linux system, you have both a new tool for doing your work and a new appreciation for a complete programming language. If you want to find out how to write Perl, you can just view the source code.

Linux HOWTOs

Don't forget about the Linux HOWTOs, which come in the commercial version of Red Hat Linux. These excellent guides to Linux are covered under the Linux Documentation Project — (LDP) — copyleft, which means that you can print them.

School days

Another way to find out more information about Unix and Linux is to take a course, perhaps at a local community college. Many colleges offer courses in Unix, and some have started using Linux to teach the Unix courses. You can do your homework on your system at home, or, if you have a notebook (laptop computer), you can work anywhere. (Jon typed text for the first edition of this book in a hotel in Auckland, New Zealand, and updated text for the second edition in the United Airlines lounge in Chicago.) What we would have given during college for the chance to do computer projects while sitting in the comfort of our own pub — er, dorm rooms. Instead, we had to sit in a room with a bunch of punch-card machines . . . well, never mind. We would have been much more comfortable and productive with a Linux system.

In the news

You can obtain additional information about the Linux operating system from mailing lists and newsgroups on the Internet. In fact, one of the first popular uses of the Internet was the Usenet information-sharing system. Usenet is similar to the World Wide Web in that it uses a set of protocols to perform a special type of communication over the general-purpose Internet. Usenet provides the ability for lets people to participate in discussions via e-mail. People post messages to a specific interest group that anyone can view and respond to.

News groups and mailing lists are dedicated to specific topics — technological and any topic that two or more people (or one person with multiple personalities) are interested in. Dozens of newsgroups and mailing lists are devoted to Linux topics. Searching these groups often provides laser-like answers to your questions. That's because it's very likely that someone else has likely encountered your problem and found a solution to it. You can also post your questions to newsgroups when necessary.

You can search for newsgroups at, for example, `www.dejanews.com` and `www.mailgate.org`. Google also provides an excellent mechanism to search groups, named Google Groups. Go to Google Groups at (`www.google.com/advanced_group_search`).

Don't neglect to directly check out the Red Hat mailing lists, at `https://listman.redhat.com/mailmain/listinfo`. This Web page provides a summary of all Red Hat groups.

User groups

User groups are springing up all over the country. Some are more active than others, but most hold meetings at least once a month. Some groups are Linux only; others are connected to a larger computer group — either Unix or a more general computer users' association. User groups are a great opportunity to ask questions. User groups also tend to stimulate new ideas and ways of doing tasks.

You can find out whether a Linux user group is in your area by checking with GLUE (Groups of Linux Users Everywhere), a service run by Specialized Systems Consultants, Inc (SSC) who are the publishers of the *Linux Journal*. You can find glue, an automated map of user groups, at this address:

```
www.ssc.com
```

When you arrive at the site, click the Resources link, which takes you to the *Linux Journal* site. Then check out the Resources area there to find out where the user group closest to you meets.

No user group in your area? Post a message at your local university or community college saying that you want to start one; other people in your area may decide to join you. Terrified at the thought of trying to start a user group? User group leaders often aren't the most technically knowledgeable members but are simply good planners. They organize the meeting space, find (or hound) speakers, send out meeting notices, locate sponsors, arrange refreshments (usually beer), and perform other organizational tasks. Sometimes, being the leader seems like a thankless job, but when a meeting goes really well, it makes all the work worthwhile. So, as a newbie to Linux, you may not know a grep from an awk, but you still may make a good chairperson.

Fixing Common Problems

Okay, enough information about finding information. This section describes how to fix several common problems. Each of the following sections outlines the problem and then describes the solution.

"I forgot my password"

Problem: You have to remember a zillion passwords at work and home. Unfortunately, you can't remember your Linux password.

Solution: The solution is simple if you have forgotten a user account password but still remember the root password. In that case, simply log in as root and reset the user password. For example, if your user name is rod, run the command **passwd rod** and enter the new password (for example) *likes coffee*.

The solution is more difficult when you forget the root password. You have to become a hacker and break in to your computer to fix the problem. Fortunately, Red Hat provides two possible solutions: Either boot into single-user mode via GRUB or boot from the first Red Hat installation disc.

"I want to boot into single-user mode via GRUB"

Turn on or restart your computer and use your cursor keys to select the Linux operation system when the GRUB boot screen appears; Linux is selected automatically if you're not using a dual-boot system (you installed only Linux). Next, press the **e** key to edit the GRUB configuration. You see three lines, the middle of which starts with the word *kernel*. Select the *kernel* line with the cursor keys when the three-line menu appears. Press the **e** key again and enter the word **single** at the end of the line. Press the Enter key and you'll return to the original GRUB window. Finally, press the **b** key to boot the system into single-user mode.

You can tell Linux to boot into non-graphical — rather than single-user — mode by substituting **3** for `single` when you're editing the GRUB boot mechanism.

"I need to rescue my computer!"

Power on or reset your computer. Change your BIOS to boot from CD-ROM, if necessary. Before your computer starts the GRUB boot system, insert the first Red Hat Linux installation CD-ROM (CD1). When the Red Hat installation process starts, type **linux rescue** at the `boot:` prompt.

Red Hat boots into single-user mode and mounts your Linux partitions. You need to edit the `/mnt/sys/image/etc/shadow` file and remove the root user's encrypted password. The root user, the first line in the file, looks similar to this line:

```
root:234l#!13@jd32#dj!(34:11922:0:999999:7:::
```

Eliminate the characters between the first and second colon to remove the password. The new line should look similar to this one:

```
root::11922:0:999999:7:::
```

Save your changes and reboot the computer. Enter **root** when prompted for the user name, and then enter an empty password. You're logged in as root, and you should immediately enter a new root password.

"I want to change the GRUB boot order"

Problem: You created a dual-boot computer with Red Hat Linux and Windows, and you want to change which one boots by default.

Solution: Modify the /etc/grub.conf file on your Linux computer. The grub.conf should look similar to this example:

```
default=0
timeout=10
splashimage=(hd0,0)/grub/splash.xpm.gz
title Red Hat Linux (2.4.x)
        root (hd0,1)
        kernel /vmlinuz-2.4.x ro root=/dev/hda7 hdb=ide-scsi
        initrd /initrd-2.4.x.img
title Windows 2000
        chainloader +1
        rootnoverify (hd0,0)
```

In this case, Linux is the operating system that boots by default, unless you select otherwise. To reverse the order, simply flip the two operating systems' positions in the file as follows:

```
default=0
timeout=10
splashimage=(hd0,0)/grub/splash.xpm.gz
title Windows 2000
        chainloader +1
        rootnoverify (hd0,0)
title Red Hat Linux (2.4.x)
        root (hd0,1)
        kernel /vmlinuz-2.4.x ro root=/dev/hda7 hdb=ide-scsi
        initrd /initrd-2.4.x.img
```

The next time you boot your computer, the order will have changed.

"My network is working, yet not working"

Problem: You have configured and checked your network connection, and it appears to be okay. But you can't connect to some or all of the machines or network services you want. You're perplexed.

Solution: Check your iptables-based firewall. Red Hat configures two different levels of iptables firewalls during the installation. This book describes several different iptables firewall configurations too. If your firewall isn't configured correctly, it prevents some or all network communications. In many cases, even if your firewall is configured correctly, it may be designed to block the type of communications you want.

Turn off your firewall with this command:

```
/etc/init.d/iptables stop
```

If your network connection instantaneously works, your firewall was most likely the culprit. In that case, you have to go modify your firewall to make it work for your needs. Don't forget to turn your firewall back on as soon as you fix the problem:

```
/etc/init.d/iptables start
```

It's beyond the scope of this book to describe how to customize an iptables firewall. However, the firewalls we construct in this book may work for you and also be easier to understand and modify. Please refer to Chapter 8 for more information about iptables-based firewalls.

"I want to make an emergency boot disk"

Problem: You skipped making an emergency boot disk when you installed Red Hat Linux.

Solution: All is not lost if you skipped making a boot disk in Chapter 3. In fact, nothing is lost because it's easy to make one. Log in to your computer as root and insert a floppy disk that you don't mind erasing (losing everything on that disk). Run this command:

```
uname -r
```

This command returns information about the version of Linux you're running. The output looks similar to the following:

```
2.4.20-8
```

Use that number to run this command:

```
mkbootdisk 2.4.18-7.80
```

You have a Red Hat Linux boot floppy when the process finishes writing to the disk. Restart your computer and press the Enter key at the `boot:` prompt. You computer then starts Red Hat Linux.

"My hard drive numbers have changed since installation"

Problem: Linux numbers hard drives each time it boots, calling SCSI hard drives names like `sda`, `sdb`, `sdc`, and `sdd`. Suppose that `sda` holds your Microsoft operating system, `sdb` holds the bulk of Linux, `sdc` holds your user files, and `sdd` holds your swap space. Now you add another hard drive, and your user files are on `sdd` and your swap space is on `sde`. The new hard drive is named `sdc` but has nothing on it. What happened?

Solution: SCSI hard drives are lettered according to the SCSI IDs set on each hard drive. Linux names the hard drives by using this ordering scheme. If you insert a new hard drive into the SCSI bus with a SCSI ID that is lower than an existing hard drive, you rename all hard drives with a SCSI ID number above the one you just installed. You should start installing your SCSI hard drives with a SCSI ID of 0, 1, 2, and so on; then put other SCSI devices at the other end of the SCSI bus (SCSI IDs 6, 5, 4, and so on).

Most SCSI controllers are set to SCSI ID 7 by default.

IDE hard drives are numbered according to the IDE controller they're on and whether they're a master or a slave on that controller. For this reason, adding a new hard drive to a set of IDE controllers doesn't change the existing names, as shown in these two tables:

Controller	Hard Drive	Linux Name
ide0	Master	hda
ide0	Slave	hdb
ide1	Master	hdc
ide1	Slave	hdd
ide2	Master	hde
ide2	Slave	hdf
ide3	Master	hdg
ide3	Slave	hdh

Controller Designation	Controller Priority
ide0	Primary controller
ide1	Secondary controller
ide2	Third controller
ide3	Fourth controller

"The ls command doesn't show files in color"

Problem: When running the ls command to show files in color, the command doesn't display files in color. (We hate that.)

Solution: You have to edit the .bashrc file in your home directory to add this line to the end of the file:

```
alias ls='ls _-color=auto'
```

Log off and then back in to reexecute your .bashrc file (assuming that you're using the bash shell), and ls shows different file types in different colors.

Problem: Your ls command lists files and directories in color.

Solution: Add the following alias to your .bashrc file:

```
alias ls=ls
```

"Linux can't find a shell script (or a program)"

Problem: You type a command name, but Linux can't find the command, even if it's in the current directory.

Solution: When you type a shell or binary command name, Linux looks for the name in specific places and in a specific order. To find out which directories Linux looks in, and in which order, type this command:

```
echo $PATH
```

You see a stream similar to the following:

```
/bin:/usr/bin:/usr/local/bin
```

Linux looks at these directories to find the command, program, or shell you want to execute. You may see more directories depending on your distribution or how your system administrator (if you have one) set up your system.

Now suppose that you create a shell or a program named bark and want to execute it (and assuming that you have set the permission bits to make bark executable by you). You have a couple of choices (well, you have more than two choices, but we're listing the safest ones). One choice is to type this line on the command line:

```
./bark
```

This line tells Linux to look in this directory (`./`) and execute `bark`.

Your second choice is to move `bark` to one of the directories shown in the PATH variable, such as `/usr/local/bin`, and then enter **bark** at the prompt again.

"When 1 start the X Window System, 1 see a gray screen"

Problem: You configured the X Window System, but when you log in as a general user (that is, not as root) and type **startx**, all you get is a gray screen with a big X in the middle. You wait a long time, but nothing happens.

Solution: First, recognize that you may have to wait a long time for a slow CPU with a small amount of main memory (about 8MB). Some machines with small amounts of memory take as long as six minutes to start X. But, assuming that you start X on a machine with a faster CPU and more memory, you may have problems with permissions on your home directory. This statement is particularly true if X works when you're logged in as root (that is, as superuser), but not when you're logged in as a general user.

To correct this problem, log in as root and go to the home directory of the user who is having problems. For this example, suppose that the login name of the user is `gabe`. After you're in the user's home directory, issue the `ls -ld` command to see who owns that directory and what the directory's permissions are:

```
cd ~gabe
ls _ld .
drwxrwx-- root bin 1024 Dec 31 16:00 .
```

In this example, the directory is owned by root and the group ownership is `bin`, which doesn't allow `gabe` to access the directory structure inside the directory. Because the shells and terminal emulators that X needs require access to that directory structure, X can't fully work.

To correct this problem, use the `chown` and `chgrp` commands to change the ownership of the `/gabe` home directory to `gabe` and to change the group ownership of the `gabe` home directory to users:

```
chown gabe  ~gabe
chgrp users ~gabe
```

Make sure that you replace the gabe login name we use in this example with the login name you're having difficulty with.

"I don't know how to make the X Window System start at boot time"

Problem: You don't want to log in to a command-line mode (such as DOS) and then type **startx**. Instead, you want to log in through the X Window System.

Solution: If you like to see a graphical interface from the beginning, change the following line in the /etc/inittab file:

```
id:3:initdefault:
```

to this:

```
id:5:initdefault:
```

Save your changes and reboot. X starts at the end of the boot process, and you can then log in through the graphical interface. To go back to the old way of booting, change the line in the /etc/inittab file back to the following:

```
id:3:initdefault:
```

and reboot the machine.

"I never seem to have the correct time"

Problem: When you boot Linux, the time is wrong, so you set it with the date command. Then you boot Windows and its time is wrong, so you reset it. When you reboot Linux, its time is wrong again.

Solution: Most Unix systems keep their time by using Universal Time (also known as Greenwich Mean Time, or GMT), but Microsoft systems keep their time as local time. When you set the time in either system, you set the CPU clock to that version of the time. Then, when you boot the other system, it interprets differently what is in the CPU clock and reports a different time.

Linux enables you to use either GMT or your local time. You make this choice when you install the system. To change your choice, follow these steps:

1. **Log in as root.**

2. **Type** timeconfig.

   The Configure Timezone dialog box appears.

3. **Select the GMT option.**

   Highlight the option by pressing the Tab key, if necessary. (You should already be there when you activate the timeconfig command.)

4. **Press the Spacebar to deselect the option. Press the Tab key until you reach the OK button and then press Enter.**

5. **Reset the time to the proper value by using the** ntpdate **command.**

   You need to point the ntpdate command at a Network Time Protocol (NTP) time server. For example, you can run the command ntpdate ntp.nasa.gov. Some ISPs maintain their own NTP server, so you may be able run the command, such as the following:

   ```
   ntpdate time.nist.gov
   ```

Chapter 19

Ten Security Vulnerabilities

*T*hey're here! The monster is under the bed. That big wooden horse is full of Greek warriors. Here's Johnny! Come into the light. One thing's for sure: The bad guys are out to get you.

Do you want the good news or the bad news first? The good news: The Internet has changed the world for the better and continues to do so in more and unforeseen ways. And the speed of change will only accelerate. The bad news: Because the Internet is constantly changing, the number of ways that someone can use the Internet to hurt you is always growing. This chapter outlines some of the more dangerous spooks that lurk out on that poorly lit electronic street.

Our purpose in this chapter is to point you in the right direction so that you can gain a general awareness of computer security. Computer security is, unfortunately, a complex subject. Because of its complexity, we cannot hope to do any more here than touch on some important aspects of security. In this chapter, we give you some specific instructions for adding security to your new Red Hat Linux computer. More importantly, we point out some of the most significant areas you should be aware of. This chapter introduces ten important security topics. You can use them as a starting point to increase your computer security.

How Many Daemons Can Dance on the Head of the Linux Process Table?

Every commercial operating system vendor wants to make its operating systems easy to install and use. Operating systems are inherently complex animals, and Linux is no exception. (Of course, we're not biased when we say that Linux is overall a simpler system than Windows, whether you measure simplicity by the number of lines of code or the transparency of its design.) Vendors walk the tightrope of making the systems easy to use while making them reasonably secure.

Ease of use and security often don't coexist well. Your operating system is much easier to use, for example, if you install and activate every software package and option. On the other hand, running every software package means that you have more potential vulnerabilities. If you install 10 doors and 20 windows in your home, you can certainly enter and leave as you please, but it also provides burglars with more opportunities to break in and do you harm. The same logic is true with your operating system: The more software you install, the more chances someone has of getting inside your computer.

We can't think of a cure-all for this dilemma. The best answer from a security viewpoint is to not provide intruders with any openings: Place your computer in a locked room with no network or external connections and turn it off. You then have a really safe system that holds the floor down.

As with most things in life, the real answer is to use your best judgment and balance security with ease of use. Run only the services you need. For example, don't run the Samba file system service if you don't want to use your Red Hat Linux computer as a (Windows) file system server. Don't run the text-based gpm service if you use the graphical X Window mode on your computer. The list is endless and beyond the scope of this book to discuss in detail. You can find more info from these sources:

- ✔ **Web sites:** Both `www.sans.org` and `www.usenix.org` deal with security issues.

- ✔ **HOWTOs:** Go to `www.redhat.com/docs/manuals/linux/RHL-8.0-Manual` and open the Customization Guide and Reference documents to access security advice.

- ✔ **Books covering security:** Browse through your local bookstore to find Linux books that discuss how to reduce services. Some good books are *Red Hat Linux Security and Optimization,* by Mohammed J. Kabir, and *Linux Security Toolkit,* by David A. Bandel, both published by Wiley Publishing, Inc.

Open the Encrypt

It's hard to trust communication media you don't completely control — such as university LANs, wireless home networks, and the Internet. Our point: Trust no one!

Any public network is potentially dangerous, especially the Internet. One way to protect yourself is to use encryption for all communication. You use encryption when you conduct credit card transactions or read remote e-mail. Secure Socket Layer (SSL) communication is the standard encryption mechanism for secure Internet browsing and e-commerce transactions.

The Secure Shell (SSH) protocol is used to conduct encrypted CLI terminal sessions and file transfers. Red Hat bundles the open source version of SSH called OpenSSH with its distributions. When you install Red Hat Linux, you automatically get the OpenSSH client. You can use OpenSSH from a terminal session by entering the command `ssh destination`. The destination is the computer you want to communicate with. You can get information about OpenSSH from `www.openssh.org`.

Using encryption is essential when you use wireless networking. Wi-Fi (also known as 802.11b) wireless networks can use built-in encryption based on the WEP protocol. WEP does have some significant security vulnerabilities, though. The only long-term answer is to either wait until the next standard comes along to fix the problem or else use OpenSSH to provide your own encryption. You're much safer if you use OpenSSH and SSL for as much of your communication as possible.

Aha! No Firewall — Very, Very Good

Broadband connections give you a quantum leap in speed and convenience when connecting to the Internet. The two most popular choices for a broadband connection are DSL and cable modems. After you start using them, you'll never go back to slow, Stone Age telephone-based modems.

But every silver lining has a dark cloud. Broadband connections give you not only fast Internet connections but also continuous ones. With a telephone-based modem, a hacker can attack only your home computer and private network while you're connected to the Internet. Using a 24/7 broadband connection means that every hacker on the Internet — that means every hacker in the world — can constantly bang on your computer and private network. That's lots of vulnerability.

Firewalls provide your number-one protection from Internet-based attacks. The modern `Netfilter/iptables` packet-filtering firewall system gives you excellent protection when it's properly configured. The Red Hat installation process installs a good `iptables`-based firewall by default, and Chapter 8 describes how to configure an even better one. You should never, ever connect to the Internet without first configuring your personal firewall.

We don't mean to imply that you're invulnerable to attack if you use a telephone-based modem to connect to the Internet. Traditional modem connections are just as vulnerable as continuous broadband connections when they're active. What we mean is that a modem that isn't connected to the Internet is a safe modem.

Keeping Up with the Software Joneses

Nobody's perfect, and that goes for operating system vendors. Even open source Linux developers and great companies like Red Hat make mistakes. Vulnerabilities are found in software systems all the time and have to be fixed.

Red Hat provides a way to keep up-to-date with current problem and security fixes through its Web site. Go to `ftp.redhat.com/pub/redhat` to find the newest and safest versions of all your system's RPM packages. You can also find out how to configure your Red Hat Linux system to update itself automatically.

"Backups? I Don't Need No Stinking Backups!"

If you don't regularly make backups of your computer's contents, you face a security vulnerability, plain and simple. You may lose some or all of your valuable information if your computer is compromised. You should back up your data as frequently as possible.

You can use one of many techniques and software for making backups, but that's stuff we couldn't possibly begin to cover. We wouldn't be able to cover Red Hat Linux if we even began to go into detail.

So we keep it simple: Archiving your home directory and copying it to another location is a simple and effective backup mechanism.

For example, the following commands use the ubiquitous Linux tape archive (`tar`) command to create an archive of your home directory. You can then use the OpenSSH `scp` command to securely copy the archive to another location, such as your ISP account or another computer you have access to. Follow these steps to create an archive of your home directory:

1. **Log in to your user account.**

2. **Run this** `tar` **command:**

```
tar czf myusername.tgz .
```

In this case, the `c` option means to use `tar` to copy the specified files and directories. The `z` option tells `tar` to compress the data. The `f` option defines the text that follows it — *myusername*.tgz — as the file to copy the files to. The single dot (`.`) says to copy to the archive all files in the current working directory.

3. **Use OpenSSH to copy the** `tar` **archive to another location:**

```
scp myusername.tgz myloginaccount@myisp.com
```

This command securely copies the `tar` archive to the account *mylogin account* at the *myisp.com* ISP.

My Buffer Overflow-ith

The most popular way hackers use to break into computers is with buffer overflows. The buffer overflow technique attempts to feed crazy streams of data to programs in order to make them behave in ways their designers never intended. (It is beyond the scope of this book to describe in detail what a queue does. Suffice it to say that Linux uses a queue to store instructions and addresses for later use.) The result of the buffer overflow is that sometimes the program provides the hacker with a shell or other open door when it fails.

The shell created by a buffer overflow is an open door to your computer. Sometimes the shell has root (superuser) privileges, and then the hacker owns your system.

Here are some simple techniques you can use to minimize buffer overflows:

✔ **The first line of defense is to simply minimize the number of services you run.** You run zero risk of compromise from a buffer overflow vulnerability in Service A if you don't run that service.

For example, the Lion worm wreaked havoc in spring 2001. Lion exercised vulnerability in the Linux sendmail and lpd printer services. Computers that didn't run those services weren't vulnerable to the Lion worm.

> ✔ **The second line of defense is to update your Red Hat Linux computer as often as possible.** Red Hat posts package updates that fix vulnerabilities as they become available. Buffer overflow fixes comprise many of the package updates. Updating your system fixes many buffer overflow vulnerabilities.

Social Engineering 1010101010

Hackers don't have to discover supertechnical tricks to break into your computer. Many wiley hackers aren't deterred when they encounter a well-protected computer or network. What does a poor hacker in these security-aware times have to do to break into your system?

Some hacker techniques don't rely on technological means. One such technique is *social engineering,* which is a fancy way of saying "I'm going to trick you or your associates into giving me information to use against you."

Social engineering can be as simple as a hacker calling you to see whether you're at home or in the office. If you're not physically present, the hacker or burglar can break in and steal the computer or its disks. Breaking into a computer if you possess it is pretty much a trivial process. Another social engineering technique hackers employ is to call a corporation's help desk and pretend to be a VIP. The poor minimum-wage slave can often be bullied or cajoled into giving out a password or other important information.

The moral of the story is to exercise good security hygiene and be careful of strangers. Don't give out information unless it's essential and you can verify the authenticity of the request.

Bad Passwords

Probably the easiest to avoid, and most often abused, vulnerability is poor or non-existent passwords. Passwords are your first line of defense. If your password is easily guessed or — even worse — blank, someone will break in.

Bad passwords are easy to fix. Start by assigning a password to every account you create — *especially* root. Then make it a habit to use "good" passwords. Passwords can be cracked by brute force because computers have become very fast. Because you connect to the Internet, hackers can steal your /etc/passwd file that contains the encrypted version of your text-based passwords and use a computer to crack them.

You should use passwords that don't use any word that can be found in a dictionary. Simple words of any language are extremely easy to crack. For example, don't use the password *redhat80*. Instead, change the *e* in *red* to *3* and the *a* in *hat* to @. Your password becomes *r3dh@t80,* which means that the cracking software will have to use brute force, rather than a mere dictionary search, to discover it.

Scan Me

Information is king when it comes to people hacking into systems and keeping them out. Hackers use knowledge about your computer and network to break into your systems. One common and powerful tool for gaining information about what type of operating system you have and the services it runs is nmap. This port-scanning tool can discover a wealth of information about individual computers and networks.

Nmap is included in the Red Hat Linux distribution. Install it by logging in as root, mounting CD2, and entering this command:

```
rpm -ivh /mnt/cdrom/RedHat/RPMS/nmap*
```

You can then scan yourself, or any computer on your private network (if you have one). If you're logged into cancun, for example, you can run this command:

```
nmap cancun
```

The nmap command probes your network interface — eth0, for example — and returns a list of services you're running. This list shows a sample result:

```
Starting nmap ( www.insecure.org/nmap/ )
Interesting ports on cancun.paunchy.net (192.168.1.1):
(The 1596 ports scanned but not shown below are in state:
         closed)
Port        State         Service
22/tcp      open          ssh
111/tcp     open          sunrpc
515/tcp     open          printer
6000/tcp    open          X11

Nmap run completed  -- 1 IP address (1 host up) scanned in 3
         seconds
```

If you're a hacker, this is good information. By knowing that the machine is running certain services, you can try to find vulnerabilities to exploit.

Another good test to run is to log in to your ISP account and scan the Internet connection your computer or private network is attached to. If your firewall is running correctly, the scan shows little or nothing. That's good. If the scan displays information about your computer and network, either your firewall isn't running correctly or it's not running at all.

You can use that information to your advantage. Seeing what the hackers see gives you the ability to plug your security holes.

1 Know Where You Logged in Last Summer

Linux is good at keeping a diary. Red Hat is configured at installation to keep logs of every user login and other technical information. Examining logs is more of an art than a science, however. We don't have any explicit techniques for determining whether your system is being attacked or has been broken into. Sorry.

Experience counts for a great deal when you're examining logs for discrepancies. The more you keep track of your system, the more you recognize its idiosyncrasies and general behavior. Red Hat checks its general-purpose logs in the /var/log directory. Check your logs frequently.

Part VI
The Appendixes

In this part . . .

This is the part of every book where you find things that just didn't fit into the flow of the chapters. This part includes the fun and exciting appendixes.

Appendix A shows you how to figure out what stuff your computer is made of. Appendixes B and C describe the Linux file system and how to use it. In Appendix D, you find out all about RPM, the Red Hat Package Manager. Finally, the contents of the companion CD-ROMs are described in Appendix E.

Appendix A

Discovering Your Hardware

*Y*ou should know as much about your computer as possible before installing Red Hat Linux. This appendix describes the basic parts that comprise a computer and shows you how to discover information about those parts.

Knowing your hardware can be interesting ("My processor is faster than your processor!"). It can also be useful if you have problems installing Red Hat Linux in Chapter 3. Understanding the bits and pieces that comprise your computer can help you install Red Hat Linux. That information also lets you know better what your new Linux computer can do. This appendix helps you get started on your path to self discovery.

Linux runs on Intel processors from the 386 on up as well as on the Digital Equipment Corporation (DEC) Alpha, Sun SPARC, Motorola, MIPS, PowerPC, and HP/PA platforms. However, the version of Red Hat Linux included with this book works on only Intel 386-, 486-, and Pentium-based computers. That shouldn't be a problem because it seems that 99.999999999999999 percent (well, maybe not quite that many) of the world's computers are Intel-based.

Breaking Down Your Computer

Computers may seem mysterious at first, but the truth is that they're not terribly complex. When you break down the parts that make up a PC, you see that each part performs a specific task. The sum of the parts equals a computer. This list outlines the subsystems that comprise a computer:

✔ **Central processing unit (CPU):** The CPU, or microprocessor, is often referred to as the brains of a computer because the CPU controls, in minute detail, everything the computer does. CPUs are controlled by software that is essentially a recipe for doing tasks as simple as detecting keyboard input or as complex as communicating across networks to display pictures in a Web browser.

The most common CPUs are now Intel Pentiums, which you're using to run your PC. Generally, the faster the CPU, the faster your computer. CPU speed is measured in *megahertz* (MHz), which means millions of cycles per second. To perform tasks such as sending e-mail, a CPU has to perform many simple tasks, or instructions. The simplest instructions require a single CPU cycle; most take several. However, the MHz measurement is a reasonably good measure of how fast a microprocessor runs.

✔ **Hard disks:** Hard disks — also referred to as hard drives — store all the permanent information on a computer. Hard disks are metal platters that store bits and bytes in tiny magnetic domains (spots). The disk spins, and a magnetic head that floats on a cushion of air reads and writes from the disk. The spinning disk allows the head to quickly access any location on the disk and also creates the air cushion.

✔ **Disk controllers:** The disk controller connects the drive to the computer's microprocessor. Several types of controllers are now commonly used: IDE, USB, FireWire, and SCSI. Most PCs come with IDE internal hard drives. However, high-performance computers tend to use SCSI-based drives because they're faster (and more expensive). IDE controllers can connect as many as four drives.

✔ **CD-ROM:** CD-ROMs store information like hard drives do, but in optical rather than magnetic form. Most PCs use IDE-based CD-ROMs. SCSI CD-ROMs are faster, just like SCSI hard disks. Because the prices of USB and FireWire CD-ROMS are dropping fast, they're becoming more common.

✔ **RAM, or Random Access Memory:** RAM is much faster than hard disks and CD-ROMs. Because RAM is used to store temporary information, programs, data, and other types of information are stored in RAM — it "forgets" everything when power to the computer is turned off.

✔ **Mouse:** What type of mouse do you have — bus, PS/2, or serial? How many buttons does it have? If you have a serial mouse, which COM port is it attached to, and which protocol (Microsoft or Logitech) does it use?

✔ **Monitor:** What are the make and model of the monitor? What are its vertical and horizontal refresh rates? You need this information only if you plan on using the graphical portion of Linux, X Window System.

✔ **Video card:** What are the make and model number of the video card or video chip set, and what is the amount of video RAM?

✔ **Network interface card (NIC):** If you have a network connection, what are the make and model number of the network interface card?

That's the rundown of computer subsystems. Each one performs a specific function; buttoned up inside a computer chassis, they work together to create the computer you're familiar with. The next two sections describe hard drives and memory in more detail.

Understanding Hard Drive Controllers

The two main types of hard drives are IDE and SCSI, and each type has its own controller. IDE is more common in PCs, and newer PCs usually have two IDE controllers rather than one. For each IDE controller, your system can have only two hard drives: a master and a slave. Therefore, a PC with two IDE controllers can have as many as four hard drives. You should know which hard drive is which. Also, if you have a Windows system you want to preserve, you should know on which hard drive it resides. The following is the normal configuration on a Windows system:

✔ The first controller's master drive is named C.

✔ The next hard drive is named D and is the slave drive on the first controller.

✔ The next hard drive is E and is the master drive on the second controller.

✔ The last hard drive is F and is the slave drive on the second controller.

Normally, Windows is located on your C drive and data is on your other drives. This lettering scheme is just one possibility; your hard drives may be set up differently and may even include CD-ROMs as drives on your IDE controllers.

Some high-end PCs have a SCSI controller on the motherboard or on a separate SCSI controller board, either in addition to or instead of the IDE controllers. Older SCSI controllers can have as many as eight devices on them, numbered from 0 to 7, including the controller. Newer SCSI controllers (known as *wide controllers*) can have as many as 16 devices, including the controller itself.

If all you have is a SCSI hard drive, drive 0 or drive 1 is usually your C drive, and others follow in order.

If you have a mixture of IDE and SCSI controllers, your C drive could be on any of them. The sections "Discovering Your Windows 9*x* or Windows Me Hardware" and "Discovering Your Windows NT, Windows 2000, or Windows XP Hardware," later in this appendix, show how to identify how many hard drives you have, what type they are, and the controllers to which they're attached.

We suggest that you consider putting Red Hat Linux on a separate hard drive, for a couple of reasons. First, you can now find 20GB hard drives for less than $100 (U.S.). Second, the task of shrinking MS-DOS and Windows to be small enough to allow Red Hat Linux to reside in its full glory on an existing hard drive is difficult at best and impossible at worst. Also, although splitting the Red Hat Linux distribution across hard drives is possible, doing so makes updating the distribution difficult later.

A Bit about Memory Bytes

Memory is the most important factor in determining how fast your computer runs. Computers use Random Access Memory (RAM) to store and access the operating system, programs, and data. The Intel processor usually has the following amount of RAM (main memory):

- ✔ Linux can run on a surprisingly small amount of memory. You can run Linux with only 16MB of memory without graphics (in X Windows, for example). Many people use old PCs with small amounts of memory as simple network servers.

- ✔ However, if you want to run Linux with graphics, you need a minimum of 32MB. With 64MB, life becomes much easier.

- ✔ With 128MB, Red Hat Linux runs multiple graphical programs, like OpenOffice, with ease.

- ✔ You need 256MB or more (many PCs now come standard with 512MB) for hard-core applications, such as VMware. VMware virtual computers need their own RAM to operate at a reasonable speed; for instance, you should allocate 128MB of memory to run a Windows 2000 virtual computer. Plan on using 512MB if you want to run multiple instances of VMware virtual computers.

You can install Red Hat Linux on most laptop computers by using the notebook's built-in CD-ROM drive, or a PCMCIA, USB, or proprietary CD-ROM drive. If you don't have any of these items, you can try to get a PCMCIA Ethernet controller and do a network installation, as long as another Linux system on the network has a CD-ROM drive installed. If that is the course you take, consult the Red Hat installation documentation at `www.redhat.com/support`. You also need a video card that Red Hat understands. Red Hat

Linux supports most video cards, and usually the only problems result from bleeding-edge notebook computers that use the latest and greatest video hardware. You can use the generic VGA, XGA, or SVGA drivers that Red Hat supplies if you can't find the specific driver.

Discovering Your Windows 9x or Windows Me Hardware

You don't have to go to Hollywood to be discovered if you're a piece of computer hardware. Windows provides the tools to use to discover your bits and pieces right at home. This section describes how to use Windows 9*x* or Windows Me for the discovery process.

If you have a Microsoft Windows 9*x* or Windows Me computer, use this section to discover and display information about your computer. We use the ubiquitous Control Panel here. Start up your Windows computer and follow these instructions:

1. **Click the Start button and choose Settings⇨Control Panel.**

2. **Double-click the System icon and then click the Device Manager tab.**

3. **At the top of the screen, select the View Devices by Connection option.**

   This step shows all components and how they relate to each other.

4. **On the Device Manager tab (from the Control Panel) of the System Properties dialog box, select the View Devices by Type option.**

   In the list, notice how a plus (+) or minus (–) sign precedes some icons. A plus sign indicates that the entry is collapsed. A minus sign indicates that the entry is expanded to show all subentries.

5. **Click the plus (+) sign to expand the list.**

   Expanding the list shows each computer subsystem. Every device that makes up your computer is shown. Right-click a device and choose the Properties option to display information about a particular device.

You can use the Web too to find out about your computer. Computer companies provide detailed information about their products on their Web sites. Go to the manufacturer's Web page and look up the model number of your computer. When you get to your page, look for the specification (or "specs") link.

Discovering Your Windows NT, Windows 2000, or Windows XP Hardware

Discovering information about Windows NT, Windows 2000, and Windows XP is similar to discovering it about Windows 9x and Windows Me. The process is the same, although getting there is a little different. The following list outlines the process.

On Windows NT and Windows 2000 computers:

1. **Click the Start button and choose Settings⇨Control Panel.**

2. **Double-click the System icon in the Control Panel window.**

3. **Click the Hardware tab when the Systems Properties window opens.**

4. **Click the Device Manager button, and the Device Manager window opens.**

5. **Click the plus sign of any hardware subsystem you want to examine.**

   Clicking the plus sign opens a submenu showing all devices of a particular type.

6. **Right-click any hardware subsystem and choose the Properties option.**

   The properties option opens a window that shows information about that particular device.

On Windows XP computers:

1. **Click the Start button and choose the My Computer option.**

   The My Computer window opens.

2. **Double-click the Control Panel icon in the My Computer option.**

3. **Double-click the System icon to open the System Properties window.**

4. **Select the Hardware tab and double-click the Device Manager button.**

   The Device Manager window opens. This window is similar to the one you see in other Windows versions.

5. **Click the plus (+) sign to display the individual devices within a subsystem.**

6. **Right-click a device to open a menu where you can choose the Properties option.**

   The Properties window opens and shows information about the device.

Appendix B

Filing Your Life Away

● ●

In This Appendix

▶ Learning about Linux files and directories

▶ Finding your way through the Linux file system

▶ Creating, moving, copying, and destroying directories and files

▶ Changing file ownership and permissions

▶ Making up your own rules

● ●

*1*n this appendix, you take your first steps through the Linux file and directory structure. Don't worry: Linux may live a structured life, but it's still flexible. With a little bit of introduction, you begin to understand the Linux way of life.

We also introduce you to file types, subdirectories, and the root (which is not evil at all) directory. You're also shown the way home — to your home directory. After you're oriented to the Linux files-and-directories structure, we show you how to make some changes, such as how to copy and move files and directories and how to destroy them.

Getting Linux File Facts Straight

Linux files are similar to Unix, DOS, Windows, and Macintosh files. All operating systems use files to store information. Files allow you to organize your stuff and keep them separate. For example, the text that comprises this appendix is stored in a file; all the other book elements are stored in their own files. Follow the bouncing prompt as we make short work of long files.

We use the command-line interface (CLI) to examine file and file system basics in this appendix. Graphical user interfaces (GUIs), such as Nautilus, are also useful, and we use them extensively in this book. However, we believe that using a CLI is better for finding out about this subject. All examples in this appendix use the GNOME Terminal Emulation Program to provide the CLI.

Storing files

We assume that you know that a *file* is a collection of information identified by a filename and that Linux can store multiple files in directories as long as the files have different names. Linux stores files with the same name in different directories.

Each directory may contain only one file with the same name.

Wonderful or not, Linux filenames can be as long as 256 characters. The filenames can contain uppercase and lowercase letters (also known as *mixed case*), numbers, and special characters, such as the underscore (_), the dot (.), and the hyphen (-). Because filenames can be composed of mixed-case names, and because each name is distinct, we call these names *case sensitive*. For example, the names *FILENAME, filename,* and *FiLeNaMe* are unique filenames of different files, but they're the same filename.

Although filenames technically can contain wildcard characters, such as the asterisk (*) and the question mark (?), using them isn't a good idea. Various command interpreters, or *shells,* use wildcards to match several filenames at one time. If your filenames contain wildcard characters, you have trouble specifying only those files. We recommend that you create filenames that don't contain spaces or other characters that have meaning to shells. In this way, Linux filenames are different from DOS and Windows filenames.

Sorting through file types

Linux files can contain all sorts of information. In fact, Linux sees as a file every device (disks, display, or keyboard, for example) except for a network interface. These five categories of files become the most familiar to you:

- ✔ **User data files:** Contain information you create. User data files, sometimes known as *flat files,* usually contain the simplest data, consisting of plain text and numbers. More complex user data files, such as graphics or spreadsheet files, must be interpreted and used by special programs. These files are mostly illegible if you look at them with a text editor because the contents of these files aren't always ASCII text. Changing these files generally affects only the user who owns the files.

- ✔ **System data files:** Are used by the system to keep track of users on the system, logins, and passwords, for example. As system administrator, you may be required to view or edit these files. As a regular user, you don't need to be concerned with system data files except, perhaps, the ones you use as examples for your own, private startup files.

- ✔ **Directory files:** Hold the names of files — and other directories — that belong to them. These files and directories are called *children.* Directories in Linux (and Unix) are just another type of file. If you're in a directory, the directory above you is called the *parent.* Isn't that homey?

When you list files with the `ls -l` command, it displays a list of files and directories. Directory files begin with the letter *d;* for example:

```
[lidia@cancun lidia]$ ls -l
drwxr-xr-x 5 lidia lidia 1024 Feb 3  2002 Desktop
drwx------ 2 lidia lidia 1024 Feb 10 2002 nsmail
```

✔ **Special files:** Represent either hardware devices (such as a disk drive, tape drive, or keyboard) or some type of placeholder that the operating system uses. The `/dev` directory holds many of these special files. You can see this directory by running this command at a command prompt:

```
ls -l /dev
```

✔ **Executable files:** Contain instructions (usually called *programs* or *shell scripts*) for your computer. When you type the name of one of these files, you're telling the operating system to *execute* the instructions. Some executable files look like gibberish, and others look like long lists of computer commands. Many of these executable files are located in `/bin`, `/usr/bin`, `/sbin`, and `/usr/sbin`.

Understanding files and directories

If you live in the Windows world, you can think of a Linux file system as one huge file folder that contains files and other file folders, which in turn contain files and other file folders, which in turn contain files and — well, you get the point. In fact, the Linux file system is generally organized in this way. One big directory contains files and other directories, and all the other directories in turn contain files and directories.

Directories and subdirectories

A directory contained, or *nested,* in another directory is a *subdirectory.* For example, the directory named `/mother` may contain a subdirectory named `/child`. The relationship between the two is referred to as parent and child. The full name of the subdirectory is `/mother/child`, which would make a good place to keep a file named `/mother/child/reunion` that contains information about a family reunion.

The root directory

In the tree directory structure of Linux, DOS, and Unix, the big directory at the bottom of the tree is the *root* directory. The root directory is the parent of all other directories (the poor guy must be exhausted) and is represented by a single `/` symbol (pronounced "slash"). From the root directory, the whole directory structure grows like a tree, with directories and subdirectories branching off like limbs.

If you could turn the tree over so that the trunk is in the air and the branches are toward the ground, you would have an *inverted tree* — which is how the Linux file system is normally drawn and represented (with the root at the top). If we were talking about Mother Nature, you would soon have a dead tree. Because the subject is computer technology, however, you have something that looks like an ever-growing, upside-down tree.

What's in a name?

You name directories in the same way as you name files, following the same rules. Almost the only way you can tell whether a name is a filename or a directory name is the way the slash character (/) is used to show directories nested in other directories. For example, usr/local means that local is in the usr directory. You know that usr is a directory because the trailing slash character tells you so; however, you don't know whether local is a file or a directory.

If you issue the ls command with the -f option, Linux lists directories with a slash character at the end, as in local/, so you know that local is a directory.

The simplest way to tell whether the slash character indicates the root directory or separate directories, or directories and files, is to see whether anything appears before the slash character in the directory path specification. If nothing appears before the slash, you have the root directory. For example, you know that /usr is a subdirectory or a file in the root directory because it has only a single slash character in front of it.

Home again

Linux systems have a directory named /home, which contains the user's home directory, where she can

- ✔ Store files
- ✔ Create more subdirectories
- ✔ Move, delete, and modify subdirectories and files

Linux system files in addition to files belonging to other users are never in a user's /home directory. Linux decides where the /home directory is placed, and that location can be changed only by a superuser (root), and not by general users. Linux is dictatorial because it has to maintain order and keep a handle on security.

Your /home directory isn't safe from prying eyes. Be sure to maintain your privacy by locking your directory. (We tell you how in the "Owning Files and Granting Permissions" section, later in this appendix.) However, anyone who logs in to your system as root can see what's in your /home directory, even if you lock it up.

Moving Around the File System with pwd and cd

You can navigate the Linux file system without a map or GPS. All you need to know are two commands: pwd and cd. (You run these commands from the command line.) However, you also need to know where to start; hence, the usefulness of the next section.

Figuring out where you are

Log in to your Red Hat Linux computer and open a GNOME Terminal Emulation Program. In this case, you log in as the example user lidia. To find out where you are in the Linux file system, simply type **pwd** at the command prompt:

```
[lidia@cancun lidia]$pwd
```

You receive this response:

```
/home/lidia
[lidia@cancun lidia]$
```

This response indicates that you're logged in as lidia and are in the /home/lidia directory. Unless your alter ego is out there, you should be logged in as *yourself* and be in the /home/*yourself* directory, where *yourself* is your login name.

The pwd command stands for *print working directory*. Your *working directory* is the default directory where Linux commands perform their actions; the working directory is where you are in the file system when you type a command. When you type the ls(1) command, for example, Linux shows you the files in your working directory. Any file actions on your part occur in your working directory unless you are root. For security reasons that we don't go into here, the root user isn't configured by default to be able to work on the current working directory. You can change this setting, but the root user generally must explicitly specify the working directory. For example, if you are root and are in the /etc directory and you want to indicate the hosts file, you must type **cat ./hosts** rather than just **cat hosts**.

Type this command:

```
ls -la
```

You see only the files in your working directory. If you want to specify a file that isn't in your working directory, you have to specify the name of the directory that contains the file in addition to the name of the file. For example, the following command lists the passwd file in the /etc directory:

```
ls -la /etc/passwd
```

Specifying the directory path

If the file you want to read is in a subdirectory of the directory you're in, you can reach the file by typing a relative filename. *Relative filenames* specify the location of files relative to where you are.

In addition to what we discuss earlier in this appendix about specifying directory paths, you need to know these three rules:

- ✔ One dot (.) always stands for your current directory.
- ✔ Two dots (..) specify the parent directory of the directory you're in.
- ✔ All directory paths that include (.) or (..) are relative directory paths.

You can see these files by using the -a option of the ls(1) command. Without the -a option, the ls(1) command doesn't bother to list the . or .. files, or any filename beginning with a period. This may seem strange, but the creators of Unix thought that having some files that are normally hidden keeps the directory structure cleaner. Therefore, filenames that are always present (. and ..) and special-purpose files are hidden. The types of files that should be hidden are those a user normally doesn't need to see in every listing of the directory structure (files used to tailor applications to the user's preferences, for example).

Specify a pathname relative to where you are; for example:

```
[lidia@cancun lidia]$pwd
/home/lidia
[lidia@cancun lidia]$ ls -la ../../etc/passwd
```

The last line indicates that to find the passwd file, you move up two directory levels (../../) and then down to /etc.

If you want to see the login accounts on your system, you can issue this command from your home directory:

```
[lidia@cancun lidia]$ ls -la ..
```

This command lists the parent directory. Because the parent directory (/home) has all the login directories of the people on your system, this command shows you the names of their login directories.

You've been looking at relative pathnames, which are relative to where you are in the file system. Filenames that are valid from anywhere in the file system are *absolute filenames*. These filenames always begin with the slash character (/), which signifies root:

```
ls -la /etc/passwd
```

Changing your working directory

You occasionally (often?) want to change your working directory. Why? Glad you asked — because doing so enables you to work with shorter relative pathnames. To do so, you simply use the cd (for change *directory*) command.

To change from your working directory to the /usr directory, for example, type this command:

```
cd /usr
```

Going home

If you type **cd** by itself, without any directory name, you return to your home directory. Just knowing that you can easily get back to familiar territory is comforting. There's no place like home.

You can also use cd with a *relative* specification; for example:

```
cd ..
```

If you're in the directory /usr/bin and type the preceding command, Linux takes you to the parent directory named /usr:

```
[lidia@cancun lidia]$ cd /usr/bin
[lidia@cancun bin]$ cd ..
[lidia@cancun usr]$
```

Here are a couple of tricks: If you type **cd ~**, you go to your home directory (the tilde symbol, **~,** is synonymous with /home/username). If you type **cd ~<*username*>**, you can go to that user's home directory. On very large systems, this command is useful because it eliminates the need for you to remember — and type — large directory specifications.

> ✔ > is known as *redirect standard output*. When you use it, you tell the computer "Capture the information that normally goes to the screen, create a file, and put the information in it."

- ✔ >> is known as *append standard output.* When you use this symbol, you tell the computer "Capture the information that would normally go to the screen and append the information to an existing file. If the file doesn't exist, create it."

- ✔ < tells the computer "Feed the information from the specified file to *standard in* (also known as *standard input*), acting as though the information is coming from the keyboard."

Manipulating Files and Directories

Linux has many ways to create, move, copy, and delete files and directories. Some features are so easy to use that you need to be careful: Unlike other operating systems, Linux doesn't tell you that you're about to overwrite a file — it just follows your orders and overwrites!

We've said it before, but we'll say it again: Make sure that you are *not* logged in as root when you go through these sections. You can unintentionally harm your computer when you're logged in as root. As root, or the superuser, you can erase any file or directory — regardless of which permissions are set. Be careful!

Creating directories

To create a new directory in Linux, you use the `mkdir` command (just like in MS-DOS). The command looks like this:

```
[lidia@cancun lidia]$mkdir newdirectory
```

This command creates a subdirectory under your current or working directory. If you want the subdirectory under another directory, change to that directory first and then create the new subdirectory.

Create a new directory named `cancun`. Go ahead — do it:

```
mkdir cancun
```

(Can you tell where we would rather be right now?)

Now create another directory named `vacation`:

```
mkdir veracruz
```

Then change the directory to put yourself in the `cancun` directory:

```
cd cancun
```

Now verify that you're in the directory cancun:

```
pwd
```

Moving and copying files and directories

The commands for moving and copying directories and files are `mv` for move and `cp` for copy. If you want to rename a file, you can use the `mv` command. No, you're not really moving the file, but in Linux (and Unix), the developers realized that renaming something was much like moving it. The format of the move command is

```
mv source destination
```

Create a file that you can practice moving. The `touch` command updates the time stamp on an existing file or creates an empty file if it doesn't. In this case, the file test doesn't exist and is created by touch.

```
touch go
```

Move the new file:

```
mv go to
```

This command leaves the file in the same directory but changes its name to `to`. The file isn't really moved — just renamed.

Now try moving the `to` file to the `veracruz` directory. To do that, you have to first move the file up and then move it into the `veracruz` directory. You can do it with one command:

```
mv to ../veracruz
```

The destination file uses the double-dot .. designation; every directory contains a double-dot directory that points to the parent directory. This command tells Linux to go up one directory level and look for a directory named `veracruz` and then put the file into that directory with the name `newgoto` because you didn't specify any other name. If you did this instead:

```
mv go ../veracruz/now
```

the `go` file would move to the `veracruz` directory named `now`. Note that in both cases (with the file maintaining its name of `go` or taking the new name `now`), your current directory is still `cancun` and all your filenames are relative to that directory.

Strictly speaking, the file still hasn't really moved. The data bits are still on the same part of the disk where they were originally. The *file specification* (the directory path plus the filename) you use to talk about the file is different, so it appears to have moved.

Removing files

The command for removing, or deleting, a file is `rm`. Using `rm` is straightforward. Create a dummy file to erase:

```
touch junk
```

You can delete the file:

```
rm junk
```

You have removed the dummy file from the current directory. To remove a file from another directory, you need to provide a relative filename or an absolute filename. For example, if you want to expunge `now` from the `veracruz` directory, you type this line:

```
rm ../veracruz/now
```

You can use metacharacters (similar in many ways to Windows wildcards) with `rm`, but please be careful if you do so! When files are removed in Linux, they are gone forever — kaput, vanished — and can't be recovered.

The following command removes *everything* in the current directory and all the directories under it that you have permission to remove:

```
[lidia@cancun lidia]$rm -r *
```

Don't do this as root (the superuser)! You should always be careful running any command as root, but be especially careful with commands that can erase entire directories and file systems.

To decrease the danger of removing lots of files inadvertently when you use wildcards, be sure to use the `-i` option with `rm`, `cp`, `mv`, and various other commands. The `-i` option means *interactive,* and it lists each filename to be removed (with the `rm` command) or overwritten (with the `mv` or `cp` command). If you answer either y or Y to the question, the file is removed or overwritten, respectively. If you answer anything else, Linux leaves the file alone.

Removing directories

You can remove not only files but also directories. If you're still following along in this chapter with the story about the handsome prince and his princess, you now have in your home directory two directories that are taking up a small amount of space. Because you're finished with them, you can delete them and recover that space for other tasks.

First, return to your home directory:

```
[lidia@cancun lidia]$ cd
```

Then remove the cancun directory:

```
[lidia@cancun lidia]$rm -rf cancun
```

Giving the rm command these options removes the cancun directory and all files and directories under it. (*Recursively* means to keep going down in the directory structure and remove files and directories as you find them. *Forcefully* means that the file should be removed if at all possible; ignore cases where rm may prompt the user for further information.)

Another command specifically for removing empty directories is named rmdir. With rmdir, the directory must be empty to be removed. If you attempt to remove the work directory without first deleting its files, the system displays this message:

```
[lidia@cancun lidia]$ rmdir veracruz
rmdir: vacation: Directory not empty
[lidia@cancun lidia]$ rm -rf veracruz
```

Owning Files and Granting Permissions

All Linux files and directories have owners and are assigned a list of permissions. This system of *ownership* and *permissions* forms the basis for restricting and allowing users' access to files. File permissions can also be used to specify whether a file is executable as a command and to determine who can use the file or command.

Files and directories are owned by user accounts. User accounts are defined in the /etc/passwd file. For example, you created the root (superuser) user account when you installed Red Hat Linux in Chapter 3 and the installation system created the superuser home directory, /root, plus several configuration files — for example, .bashrc. The root user owns all those files and directories. If you created a regular user account — for example, lidia — that user's home directory and configuration files are all owned by lidia. Users can access and modify any files or directories they own.

Files and directories all have group ownership in addition to user ownership. Groups are defined by the /etc/group file and provide a secondary level of access. For example, you can assign group ownership to files you own and allow other users who belong to the group to access those files.

Files and directories are assigned permissions that permit or deny read, write, and execute access. Permissions are assigned to the owner, group, and anyone of the file or directory. The owner, group, and anyone permissions are independent of each other.

Using the ls command with the -l option allows you to see the file's permissions, along with other relevant information, such as who owns the file, which group of people have permission to access or modify the file, the size of the file or directory, the last time the file was modified, and the name of the file.

First, create a file and then list it:

```
[lidia@cancun lidia]$ touch gotowork
[lidia@cancun lidia]$ ls -l gotowork
-rw-rw-r-- owner group 0 Feb 3  16:00 gotowork
```

The -rw-rw-r- characters are the permissions for the gotowork file: The owner is you, and the group is probably you but may be someone or something else, depending on how your system is set up and administered.

You may be wondering how you can become an owner of a file. Well, you're automatically the owner of any file you create, which makes sense. As the owner, you can change the default file permissions — and even the ownership. If you change the file ownership, however, *you* lose ownership privileges.

To change the ownership of a file or a directory, use the chown command. (Get it? chown — change ownership.) In general, you have to be root to do this.

Suppose that you have decided to settle down and lead a more contemplative life, one more in line with a new profession of haiku writing. Someone else will have to plan the weekend sprees and all-night bashes. So you give up ownership of the gotowork file:

```
[lidia@cancun lidia]$chown root gotowork
```

This command changes the ownership of gotowork to root. If you want to change it back, you can use the chown command, but you have to do it as root.

Files and users all belong to *groups*. In the gotowork example, the group is users. Having groups enables you to give large numbers of users — but not all users — access to files. Group permissions and ownership are handy for making sure that the members of a special project or workgroup have access to files needed by the entire group.

To see which groups are available to you on your system, take a look at the /etc/group file. To do so, use the more command. You see a file that looks somewhat like this:

```
root::0:root
bin::1:root,bin,daemon
...
nobody::99:
users::100:
floppy:x:19:
.....
your_user_name::500:your_user_name
```

where *your_user_name* is the login name you use for your account. Please remember that the file doesn't look exactly like this — just similar. The names at the beginning of the line are the group names. The names at the end of the line (such as root, bin, and daemon) are user-group names that can belong to the user-group list.

To change the group the file belongs to, log in as root and use the chgrp command. Its syntax is the same as that of the chown command. For example, to change the group that gotowork belongs to, you issue this command:

```
[lidia@cancun lidia]$chgrp newgroupname gotowork
```

Red Hat assigns a unique group to each user. For example, when you add the first user to your system, that user gets the user ID and group ID of 500. The next user receives the user ID and group ID of 501, and so on. This system gives you lots of control over who gets what access to your files.

Making Your Own Rules

You, as the owner of a file, can specify permissions for reading, writing to, or executing a file. You can also determine who (yourself, a group of people, or everyone in general) can do these actions on a file. What do these permissions mean? Read on (you have our permission):

- ✔ **Read permission:** You can read the file. For a directory, read permission allows the ls command to list the names of the files in the directory. You must also have execute permission for the directory name to use the -l option of the ls command or to change to that directory.

- ✔ **Write permission:** You can modify the file. For a directory, you can create or delete files inside that directory.

- ✔ **Execute permission:** You can type the name of the file and execute it. You can't view or copy the file unless you also have read permission. Files containing executable Linux commands, called *shell scripts,* must therefore be both executable and readable by the person executing them. Programs written in a compiled language, such as C, however, must have only executable permissions, to protect them from being copied where they shouldn't be copied.

For a directory, execute permission means that you can change to that directory (with cd). Unless you also have read permission for the directory, `ls -l` doesn't work. You can list directories and files in that directory, but you can't see additional information about the files or directories by using just an `ls -l` command. This arrangement may seem strange, but it's useful for security.

The first character of a file permission is a hyphen (-) if it's a file; the first character of a directory is d. The nine other characters are read, write, and execute positions for each of the three categories of file permissions:

✔ Owner (also known as the user)

✔ Group

✔ Others

Your `gotowork` file, for example, may show these permissions when listed with the `ls -l gotowork` command:

```
-rw-rw-r--
```

The hyphen (-) in the first position indicates that it's a regular file (not a directory or other special file). The next characters (rw-) are the owner's permissions. The owner can read and write to the file but can't execute it. The next three characters (rw-) are the group's permissions. The group also has read-write access to the file. The last three characters (r-) are the others' permissions, which are read-only.

[-][rw-][rw-][r-] illustrates the four parts of the permissions: the file type followed by three sets of triplets, indicating the read, write, and execute permissions for the owner, group, and *other* users of the file (meaning *everyone else*).

You can specify most file permissions by using only six letters:

✔ **ugo,** which stands for — no, not a car — user (or owner), group, and other

✔ **rwx,** which stands for read, write, and execute

These six letters, and some symbols, such as the equal sign (=) and commas, are put together into a specification of how you want to set the file's permissions.

The command for changing permissions is chmod. The syntax for the command is

```
chmod specification filename
```

Change the mode of gotowork to give the user the ability to read, write, and execute the file:

```
chmod u=rwx gotowork
```

That was easy enough, wasn't it? What if you want to give the group permission to only read and execute the file? You execute this command:

```
chmod g=rx gotowork
```

Note that this command doesn't affect the permissions for owner or other — just the group's permissions.

You can set the permission bits in other ways. But because this way is so simple, why use any other?

Appendix C

Becoming a Suit: Managing the Red Hat Linux File System

- -

In This Appendix

▶ Mounting and unmounting a file system

▶ Rehabilitating corrupted files

▶ Increasing disk space with a new drive

- -

*M*anaging the Linux file system isn't a complex job, but it's an important one. You have the responsibility of managing the Red Hat Linux file system and ensuring that users (even if you're the only user) have access to secure, uncorrupted data. You're the manager (yes, a *suit*) of your file system.

This chapter introduces you to managing your Linux file system. Consider yourself a management trainee. When you're done reading this chapter, feel free to take a nice, long, expensive lunch.

Mounting and Unmounting

Red Hat Linux, and other Unix-like operating systems, use files in ways that are different from MS-DOS, Windows, and Macintosh operating systems. In Linux, *everything* is stored as files in predictable locations in the directory structure; Linux even stores commands as files. Like other modern operating systems, Linux has a tree-structured, hierarchical directory organization called a *file system*.

All user-available disk space is combined into a single directory tree. The base of this system is the *root directory* (not to be confused with the root user), designated with a slash, /. A file system's contents are made available to Linux by using the mounting process. *Mounting* a file system makes Linux aware of the files and directories it contains. This process is just like mounting a horse — except that no horse is involved.

File systems can be *mounted* or *unmounted,* which means that file systems can be connected to or disconnected from the directory tree. The exception is the *root file system,* which is always mounted on the root directory when the system is running and can't be unmounted. Other file systems may be mounted as needed, such as systems contained on another hard drive, a floppy disk, Zip disks, USB disks, or a CD-ROM.

Mounting Windows files from a floppy disk

Mounting provides a good example of the difference between Linux and MS-DOS/Windows. If you use a floppy disk or CD with Windows, you just insert it into the drive and you have immediate access to it. With Linux, you must insert the floppy disk into the drive and then explicitly mount it. Sounds complicated? Not really.

You can mount a Windows disk (hard drive or floppy disk) on your Linux computer. You can then transfer files from one operating system to the other. We concentrate in this section on describing how to mount a Windows floppy disk. These steps show you how to mount this type of disk:

1. **Insert a Windows MS–DOS-formatted floppy disk (FAT or FAT32, but not NTFS) into the drive.**

2. **Click the GNOME Menu button and choose System Tools⇨Disk Management. Enter the root password if requested.**

   The User Mount Tool window appears, as shown in Figure C-1.

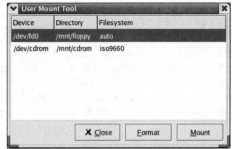

Figure C-1:
The User
Mount Tool
window.

3. **Select the floppy disk and click the Mount button.**

   The floppy disk mounts, usually in only a few seconds.

   You know that the floppy disk has mounted successfully when a floppy disk icon is displayed on the left of the screen.

4. **You can now read and write to the floppy disk (unless the read-only tab on the disk is set).**

   Refer to Appendix B for more information about opening, reading, writing, changing, saving, and deleting files.

5. **Click the Exit button to leave the utility.**

Red Hat Linux and GNOME are configured to automatically start the process that mounts your floppy disk or CD when you insert it into the drive. We present the manual method here to show you how the process works.

To manually mount the floppy in the command-line interface, log in as root, open the terminal window, and run this command:

```
mount _t msdos /dev/fd0 /mnt/floppy
```

A directory used as a mount point is just like any other directory — it can store files and other directories. However, you can't see or use any files or directories stored in a directory used as a mount point until the file system mounted on that directory is unmounted. For more on unmounting files, see the following section.

Unmounting file systems

Unmounting a Linux file system is a little simpler than mounting one. Because the file system is already mounted, you don't have to specify any options or other information. You just have to tell the Red Hat disk management druid to unmount the file system.

Be careful, though. You never want to unmount a hard-drive-based file system, such as /, /usr, or /home. This action sends your Red Hat Linux computer into Never-Never Land. On the other hand, you have to unmount a removable drive, such as a CD-ROM or floppy drive, before removing it. You can also safely unmount a Windows partition because Red Hat Linux doesn't use it for any system-based purpose; you mount a Windows partition only when you're using that operating system.

To unmount a file system, follow these steps:

1. **Log in as root.**

2. **Click the Main Menu button and choose System Tools⇨Disk Management. Enter the root password if requested.**

   The User Mount Tool window appears.

3. **Click the button to the right of the file system in which you're interested.**

   The button indicates whether the file system is mounted or unmounted.

Understanding user rights and permissions

This chapter explains how to mount and unmount a file system from a floppy disk. However, these instructions assume that you're mounting a *vanilla* (your average PC) system. You can specify other options. Here's a short description of each option:

Read-only: The file system is mounted as read-only. You can't write to the file system.

User mountable: When this option is set, any user in addition to root can mount the partition. This option is useful when regular users must be able to mount devices, such as CDs and floppy disks.

Mountable by device owner: A regular user who owns the device file (for example, /dev/fd0) can mount the file system.

Not mount at boot time: Red Hat Linux doesn't automatically mount the file system when it boots.

No program allowed to execute: A regular user isn't allowed to execute files found on a file system. You may want to allow a regular user to mount a device (such as a CD) but not execute programs on the device for security reasons.

No special device file support: The device files in the /dev directory are created with specific permissions in order to enhance system security. This option prevents other, nonsecure device files from being used to mount a file system.

No setuid programs allowed: This option is an important security feature. When an executable Linux file has its setuid bit set, any regular user who belongs to the same group can run it. If root owns the file, then whatever that file does is done with all the power of root. Files with setuid permission often present big security holes. Setting this option prevents any files on the file system from exercising their setuid privileges.

User quota enabled: This option enables Linux quotas to be exercised. Quotas allow limits to be set on what resources individual users can access.

Group quota enabled: This option enables quotas to be set for groups.

After a few seconds, the button changes from Unmount to Mount to show that it has been unmounted.

4. Click the Exit button to leave the utility.

The file system is unmounted. If the file system was a removable type, such as a floppy disk or CD, you can remove it. Otherwise, the file system is simply not available for use until you remount it.

You can run the eject command from a bash shell to eject a CD from its drive. You have to unmount the CD first and then enter the eject command. Otherwise, to eject a CD, you must unmount it and then press the eject button on the CD-ROM drive. In either case, you can't eject the CD until you've unmounted it.

Sending Corrupted File Systems to Reform School: fscking Your Filesystem

You can *corrupt* file systems by turning off your computer without properly shutting down Red Hat Linux. The result? The file doesn't open or the data in the file is all scrambled up. Corruption can also occur because of a driver error or a hardware crash. The type of corruption that occurs when you incorrectly turn off your computer is generally not serious. You shouldn't push fate, however, and you should avoid even mild corruption.

The `fsck` (*file system check*) utility checks Linux file systems. The `fsck` utility reports errors and makes some repairs. Usually, the `fsck` program is called to duty automatically whenever your system boots. This way, if your system crashes, `fsck` checks out all the file systems that were mounted at the time of the system crash.

You can run `fsck` manually, as opposed to having the boot process run it automatically. In some cases, you must run it manually because it needs to prompt you during the process.

Unfortunately, `fsck` doesn't always do the trick; for example:

- ✔ `fsck` can't find (let alone repair) corrupted data that's located in a structurally intact file.
- ✔ With the exception of the root file system, `fsck` runs only on unmounted file systems.
- ✔ You must make sure that the system is in single-user mode to use `fsck` on the root file system.

Here's the syntax you use to run the `fsck` command manually:

```
fsck (options) filesystem
```

The word *filesystem* here names the device driver (or *block special file,* in technical geekspeak) that connects Linux to the file system. If *filesystem* is omitted, the `fsck` utility checks all the file systems listed in the `/etc/fstab` file configuration file. If the `fsck` utility finds any errors, it prompts you for input on what to do about the errors. For the most part, you simply agree with whatever the program suggests. The `fsck` command has these options:

- ✔ **p:** Preens the file system. Performs automatic repairs that don't change the contents of files
- ✔ **n:** Answers No to all prompts and lists only problems; doesn't repair them

> ✔ **y:** Answers Yes to all prompts and repairs damage regardless of severity
>
> ✔ **f:** Forces a file system check

Many people run the `fsck` command with the `-y` option. If you run `fsck` with the `-p` option, Linux performs some steps automatically, placing lost files in the `lost+found` directory, deleting zero-length files, and placing missing blocks back on the list of free blocks. (*Free blocks* are still available for filling with data, among other things.)

`fsck` can cause problems with your disk. The best way to ensure that `fsck` doesn't cause damage is to run it when your computer is operating in single-user mode. Change the state of your computer to single-user mode by running the `init -s` command.

Increasing Drive Space

Sooner or later, you're likely to want to add more hard drive storage to your Linux system to hold more programs and data or to enable more users to log in.

The first step to increasing your drive space is to add a new disk drive. The following tasks are required in order to add a drive to your system (regardless of whether the drive is an IDE, SCSI, or FireWire, for example) and make it accessible to users:

> ✔ Physically attach the disk drive to your computer system. Be careful to turn off the power to your computer and monitor. Disconnect the power cable. Be careful to not cut yourself when reaching into the computer. You should also use the antistatic strap that comes with the hard drive; follow the instructions included with the strap.
>
> ✔ Provide a suitable device driver for the drive's controller in Linux.
>
> ✔ Define at least one partition (see the following section).
>
> ✔ Create the block special files for the partitions.
>
> ✔ Create a Linux file system (or systems) on any partitions to be used for user files.
>
> ✔ Enter the new file systems into `/etc/fstab`, the configuration file.
>
> ✔ Mount the file systems. (You may have to make a directory for a mount point.)

The following sections guide you through the process of creating a drive partition and configuring a hard drive, a floppy drive, and a CD-ROM drive after they're physically installed.

Creating a drive partition

You have to partition your new hard drive after you've added it to your Linux computer. The *drive partition* is the basic file storage unit of Linux. Follow these general steps to create a drive partition:

1. **Create the file systems on the drive partitions.**

2. **Combine the file systems to form a single directory tree structure.**

   The directory tree structure can be on one drive or spread across many.

3. **Define the drive partitions.**

   You can define drive partitions when adding a new drive, or you can do it later.

   In most cases, Linux defines drive partitions during the original Linux installation. You may divide a drive into one, two, four, or more partitions, each of which may contain a file system or be used as a swap partition. *Swap partitions* allow very large programs or many small programs to run, even if they take up more memory than you have as RAM in your computer. The total of all your swap partitions and RAM is called *virtual memory*.

4. **Create a file system.**

   The file system occupies a single space on the drive that has a unique block special file (device) name. This unique name accesses the file system regardless of whether the data is stored on all or only part of a physical drive or is an aggregation of multiple physical drives.

Adding and configuring a hard drive

The business of adding a hard drive to your microcomputer can be broken down into two steps:

1. Physically add the hard drive.

2. Logically make Linux aware of it.

Describing the first step is beyond the scope of this book because your drive may be connected with an IDE, SCSI, FireWire, or USB interface and because the setup of the physical drive is dependent on the rest of the hardware in the system. We suggest that you consult the hardware manual that came with your system or have a computer reseller install your new hard drive. The Linux system is complicated by the fact that several operating systems — such as DOS, Linux, and SCO Unix — may share the same hard drive.

To complete all the steps necessary to install and configure your new drive, you must know the total formatted drive capacity and the number of heads and cylinders, among other details. You can usually find this information in the documentation from the manufacturer or from the computer's BIOS.

You may want to keep a record of the data from the partition table (as displayed by fdisk), such as

✔ Partition numbers

✔ Type

✔ Size

✔ Starting and ending blocks

Installing a drive

After the drive is attached to the system, Linux should recognize it when you boot. To review the booting messages in a slower fashion than they're displayed, use the dmesg command.

Here's what to look for:

✔ If you added a new IDE drive, look for the mention of a new hd*x* drive, where the *x* is replaced with the letter *b, c, d,* or *e.* This information tells you that your kernel saw the new hard drive as it booted and that rebuilding the kernel isn't necessary in order to add this drive.

The messages for an IDE drive may look like this:

```
hdb: HITACHI_DK227A-50, 4789MB w/512KB Cache,CHS=610/
      255/63
```

Sometime later, a message appears that looks like the following line, which describes the existing partitions (if any) on the new drive:

```
hdb: hdb1 hdb2 < hdb5 hdb6 hdb7 hdb8 >
```

✔ For instance, if you're adding a new SCSI disk drive, you see a boot message indicating a new disk drive that has the designation sd*x,* where the *x* is a letter. In the IDE or SCSI case, you may see other messages with additional information.

A SCSI disk drive has messages that look like this:

```
SCSI device sdb: hdwr device= .......
  sdb: sdb1
```

If you see these messages, the kernel has seen your new drive and you don't have to rebuild the kernel to use the new drive.

The Linux distribution on the companion CD-ROMs features block special files for each of eight IDE disks (hda–hdh) with nine partitions each (1–9). Linux also has block special files for seven SCSI hard drives (sda–sdg), which can have eight partitions each (1–8). In addition, Linux has a block special file for a SCSI CD-ROM (scd) with eight partitions (0–7). If you have lots of drives, or if your Linux distribution doesn't have enough block special files for your drive, you may have to create one or more additional block special files for the device, like this:

```
cd /dev; makedev sdg
```

This command creates the device driver (called a *block special file*) for SCSI drive 7. Note that in both IDE and SCSI drives, the letters and drive numbers correspond: *a* is for the first disk, *b* is for the second disk, and so on.

If you add a SCSI disk drive with a lower ID number than the one you already have, the new disk drive takes on that number. Suppose that you have SCSI disk drives with hardware ID numbers of 0, 2, and 3. Linux gives these drives the names sda, sdb, and sdc, respectively. You make your partitions and your file systems and create your entries in /etc/fstab to show where you want the file systems mounted. Then, you get a new disk drive and set the hardware ID number to 1. When you reboot, the new disk drive gets the sdb designation and the disk drives with ID numbers of 2 and 3 are renamed to sdc and sdd, respectively. You must now at least change your /etc/fstab table. For this reason, we recommend that you add SCSI disk drives to your system, starting with ID 0 and working up the number chain, with no gaps in the numbering.

Partitioning a drive

You can use fdisk to partition the drive after you've added it to your computer. You need to partition a disk before formatting it (adding a file system). For example, if you want to invoke fdisk for partitioning the first IDE drive, you type this command:

```
fdisk /dev/hda
```

Using fdisk isn't too difficult; you can partition the drive fairly easily. We don't discuss it in this book, but you can find out more information at www.redhat. com/docs/manuals/linux/RHL-7.3-Manual/install-guide/.

Making the file system

Every drive partition is simply an empty space with a beginning and an end. Unless the partition is being used for swap space, you have to put some type of file system on the partition before it can become useful. The mkfs (for *make* f*i*le *s*ystem) command is used to create the file system on the partition. Normally, the file system is a native Linux file system, which, at this time, is called ext3. The Linux version of mkfs has been nicely streamlined and requires hardly any input.

To create a file system on the disk drive partition sda1, for example, type this command:

```
mkfs -t ext3 /dev/sda1
```

Or, for an IDE drive, type this command:

```
mkfs -t ext3 /dev/hda1
```

If you want to create an MS-DOS file system on the drive partition, you use this command:

```
mkfs -t msdos /dev/sda2
```

Be careful to type these commands precisely. You can easily format the entire disk if you make a mistake. For example, typing mkfs -t ext /dev/sda formats the whole disk. The difference is that sda2 specifies a single partition, whereas sda means the whole disk.

You can continue to execute mkfs commands to create file systems for every partition on your new drive. Or, you can leave some partitions without file systems (for future use), as long as you remember to perform the mkfs command on them before trying to attach them to your file system, by using the mount command or the /etc/fstab table.

Congratulations! Your drive has been physically added to your system and partitioned, and you've added file systems to it. Now the drive is ready to join the rest of the file system; simply use either the mount command or the /etc/fstab file, which we describe earlier in this chapter.

Appendix D

Revving Up RPM

- -

- -

*T*his appendix introduces you to the Red Hat Package Manager (RPM). Red Hat, Inc., developed RPM in conjunction with another Linux distributor, Caldera Systems. RPM makes a grand effort to reduce the amount of work you have to do when you install software. In other words, RPM makes installing, updating, and removing software an automatic process. Woo-hoo!

Other package managers are available, but RPM has become the most popular system for installing, modifying, and transporting Linux software. This handy-dandy tool is a big reason that Red Hat is the de facto Linux distribution leader. Motor through this chapter to find out everything you need to know about RPM.

Introducing RPM

One of the primary reasons that the Red Hat Linux distribution became popular was that it added value for its customers with technologies such as Red Hat Package Manager (RPM).

All the software that was installed during the Red Hat installation process is stored in RPM's giving format, called packages. *Packages* are a collection of individual software (applications, libraries, and documentation, for example) contained in one file.

The package-management concept has been around for quite a while, with all the major Unix vendors supplying their own systems. The idea is to distribute software in a single file and have a package manager do the work of installing, or uninstalling, and managing the individual files. The Linux world has benefited greatly from this system, which simplifies the distribution and use of software.

You *could* install software without RPM, but we're not sure why you would want to — the RPM package contains everything you need to install and run an application. For example, if you didn't have the RPM package, installing Mozilla would work a little something like this: You would have to install the individual pieces that make up the Mozilla system, which can require dozens or more steps. You can also install, update, or uninstall RPM software. (See the following section, "Taking a Look at What RPM Does," for details.)

We remember, back in the day, when we used the Linux operating system for the first time. We had to install all the software using the dreaded tape archive system (tar). Trust us: installing, maintaining, and upgrading Linux with tar was a difficult task. RPM has made life easy.

The `/mnt/cdrom/RedHat/RPMS` directory contains all the RPM packages.

Taking a Look at What RPM Does

RPM performs three basic functions: It installs, upgrades, and removes packages. In addition to these functions, it can find out all sorts of information about installed and yet-to-be-installed packages. (All this, and it washes windows, too.) Here's a brief rundown of each function:

- **Installing packages:** RPM installs software. Software systems such as Mozilla have files of all types that must be put into certain locations in order to work properly. For example, under Red Hat, some (but not all) of the Mozilla files need to go into the `/usr/bin` directory. RPM performs this organizational stuff automatically without any fuss or muss.

  RPM not only installs files into their proper directories but also performs tasks such as creating the directories and running scripts to do the things that need to be done. (It's such a tidy and organized little scamp.)

- **Upgrading packages:** Gone are the days when updating a system was worse than going to the dentist. RPM acts like the personal Linux assistant you wish you had by updating existing software packages for you. RPM also keeps track of, in a database of its own, all the packages you have installed. When you upgrade a package, RPM does all the bookkeeping chores and replaces only the files that need to be replaced. It also saves the configuration files it replaces.

- **Removing packages:** The package database the RPM keeps is also useful in removing packages. To put it simply, RPM takes out the trash.

(Housekeeping was never so easy.) RPM goes to each file and uninstalls it. Directories belonging to the package are also removed when no files from other packages occupy them.

✔ **Querying packages and files:** RPM can also give you a great deal of information about a package and its files. You can use the query function to find out the function of a package and which files belong to it. RPM can also work on the RPM packages themselves, regardless of whether they have been installed.

✔ **Verifying packages:** RPM can validate an installed package against a `checksum` (a computer fingerprint) to see whether and how it has been changed. This feature is useful for security reasons. If you suspect that a file or system has been hacked, you can use RPM to find out how it has changed.

RPM packages often include configuration files as part of their installation. If you erase an RPM package, those configuration files are deleted but instead are renamed by appending the suffix `.rpmsave` to the end of the original file-name. For instance, removing the Kerberos package, `krbafs`, saves the configuration file by renaming `/etc/krb.conf` to `/etc/krb.conf.rpmsave`.

When you remove a package, RPM removes the associated files and directories. RPM cleans up after itself — what Martha Stewart would definitely call a "good thing."

Using the Red Hat Package Manager

Red Hat Linux provides a tool named the Package Manager for working with RPM packages. The Package Manager graphical tool provides all the functions for managing RPMs. It's like putting automatic transmission on a car — the Package Manger does the shifting for you.

Okay, the Package Manager does the shifting for you, but you still have to drive it. The Package Manager provides easy access to RPM functions, such as install, upgrade, uninstall, query, and verify. The following sections describe how to use the Package Manager to rev up your RPM.

To start the Package Manager, click the GNOME Menu button and choose System Settings⇨Packages. If you aren't logged in as root, type the root password in the Input window when you're prompted. A progress window appears briefly while the Package Manager determines which packages you have installed. After "thinking," the Package Management window appears.

The Package Manager displays all the Red Hat package groups that are installed by default on your system. Individual packages are organized into groups, such as the X Window System and GNOME. When the check box to the left of a group is active, designated by a plus sign (+), one or more packages from that group is installed. The number to the right of the package group shows how many packages of the total number in that group are installed.

Clicking the Details option opens the GNOME Desktop Environment Package Details window, which shows all the base and optional packages in the group; short, one-line descriptions of each package are also displayed next to each package. Base packages are always installed with a package group. Optional packages are, well, optionally installed.

This may be a *For Dummies* book, but you, of course, are no dummy. It's obvious what the GNOME RPM buttons, displayed along the top of the GNOME RPM window, are used for. The following sections describe how to use them for their intended functions.

Installing an RPM package from a CD-ROM

When you install your Red Hat Linux system, all the software that is copied to your hard drive from the CD-ROM comes from RPM packages. When you want to add additional software from the companion CD-ROM or an RPM repository, such as www.freshmeat.net, or from Red Hat at www.redhat.com, you can do so by using the Install button. To install an RPM package from a CD-ROM, follow these steps:

1. **Start the Package Manager by clicking the GNOME Menu button and choosing System Settings⇨Add/Remove Applications.**

   Enter the root password in the Information window if you're prompted.

   The Package Management window opens.

2. **Select the package group you want to install.**

   For instance, if you want to install extra skins for XMMS, you have to scroll down to the Sound and Video package group. The short description next to the package group says "From CD recording to playing audio CDs and multimedia files," which indicates that you're on the right path.

3. **Click the Details button to locate the package (or packages) to install.**

   The Sound and Video Package Details window opens.

4. **Select the radio button next to the xmms-skins package.**

5. **Click the Close button to return to the Package Management window.**

6. **Click the Update button, and the Preparing Systems Update window opens.**

   The Package Manager determines which (if any) additional packages are needed by the package you're installing. After the dependencies are determined, the Completed System Preparation window displays the number of packages that will be installed and how much disk space they require.

   You can click the Show Details buttons to see a list of packages queued for installation.

7. **Click the Continue button.**

   The Information window opens and you're prompted to insert the necessary CDs. In this example, you're asked to insert CD2

8. **Insert CD2 and click OK.**

   The System Update Progress Installing window shows a progress meter.

9. **Insert additional CDs, if prompted, and click the OK button in the Information window.**

10. **After the installation process is finished, the System Update Process window shows the Update Complete message.**

11. **Click the OK button to return to the Package Management window.**

Until the advent of the RPM (and the Debian package manager on Debian Linux systems), Linux software was distributed only by tar archives, which are sometimes referred to as _tarballs,_ or more descriptively, _hairballs._ The tar file storage mechanism stores one or more files in a single file in a tar format. A tar file has the `.tar` file suffix; if the tar file is compressed, it has a suffix like `.tgz` or `.tar.gz`. Using the tar-based distribution system is sufficient if your software doesn't change often and you're young. But when you need to upgrade or change software or work with complex software systems, tar becomes quite difficult to work with. Rather than spend your life spitting up hairballs, use systems such as RPM to greatly simplify your life.

Removing an RPM package

You can remove Red Hat packages as easily as you install them. Use the RPM erase (`-e`) function, which is the opposite of the install (`-i`) function. The Package Manager removes a package when you unselect an installed package. These steps describe how the remove a package:

1. **Click the GNOME Menu button and choose System Settings⇨Add/Remove Applications.**

2. **Enter the root password in the Information window if prompted.**

   The Package Management window opens.

3. **Select the package group that contains the package you want to remove.**

   For instance, if you want to remove a package in the Development Tools group, click the radio button to the left of the `Mail Server` group if it's blank.

   (Leave the radio button alone if it's already selected.)

4. **Click the Details button to view the package you're interested in removing.**

5. **Click the radio button next to the package, such as `res`, that you want to remove.**

6. **Click the Close button.**

   You return to the Add or Remove Packages window.

7. **Click the Update button.**

   The Completed System Preparation window opens.

8. **Click the Continue button in the Completed System Preparation window.**

   The package (or packages) is removed.

9. **After the package-removal process finishes, click the OK button in the Update Complete window.**

   You return to the Add or Remove Packages window.

Be sure that you really want to get rid of the package because when you remove a package, it's gone — as in *gone*. Okay, okay, maybe we're being a little dramatic. You can always go online to a site like `www.freshmeat.net` or to `www.redhat.com`. From there, you can download more packages to install. We recommend that you do that. Some new tool is always coming out that can help optimize your Red Hat Linux computing experience.

Manually Shifting with RPM

The first part of this chapter concentrates on using the Red Hat Package Manager to install and remove packages. But you also have the option using the `rpm` command. It provides additional features for installation and removal functions. You can use `rpm` to install, update, remove, and query packages.

This section provides several examples of how to use the manual `rpm` command.

Manually installing and upgrading packages

The RPM -i parameter indicates that an installation will take place. You can add verbose mode (which provides additional information) by using the -v option. (Note that you can combine options into a single group; for example, -i -v can become -iv.) Follow these instructions to install and upgrade packages:

1. **Log in as root and insert CD2 in the CD-ROM drive.**

2. **Open a terminal emulator window by clicking the terminal icon in the GNOME Panel (see Chapter 4 for instructions).**

   The GNOME Terminal emulator window opens.

3. **To add the package, type this command from a terminal window:**

```
rpm -iv /mnt/cdrom/RedHat/RPMS/xmms-skins*
```

Alternatively, you can upgrade a package that has already been installed on your system. Substitute the RPM upgrade option, -U, in place of the install option, -i. For instance, the following command updates the package:

```
rpm -Uv /mnt/cdrom/RedHat/RPMS/xmms-skins*
```

The files that constitute the newer XMMS skins package overwrite the older version. Existing configurations, however, are saved by adding the .rpmsave suffix to the configuration file.

Manually removing packages

RPM packages are good residents on your computer because they lend themselves to easy removal. The rpm command permits you to remove packages via the erase (-e) function.

Suppose that you're not so fond of the Mozilla e-mail client because you like the Evolution client better. No problem: Go ahead and remove the Mozilla mail package.

To remove an RPM package, follow these steps:

1. **Log in as root and insert CD2 in the CD-ROM drive.**

2. **Open a terminal emulator window by clicking the terminal icon in the GNOME Panel (see Chapter 4 for instructions).**

   The GNOME Terminal emulator window opens.

3. **Enter this command to find the name of the package to remove:**

```
rpm -qa | grep mozilla
```

You should see these results:

```
mozilla-nss-1.0.1-10
mozilla-1.0.1-10
mozilla-nspr-1.0.1-10
mozilla-psm-1.0.1-10
mozilla-mail-1.0.1-10
```

You need to know the name of the package before you can remove it. We use this step to display all the installed Mozilla packages in order to find the name of the package.

4. **Enter this command to remove the Mozilla e-mail client:**

```
rpm -e mozilla-mail
```

Note that we don't specify the version of the Mozilla-mail package. You need to use only the name of the package, not the version.

If you remove a package and realize that you didn't want to, in most cases you've done very little harm. The beauty of installing everything on your Red Hat Linux computer from RPM packages is that you can easily reinstall any package.

Sometimes, however, other package files occupy the same directories of the package you want to delete. In these cases, you get a message saying that the directory can't be deleted because it isn't empty.

Getting information about an RPM package

After installing a package (for example, pilot-link), you can find out information about the contents of the package by using the gnorpm query function. To use this function, follow these steps:

1. **Log in as root.**

2. **Open a terminal emulator window by clicking the terminal icon in the GNOME Panel (see Chapter 4 for instructions).**

The GNOME Terminal emulator window opens.

3. **Enter this command to find the name of the package to query:**

```
rpm -qa | grep mozilla
```

You should see these results:

```
mozilla-nss-1.0.1-24
mozilla-nspr-1.0.1-24
mozilla-mail-1.0.1-24
mozilla-1.0.1-24
mozilla-psm-1.0.1-24
```

4. **Enter the following query command to get information about the basic Mozilla package:**

```
rpm -qi mozilla
```

The combination of the query (-q) command and query option (i) tells RPM to display a summary of the package.

Appendix E

About the CD-ROMs

The CD-ROMs that come with this book contain the Publisher's Edition distribution of Red Hat Linux 9. This appendix describes the minimum computer configuration you need in order to install Red Hat Linux and also some of what you get on the companion CD-ROMs.

Although the CD-ROMs contain the Linux kernel and many supporting GNU programs and applications, they don't carry some utilities and applications described in the book. You must download utilities such as FIPS.EXE from the Red Hat Web site (www.redhat.com) or purchase the full boxed set of CDs. You can also download commercial applications, such as VMware and RealPlayer, from their respective Web sites.

System Requirements

Make sure that your computer meets the minimum system requirements listed here and in Chapter 3. More resources are needed for a graphical workstation. If your computer doesn't match up to most of these requirements, you may have problems installing and running Red Hat Linux:

- A Pentium-class PC with a 200MHz or faster processor recommended.

- For the best performance using the X Window System, we recommend at least 64MB, and preferably 128MB, of main memory. You can never have too much memory, and these numbers are the least amount you should have.

- Red Hat provides several installation classes that install different bundles of software. The installation classes take up different amounts of space, of course. The basic installation, Personal Desktop, takes a little less than 2GB of disk space. The Workstation installation consumes roughly 2.2GB; we use this method in Chapter 3. We recommend that your computer have a minimum of 2.5GB. That much space leaves you with about 250MB to play with when using our installation instructions.

- A CD-ROM drive, (and, optionally, a 3¼-inch floppy disk drive plus a blank 3¼-inch disk), a multisync monitor, an internal IDE or SCSI hard drive, a keyboard, and a mouse.

The instructions for installing the Red Hat Linux operating system from the CDs are detailed in Part I. After you install the software, return the CDs to their plastic jacket, or another appropriate place, for safekeeping.

What You Find

You can download the installation manual from the Red Hat Web site (`www.redhat.com/support`). The CDs don't contain the Linux source code and some utilities that come with the full Red Hat Linux distribution. You can download the full distribution from `www.redhat.com/download/mirrors. html` if you have a broadband Internet connection. You can also use the coupon at the back of this book (plus some dinero) to obtain the extra CDs that contain the extra stuff.

You may view much of the documentation on these CDs through an HTML viewer, such as Mozilla, which is also included on the CDs; or you may print it. You can also view most of the documentation from other operating systems, such as DOS, Windows, or Unix.

The CD-ROMs have a nearly full implementation of Linux, and to list all the accompanying tools and utilities would take too much room. Briefly, the CDs include most of the software so that you can

✔ Access the Internet

✔ Write programs in several computer languages

✔ Create and manipulate images

✔ Create, manipulate, and play back sounds (if you have a sound card)

✔ Play certain games

✔ Work with electrical design

For more information about Red Hat Linux agreements and installation, see the pages at the end of this book following the index.

If You Have Problems (Of the CD Kind)

We tried our best to test various computers with the minimum system requirements. Alas, your computer may differ, and Linux may not install or work as stated.

The two likeliest problems are that you don't have enough RAM for the programs you want to use or you have some hardware that Linux doesn't support. Luckily, the latter problem occurs less frequently each day as more hardware is supported by Linux.

You may also have one or more FireWire, USB, or SCSI hard drives that use a driver (called a *kernel module* in Linux parlance) not supported by Linux or a controller that is simply too new for the Linux development team to have given it the proper support at the time these CDs were pressed.

If you have trouble with the CD, please call the Wiley Publishing Customer Care phone number: 800-762-2974. Outside the United States, call 1-317-572-3994. You can also contact Customer Service by e-mail at `techsupdum@wiley.com`. Wiley Publishing, Inc. provides technical support only for installation and other general quality-control items; for technical support for the applications themselves, consult the program's vendor or author.

Index

Notes

Notes

Notes

Notes

FOR DUMMIES®

The easy way to get more done and have more fun

PERSONAL FINANCE

0-7645-5231-7

Personal Finance FOR DUMMIES

Investing FOR DUMMIES

0-7645-2431-3

Home Buying FOR DUMMIES

0-7645-5331-3

Also available:

Estate Planning For Dummies
(0-7645-5501-4)

401(k)s For Dummies
(0-7645-5468-9)

Frugal Living For Dummies
(0-7645-5403-4)

Microsoft Money "X" For Dummies
(0-7645-1689-2)

Mutual Funds For Dummies
(0-7645-5329-1)

Personal Bankruptcy For Dummies
(0-7645-5498-0)

Quicken "X" For Dummies
(0-7645-1666-3)

Stock Investing For Dummies
(0-7645-5411-5)

Taxes For Dummies 2003
(0-7645-5475-1)

BUSINESS & CAREERS

Accounting FOR DUMMIES

0-7645-5314-3

Grant Writing FOR DUMMIES

0-7645-5307-0

Resumes FOR DUMMIES

0-7645-5471-9

Also available:

Business Plans Kit For Dummies
(0-7645-5365-8)

Consulting For Dummies
(0-7645-5034-9)

Cool Careers For Dummies
(0-7645-5345-3)

Human Resources Kit For Dummies
(0-7645-5131-0)

Managing For Dummies
(1-5688-4858-7)

QuickBooks All-in-One Desk Reference For Dummies
(0-7645-1963-8)

Selling For Dummies
(0-7645-5363-1)

Small Business Kit For Dummies
(0-7645-5093-4)

Starting an eBay Business For Dummies
(0-7645-1547-0)

HEALTH, SPORTS & FITNESS

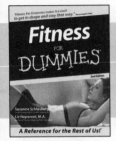

Fitness FOR DUMMIES

0-7645-5167-1

Golf FOR DUMMIES

0-7645-5146-9

Diabetes FOR DUMMIES

0-7645-5154-X

Also available:

Controlling Cholesterol For Dummies
(0-7645-5440-9)

Dieting For Dummies
(0-7645-5126-4)

High Blood Pressure For Dummies
(0-7645-5424-7)

Martial Arts For Dummies
(0-7645-5358-5)

Menopause For Dummies
(0-7645-5458-1)

Nutrition For Dummies
(0-7645-5180-9)

Power Yoga For Dummies
(0-7645-5342-9)

Thyroid For Dummies
(0-7645-5385-2)

Weight Training For Dummies
(0-7645-5168-X)

Yoga For Dummies
(0-7645-5117-5)

Available wherever books are sold.
Go to www.dummies.com or call 1-877-762-2974 to order direct.

FOR DUMMIES®

A world of resources to help you grow

HOME, GARDEN & HOBBIES

0-7645-5295-3

0-7645-5130-2

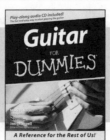

0-7645-5106-X

Also available:

Auto Repair For Dummies
(0-7645-5089-6)

Chess For Dummies
(0-7645-5003-9)

Home Maintenance For Dummies
(0-7645-5215-5)

Organizing For Dummies
(0-7645-5300-3)

Piano For Dummies
(0-7645-5105-1)

Poker For Dummies
(0-7645-5232-5)

Quilting For Dummies
(0-7645-5118-3)

Rock Guitar For Dummies
(0-7645-5356-9)

Roses For Dummies
(0-7645-5202-3)

Sewing For Dummies
(0-7645-5137-X)

FOOD & WINE

0-7645-5250-3

0-7645-5390-9

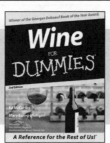

0-7645-5114-0

Also available:

Bartending For Dummies
(0-7645-5051-9)

Chinese Cooking For Dummies
(0-7645-5247-3)

Christmas Cooking For Dummies
(0-7645-5407-7)

Diabetes Cookbook For Dummies
(0-7645-5230-9)

Grilling For Dummies
(0-7645-5076-4)

Low-Fat Cooking For Dummies
(0-7645-5035-7)

Slow Cookers For Dummies
(0-7645-5240-6)

TRAVEL

0-7645-5453-0

0-7645-5438-7

0-7645-5448-4

Also available:

America's National Parks For Dummies
(0-7645-6204-5)

Caribbean For Dummies
(0-7645-5445-X)

Cruise Vacations For Dummies 2003
(0-7645-5459-X)

Europe For Dummies
(0-7645-5456-5)

Ireland For Dummies
(0-7645-6199-5)

France For Dummies
(0-7645-6292-4)

London For Dummies
(0-7645-5416-6)

Mexico's Beach Resorts For Dummies
(0-7645-6262-2)

Paris For Dummies
(0-7645-5494-8)

RV Vacations For Dummies
(0-7645-5443-3)

Walt Disney World & Orlando For Dummies
(0-7645-5444-1)

Available wherever books are sold. Go to www.dummies.com or call 1-877-762-2974 to order direct.

FOR DUMMIES®

Plain-English solutions for everyday challenges

COMPUTER BASICS

0-7645-0838-5

0-7645-1663-9

0-7645-1548-9

Also available:

PCs All-in-One Desk Reference For Dummies (0-7645-0791-5)

Pocket PC For Dummies (0-7645-1640-X)

Treo and Visor For Dummies (0-7645-1673-6)

Troubleshooting Your PC For Dummies (0-7645-1669-8)

Upgrading & Fixing PCs For Dummies (0-7645-1665-5)

Windows XP For Dummies (0-7645-0893-8)

Windows XP For Dummies Quick Reference (0-7645-0897-0)

BUSINESS SOFTWARE

0-7645-0822-9

0-7645-0839-3

0-7645-0819-9

Also available:

Excel Data Analysis For Dummies (0-7645-1661-2)

Excel 2002 All-in-One Desk Reference For Dummies (0-7645-1794-5)

Excel 2002 For Dummies Quick Reference (0-7645-0829-6)

GoldMine "X" For Dummies (0-7645-0845-8)

Microsoft CRM For Dummies (0-7645-1698-1)

Microsoft Project 2002 For Dummies (0-7645-1628-0)

Office XP For Dummies (0-7645-0830-X)

Outlook 2002 For Dummies (0-7645-0828-8)

Get smart! Visit www.dummies.com

- **Find listings of even more *For Dummies* titles**

- **Browse online articles**

- **Sign up for Dummies eTips™**

- **Check out *For Dummies* fitness videos and other products**

- **Order from our online bookstore**

Available wherever books are sold. Go to www.dummies.com or call 1-877-762-2974 to order direct.

FOR DUMMIES®

Helping you expand your horizons and realize your potential

INTERNET

0-7645-0894-6

0-7645-1659-0

0-7645-1642-6

Also available:

America Online 7.0 For Dummies
(0-7645-1624-8)

Genealogy Online For Dummies
(0-7645-0807-5)

The Internet All-in-One Desk Reference For Dummies
(0-7645-1659-0)

Internet Explorer 6 For Dummies
(0-7645-1344-3)

The Internet For Dummies Quick Reference
(0-7645-1645-0)

Internet Privacy For Dummies
(0-7645-0846-6)

Researching Online For Dummies
(0-7645-0546-7)

Starting an Online Business For Dummies
(0-7645-1655-8)

DIGITAL MEDIA

0-7645-1664-7

0-7645-1675-2

0-7645-0806-7

Also available:

CD and DVD Recording For Dummies
(0-7645-1627-2)

Digital Photography All-in-One Desk Reference For Dummies
(0-7645-1800-3)

Digital Photography For Dummies Quick Reference
(0-7645-0750-8)

Home Recording for Musicians For Dummies
(0-7645-1634-5)

MP3 For Dummies
(0-7645-0858-X)

Paint Shop Pro "X" For Dummies
(0-7645-2440-2)

Photo Retouching & Restoration For Dummies
(0-7645-1662-0)

Scanners For Dummies
(0-7645-0783-4)

GRAPHICS

0-7645-0817-2

0-7645-1651-5

0-7645-0895-4

Also available:

Adobe Acrobat 5 PDF For Dummies
(0-7645-1652-3)

Fireworks 4 For Dummies
(0-7645-0804-0)

Illustrator 10 For Dummies
(0-7645-3636-2)

QuarkXPress 5 For Dummies
(0-7645-0643-9)

Visio 2000 For Dummies
(0-7645-0635-8)

Available wherever books are sold. Go to www.dummies.com or call 1-877-762-2974 to order direct.

FOR DUMMIES®

SELF-HELP, SPIRITUALITY & RELIGION

0-7645-5302-X

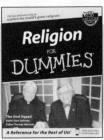
0-7645-5418-2

0-7645-5264-3

Also available:

The Bible For Dummies
(0-7645-5296-1)

Buddhism For Dummies
(0-7645-5359-3)

Christian Prayer For Dummies
(0-7645-5500-6)

Dating For Dummies
(0-7645-5072-1)

Judaism For Dummies
(0-7645-5299-6)

Potty Training For Dummies
(0-7645-5417-4)

Pregnancy For Dummies
(0-7645-5074-8)

Rekindling Romance For Dummies
(0-7645-5303-8)

Spirituality For Dummies
(0-7645-5298-8)

Weddings For Dummies
(0-7645-5055-1)

PETS

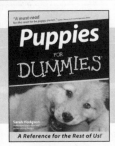
0-7645-5255-4

0-7645-5286-4

0-7645-5275-9

Also available:

Labrador Retrievers For Dummies
(0-7645-5281-3)

Aquariums For Dummies
(0-7645-5156-6)

Birds For Dummies
(0-7645-5139-6)

Dogs For Dummies
(0-7645-5274-0)

Ferrets For Dummies
(0-7645-5259-7)

German Shepherds For Dummies
(0-7645-5280-5)

Golden Retrievers For Dummies
(0-7645-5267-8)

Horses For Dummies
(0-7645-5138-8)

Jack Russell Terriers For Dummies
(0-7645-5268-6)

Puppies Raising & Training Diary For Dummies
(0-7645-0876-8)

EDUCATION & TEST PREPARATION

0-7645-5194-9

0-7645-5325-9

0-7645-5210-4

Also available:

Chemistry For Dummies
(0-7645-5430-1)

English Grammar For Dummies
(0-7645-5322-4)

French For Dummies
(0-7645-5193-0)

The GMAT For Dummies
(0-7645-5251-1)

Inglés Para Dummies
(0-7645-5427-1)

Italian For Dummies
(0-7645-5196-5)

Research Papers For Dummies
(0-7645-5426-3)

The SAT I For Dummies
(0-7645-5472-7)

U.S. History For Dummies
(0-7645-5249-X)

World History For Dummies
(0-7645-5242-2)

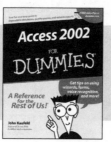

redhat ®

www.redhat.com

GNU GENERAL PUBLIC LICENSE

Version 2, June 1991
Copyright © 1989, 1991 Free Software Foundation, Inc.
59 Temple Place - Suite 330, Boston, MA 02111-1307, USA

Preamble

The licenses for most software are designed to take away your freedom to share and change it. By contrast, the GNU General Public License is intended to guarantee your freedom to share and change free software—to make sure the software is free for all its users. This General Public License applies to most of the Free Software Foundation's software and to any other program whose authors commit to using it. (Some other Free Software Foundation software is covered by the GNU Library General Public License instead.) You can apply it to your programs, too.

When we speak of free software, we are referring to freedom, not price. Our General Public Licenses are designed to make sure that you have the freedom to distribute copies of free software (and charge for this service if you wish), that you receive source code or can get it if you want it, that you can change the software or use pieces of it in new free programs; and that you know you can do these things.

To protect your rights, we need to make restrictions that forbid anyone to deny you these rights or to ask you to surrender the rights. These restrictions translate to certain responsibilities for you if you distribute copies of the software, or if you modify it.

For example, if you distribute copies of such a program, whether gratis or for a fee, you must give the recipients all the rights that you have. You must make sure that they, too, receive or can get the source code. And you must show them these terms so they know their rights.

We protect your rights with two steps: (1) copyright the software, and (2) offer you this license which gives you legal permission to copy, distribute and/or modify the software.

Also, for each author's protection and ours, we want to make certain that everyone understands that there is no warranty for this free software. If the software is modified by someone else and passed on, we want its recipients to know that what they have is not the original, so that any problems introduced by others will not reflect on the original authors' reputations.

Finally, any free program is threatened constantly by software patents. We wish to avoid the danger that redistributors of a free program will individually obtain patent licenses, in effect making the program proprietary. To prevent this, we have made it clear that any patent must be licensed for everyone's free use or not licensed at all.

The precise terms and conditions for copying, distribution and modification follow.

TERMS AND CONDITIONS FOR COPYING, DISTRIBUTION, AND MODIFICATION

0. This License applies to any program or other work which contains a notice placed by the copyright holder saying it may be distributed under the terms of this General Public License. The "Program", below, refers to any such program or work, and a "work based on the Program" means either the Program or any derivative work under copyright law: that is to say, a work containing the Program or a portion of it, either verbatim or with modifications and/or translated into another language. (Hereinafter, translation is included without limitation in the term "modification".) Each licensee is addressed as "you".

   Activities other than copying, distribution and modification are not covered by this License; they are outside its scope. The act of running the Program is not restricted, and the output from the Program is covered only if its contents constitute a work based on the Program (independent of having been made by running the Program). Whether that is true depends on what the Program does.

1. You may copy and distribute verbatim copies of the Program's source code as you receive it, in any medium, provided that you conspicuously and appropriately publish on each copy an appropriate copyright notice and disclaimer of warranty; keep intact all the notices that refer to this License and to the absence of any warranty; and give any other recipients of the Program a copy of this License along with the Program.

   You may charge a fee for the physical act of transferring a copy, and you may at your option offer warranty protection in exchange for a fee.

2. You may modify your copy or copies of the Program or any portion of it, thus forming a work based on the Program, and copy and distribute such modifications or work under the terms of Section 1 above, provided that you also meet all of these conditions:

   a) You must cause the modified files to carry prominent notices stating that you changed the files and the date of any change.

   b) You must cause any work that you distribute or publish, that in whole or in part contains or is derived from the Program or any part thereof, to be licensed as a whole at no charge to all third parties under the terms of this License.

   c) If the modified program normally reads commands interactively when run, you must cause it, when started running for such interactive use in the most ordinary way, to print or display an announcement including an appropriate copyright notice and a notice that there is no warranty (or else, saying that you provide a warranty) and that users may redistribute the program under these conditions, and telling the user how to view a copy of this License. (Exception: if the Program itself is interactive but does not normally print such an announcement, your work based on the Program is not required to print an announcement.)

   These requirements apply to the modified work as a whole. If identifiable sections of that work are not derived from the Program, and can be reasonably considered independent and separate works in themselves, then this License, and its terms, do not apply to those sections when you distribute them as separate works. But when you distribute the same sections as part of a whole which is a work based on the Program, the distribution of the whole must be on the terms of this License, whose permissions for other licensees extend to the entire whole, and thus to each and every part regardless of who wrote it.

Thus, it is not the intent of this section to claim rights or contest your rights to work written entirely by you; rather, the intent is to exercise the right to control the distribution of derivative or collective works based on the Program.

In addition, mere aggregation of another work not based on the Program with the Program (or with a work based on the Program) on a volume of a storage or distribution medium does not bring the other work under the scope of this License.

3. You may copy and distribute the Program (or a work based on it, under Section 2) in object code or executable form under the terms of Sections 1 and 2 above provided that you also do one of the following:

   a) Accompany it with the complete corresponding machine-readable source code, which must be distributed under the terms of Sections 1 and 2 above on a medium customarily used for software interchange; or,

   b) Accompany it with a written offer, valid for at least three years, to give any third party, for a charge no more than your cost of physically performing source distribution, a complete machine-readable copy of the corresponding source code, to be distributed under the terms of Sections 1 and 2 above on a medium customarily used for software interchange; or,

   c) Accompany it with the information you received as to the offer to distribute corresponding source code. (This alternative is allowed only for noncommercial distribution and only if you received the program in object code or executable form with such an offer, in accord with Subsection b above.)

The source code for a work means the preferred form of the work for making modifications to it. For an executable work, complete source code means all the source code for all modules it contains, plus any associated interface definition files, plus the scripts used to control compilation and installation of the executable. However, as a special exception, the source code distributed need not include anything that is normally distributed (in either source or binary form) with the major components (compiler, kernel, and so on) of the operating system on which the executable runs, unless that component itself accompanies the executable.

If distribution of executable or object code is made by offering access to copy from a designated place, then offering equivalent access to copy the source code from the same place counts as distribution of the source code, even though third parties are not compelled to copy the source along with the object code.

4. You may not copy, modify, sublicense, or distribute the Program except as expressly provided under this License. Any attempt otherwise to copy, modify, sublicense or distribute the Program is void, and will automatically terminate your rights under this License. However, parties who have received copies, or rights, from you under this License will not have their licenses terminated so long as such parties remain in full compliance.

5. You are not required to accept this License, since you have not signed it. However, nothing else grants you permission to modify or distribute the Program or its derivative works. These actions are prohibited by law if you do not accept this License. Therefore, by modifying or distributing the Program (or any work based on the Program), you indicate your acceptance of this License to do so, and all its terms and conditions for copying, distributing or modifying the Program or works based on it.

6. Each time you redistribute the Program (or any work based on the Program), the recipient automatically receives a license from the original licensor to copy, distribute or modify the Program subject to these terms and conditions. You may not impose any further restrictions on the recipients' exercise of the rights granted herein. You are not responsible for enforcing compliance by third parties to this License.

7. If, as a consequence of a court judgment or allegation of patent infringement or for any other reason (not limited to patent issues), conditions are imposed on you (whether by court order, agreement or otherwise) that contradict the conditions of this License, they do not excuse you from the conditions of this License. If you cannot distribute so as to satisfy simultaneously your obligations under this License and any other pertinent obligations, then as a consequence you may not distribute the Program at all. For example, if a patent license would not permit royalty-free redistribution of the Program by all those who receive copies directly or indirectly through you, then the only way you could satisfy both it and this License would be to refrain entirely from distribution of the Program.

   If any portion of this section is held invalid or unenforceable under any particular circumstance, the balance of the section is intended to apply and the section as a whole is intended to apply in other circumstances.

   It is not the purpose of this section to induce you to infringe any patents or other property right claims or to contest validity of any such claims; this section has the sole purpose of protecting the integrity of the free software distribution system, which is implemented by public license practices. Many people have made generous contributions to the wide range of software distributed through that system in reliance on consistent application of that system; it is up to the author/donor to decide if he or she is willing to distribute software through any other system and a licensee cannot impose that choice.

   This section is intended to make thoroughly clear what is believed to be a consequence of the rest of this License.

8. If the distribution and/or use of the Program is restricted in certain countries either by patents or by copyrighted interfaces, the original copyright holder who places the Program under this License may add an explicit geographical distribution limitation excluding those countries, so that distribution is permitted only in or among countries not thus excluded. In such case, this License incorporates the limitation as if written in the body of this License.

9. The Free Software Foundation may publish revised and/or new versions of the General Public License from time to time. Such new versions will be similar in spirit to the present version, but may differ in detail to address new problems or concerns.

   Each version is given a distinguishing version number. If the Program specifies a version number of this License which applies to it and "any later version", you have the option of following the terms and conditions either of that version or of any later version published by the Free Software Foundation. If the Program does not specify a version number of this License, you may choose any version ever published by the Free Software Foundation.

10. If you wish to incorporate parts of the Program into other free programs whose distribution conditions are different, write to the author to ask for permission. For software which is copyrighted by the Free Software Foundation, write to the Free Software Foundation; we sometimes make exceptions for this. Our decision will be guided by the two goals of preserving the free status of all derivatives of our free software and of promoting the sharing and reuse of software generally.

Wiley Publishing, Inc.
Linux Source Code Mail-In Coupon

To allow us to offer this book at the list price, we provide separately the Linux source code. You may use this fulfillment offer to receive the source code on CD-ROMs. If you want the source code sent to you, please:

1. Complete the coupon.

2. Include a check or money order for $8.99 (U.S. funds) for orders shipping within the U.S. or $16.99 (U.S. funds) for orders outside the U.S.

3. Send it to us at the address listed at the bottom of the coupon.

Name _____

Company _____

Address_____

City _____**State** _____**Postal Code** _____

Country_____

E-mail _____**Telephone** _____

❑ Check here to find out what we're up to by joining our email list — a convenient way to receive news about our products and events as well as about special discount offers

Return this coupon with the appropriate US funds to:

Wiley Publishing, Inc.
Media Development Department
Red Hat Linux 9 For Dummies 539906 Fulfillment
10475 Crosspoint Blvd.
Indianapolis, IN 46256

Terms: Void where prohibited or restricted by law. Allow 2-6 weeks for delivery. Wiley is not responsible for lost, stolen, late, or illegible orders. For questions regarding this fulfillment offer, please e-mail us at MediaDev@wiley.com.